HEALTHY FOOD

FOR

HEALTHY CHILDREN

HEALTHY FOOD

FOR

HEALTHY CHILDREN

GAIL DUFF

Conran Octopus

Recipes suitable for children on allergy diets are indicated by
the symbols that appear under the recipe titles.
The key is as follows:

D	E	G	W
Dairy-free	Egg-free	Gluten-free	Wheat-free

Further information, advice and recipes are given in
Chapter Ten.

The child in this book is referred to as 'he' and 'she' in
alternate chapters throughout, but in all cases the advice
applies equally to both sexes.

First published in 1986 as
Good Food – Healthy Children by
Conran Octopus Limited
37 Shelton Street
London WC2H 9HN

This paperback edition published 1989

Editor by Charyn Jones
Illustrations by Carol Wilhide

Photography by Julie Fisher

ISBN 1 85029 183 7

Typeset by Servis Filmsetting Ltd, Manchester
Produced by Mandarin Offset
Printed and bound in Hong Kong

PREFACE

I was in my mid-thirties when I decided that the time had come to start a family. I had never really turned my mind to the condition of pregnancy before, despite many years as a professional cookery writer, and it was only after much research that I started to formulate ideas about diet and nutrition and how it might affect me and my growing baby. Nine healthy and happy months later I gave birth to Lucy, and all my careful attention to what I ate seemed to be vindicated. Armed with further research into nutrition for growing babies and children, I set out to devise a diet for Lucy that would see her through from weaning to going to school. This book is an attempt to share with other parents my own very rewarding experience of cooking for a growing family.

All the foods I use fall roughly into the category of 'wholefood', a term that can be very off-putting if you are unfamiliar with it. Wholefoods are simply those that are fresh, unprocessed, and as near to their natural state as possible: for example, fresh meat and fish, nuts, eggs, cheese, fruit and vegetables and wholewheat flour. Most children would have no quarrel with any of these foods, but many parents encounter problems when they try to limit their child's intake of sugary foods and sweets: for sugar is empty of all nutrients except calories, and however much children love its sweet taste it is not of any nutritional benefit to them. To solve the problem, I have shown how you can substitute other ingredients for sugar, ingredients that are rich in nutrients and which also supply children with the calories they need and the sweetness they like. You will soon see that a diet without added sugar does not mean giving up favourite puddings and rich cakes – far from it.

This book is all about your healthy children and how to keep them that way. I hope it will enable you to feed your family good food that will interest and satisfy them – food that they will enjoy eating and that you know is appropriate to their nutritional needs.

CONTENTS

CONTENTS

CHAPTER ONE

BEGINNING WITH THE BASICS
An Introduction to the Wholefood Larder

This chapter is a brief guide to the wide
range of ingredients normally included in a wholefood diet.
Today's awareness of the effects of diet on health means that such
ingredients are no longer hard to find. You will usually be able to
buy the wholefoods described here in supermarkets, pharmacies,
healthfood and wholefood shops, but should you have any
difficulty a list of suppliers of the less common
ingredients and foods appears on page 156.

Fruit

Fruit is usually the first solid food
that a young baby is given. Fresh
fruit is a good source of natural
sweetness and is an ideal snack food.
Fruit between meals is not as filling
as sweets and cakes and so does not
reduce appetite, and it will supply a
wide range of vitamins and minerals,
particularly vitamin C, plus natural
fibre.

Fruit should be eaten as fresh as
possible, and it is best bought every
week rather than in bulk. Apples,
pears and citrus fruits are best stored
in a cool, dark larder, soft fruits and
stone fruits in the bottom of the
refrigerator. Soft fruits don't keep
well for longer than two days.

Freezing destroys some of the
vitamins in fruit and affects the
texture. Tinned fruits also undergo a
vitamin loss during processing,
although the type that have been
tinned in natural juices are an
excellent stand-by. They can be made
into low-sugar desserts or served
direct from the tin. Don't rely on
processed or frozen fruits as your sole
source of fruit. Encourage your family
to eat fresh fruit as often as possible
and treat the tinned and frozen ones
as a convenience ingredient.

Dried Fruit

Dried fruit is a concentrated form of
natural sweetness. It has a high
mineral content and supplies plenty of
fibre and varying amounts of vitamins
A and B. Dried fruit can be added to
fresh fruits during cooking to give
additional sweetness, mixed with nuts,
or eaten alone as a sweet treat (pages
92–3). However, dried fruits cause
tooth decay just as surely as do boiled
sweets.

Sometimes the dried fruits may
have been coated with a mineral oil;
this is thought by some to be harmful,

particularly if a lot of dried fruit is consumed, as would be the case in a low-sugar diet. If the pack lists 'edible oil' or something similar in the list of ingredients, rinse the fruit in a collander under running warm water for about a minute. Drain and pat dry with kitchen paper.

Dried fruit will keep for several months but it is best if you consume it within about a month. After this time, the fruit may dry out or develop a sugary bloom.

Vegetables

Fresh vegetables are an essential part of everyone's diet, and it is best to eat several different types every day so that you get the widest possible range of all the vitamins and minerals they provide. If you can, do your vegetable shopping at least twice a week to ensure freshness.

To rid vegetables of any chemical residue or dirt, wash them before you prepare and cook them, but don't leave them soaking in cold water – the vitamins will quickly dissolve away. Take care not to overprepare vegetables by peeling or trimming them unnecessarily. Peel root vegetables only when necessary and cook potatoes in their skins: check them first for green patches, which are poisonous and should be removed. If the potatoes are to be mashed, boil them first and take the thin layer of skin off afterwards. You will find the skins slough off easily, involving far less work than peeling them raw. It is also beneficial because much of the fibre, iron, vitamin C and protein lies just under the skin of the potato and is removed by the peeler.

Never overcook vegetables as you can destroy all their nutrients: cook

CHILDREN IN THE KITCHEN

Once you have children, your kitchen is no longer your own. They open doors, eat your carefully weighed ingredients, fall off chairs and demand drinks just at the moment when your sauce needs attention. They want to get their fingers in every mixture. You can't prevent this – unless you ban them from the kitchen – but you can make life safer and cooking more enjoyable for all of you. Try to make the preparation of food fun as well as a necessity and you will all have a better time than if you make the children feel that they are a nuisance.

There is one corner cupboard in my kitchen that has no catch. This one contains the cake tins, collanders and jelly moulds of all shapes and sizes. When my daughter Lucy was young, she had a wonderful time taking everything out, banging it around and scattering it all over the floor. The kitchen looked a shambles but I was able to carry on uninterrupted. Other good kitchen toys include small amounts of coloured beans securely taped into see-through plastic pots, small plastic bowls and wooden spoons. One word of warning though: check all your tins first to make sure that there are no sharp edges.

As children get older, they will want to know what you are doing and will be asking questions constantly. Answer them or your children will only seek other ways to demand your attention. If you grow your own vegetables, take the children into the garden to help you collect some. Tell them what you are making. Show them the ingredients that go into a recipe. Let them see the dish before it goes into the oven

The most important thing to consider is the safety angle:

- Turn all saucepan handles away from the edges of the cooker or worktop
- Fit a guard round the top of your cooker
- Make sure the lead of the electric kettle is not dangling
- Do not carry containers of hot liquid near your child
- Keep food mixers unplugged and out of reach
- Do not leave sharp knives within reach and throw all opened tins away as soon as they have been emptied
- Fit safety catches to all your ground-level cupboard doors
- Store bleach, disinfectants and household cleaners high up and well out of a child's reach
- If you have electric sockets at ground level, fit safety caps.

and when it comes out. All this will help to give them an interest in food, and when it comes to eating it they will be more curious to see what the end result tastes like.

By the age of eighteen months, children are ready to 'help' with stirring and mixing. Once your child has helped in the kitchen, nothing will ever be quite perfect again. Loaves will be lopsided because they have been punched too hard on one side, and cakes may contain a little too much bicarbonate of soda or only half an egg because the other half has been dropped on the floor! You will have to leave some mixture behind so that the bowl can be licked. But it is surprising just how little these things really matter. What does matter is a happy child with a healthy, but not obsessive, interest in food.

The kitchen becomes an important place at times of traditional festivals. Mince pies, puddings and cakes at Christmas, pancakes on Shrove Tuesday, hot cross buns and simnel cake at Easter and pumpkin pies at Hallowe'en are all part of our heritage. Children can join in by putting the fillings in the pies, stirring the pudding, helping to decorate the cakes, beating the pancakes and putting the crosses on the buns. All this helps to make food interesting and fun, and as a result it will be all the more readily eaten and enjoyed.

them until they are just tender but not mushy. Steaming is the best method, both because it minimizes loss of valuable nutrients and because it preserves the texture of the vegetables. Keeping vegetables warm for long periods or reheating them will cause vitamins to disappear, so eat them freshly cooked whenever you can.

Frozen vegetables have generally lost only small amounts of vitamins, but use them within six months. Tinned vegetables have lost significant amounts of nutrients and are usually preserved in salted and sugared water. They should never be relied on as a main vegetable supply.

Meat

The question I am frequently asked is, 'How can you eat a wholefood diet and still eat meat?' Meat is an excellent source of protein, B vitamins and iron. It is best not to eat meat every day – three or four times a week is quite enough – but there is no need to give it up altogether on dietary grounds alone.

If you choose to eat meat, buy it as lean as you can and cut off any extra fat before cooking. Eat a range of different meats and, if possible, include liver and kidneys regularly for their high iron and vitamin B content.

If possible, avoid processed meats. These often have a high fat and salt content and may contain colourings, preservatives, flavourings and other added ingredients. If you like fresh sausages, buy the best quality, but remember that all sausages have high levels of fat: try to eat them only infrequently.

Many people are becoming increasingly concerned about the residues of chemical growth promoters in meat. There are producers who rear meat by completely natural methods: for a list of addresses see page 156.

Fish

Fish is another excellent source of protein and there are two main types – white and oily. White fish is one of the few foods that contain iodine and oily fish is an excellent source of vitamins A and D.

Buy fresh fish whenever you can – it is just as easy to cook as frozen. A handy stand-by, however, is frozen cod steaks without crumbs or batter.

Pulses

This is the term used to cover all the different types of dried beans, lentils and split peas. They are a good source of protein, vitamins, iron, potassium, calcium and fibre. As a vegetable rather than an animal protein, pulses do not contain all the amino acids that our bodies need (page 20), so they should be combined in a meal with a whole grain. Beans on wholewheat toast is the simplest example, but pulses can also be combined with

brown rice, wholewheat pasta or pastry.

Pulses will keep for a long time in an airtight container, but do not keep them for more than a year as the skins will start to toughen.

Beans must be boiled for at least ten minutes during some stage of their cooking period to make them quite safe for eating (they can, if not cooked properly, cause stomach upsets). They should either be soaked overnight (remove any that float), brought to the boil, boiled for ten minutes and drained; or put into a saucepan of water, brought to the boil, boiled for ten minutes, then taken from the heat, soaked for two hours and finally drained. After either of these processes they will be ready for further cooking until tender. All beans vary as to their cooking time – as little as 50 minutes for the smaller, softer types and as long as two hours or more for chickpeas (garbanzos). Do not add salt to the cooking water as this toughens the skins, or soda, as this will destroy vitamins.

Once beans have been cooked they can be mixed with vegetables and herbs to make satisfying main dishes, added to meat dishes or made into delicious salads.

Lentils need no soaking and most will cook within 50 minutes. The split red type are best for soups and stews. Whole green or brown lentils can be used for main dishes in the same way as beans.

Nuts

Nuts are rich in minerals and contain varying amounts of B vitamins and vitamins C, D and E. They can be used as the main protein part of a meal, as additions to salads and desserts, or as tasty snacks between meals. Finely ground, they can be

APPROXIMATE COOKING TIMES FOR PULSES		
Variety	Saucepan	Pressure cooker
Aduki beans	45 mins	20 mins
Black-eye beans	45 mins	30 mins
Butter beans	1½ hours	35 mins
Cannellini beans	1 hour	20 mins
Haricot beans	1 hour	20 mins
Kidney beans	1¼ hours	25 mins
Chickpeas	1½–2 hours	30 mins
Split peas	30 mins	15 mins
Mung beans	45 mins	15 mins
Red lentils	20 mins	10 mins
Pinto beans	1¼ hours	25 mins

added to cake mixtures, used to make cake decorations, or mixed into foods for a young baby. Store shelled nuts in airtight containers in a dark cupboard for no longer than one month.

Processing Almonds Some of the recipes in this book call for blanched or ground almonds. These will be more moist if you process them yourself. To blanch almonds, put them into a shallow pan and cover them with cold water. Bring to the boil, drain and immediately squeeze them from their skins. To grind them, put about 2 tablespoonfuls at a time into a coffee grinder. Store in the refrigerator. If you do buy nuts ready processed, use them within two weeks.

Tahini is also known as sesame paste and is a nut butter, like peanut butter, but made from ground sesame seeds. It is smoother than peanut butter with a creamy, nutty flavour. There are two types: light grey (called white) and dark grey (called grey). Of the two, the white has the better flavour. Tahini is used to flavour and moisten dishes and as a principal ingredient in spreads (page 121). Tahini can be bought in small jars or large tubs. It will keep for up to a year in the refrigerator but may have to be stirred occasionally as the oil tends to float to the top.

——— Grains and Rice ———

The heart of the wholefood kitchen is the flour bin: in it there should ideally be a good supply of wholewheat (also called wholemeal) flour. Wholewheat flour comprises 100 per cent of the wheat grain and contains fibre, B vitamins, vitamin E, iron and calcium, all in the correct proportions to be of most use to your body. White flour (70 per cent of the grain) contains a little fibre; most of the vitamins and minerals have been removed and some put back artificially. There is no need at all to use white flour. Wholewheat flour can be used for all the baking, thickening or coating that you will need to do. Besides being a healthier product, it also has an excellent flavour. Flours are sometimes labelled according to the percentage of the grain. For example, '85%' flour is 85 per cent of the grain. It contains most of the wheatgerm, but 15 per cent of the fibre (in the form of the bran that covers the wheat grain) has been removed.

As soon as a wheat grain is ground it begins to deteriorate nutritionally, so it is best not to keep wholewheat flour for longer than a month. After this time the oil contained in it may become rancid. Resist the temptation to buy in bulk if you do not think you will be able to use it up in time, and store in a cool, dry place.

Bread Whenever you can, buy wholewheat bread for all the family or make your own (page 104). This is made with wholewheat flour and so contains all the goodness and fibre of the wheat grain. Make sure that the wrapper actually states wholewheat or wholemeal: if it says simply 'brown' you may be buying a loaf made from coloured white flour. Wheatgerm breads are made from flour that has had most of the bran taken away and extra wheatgerm added. Granary bread is made from flour that has had some of the bran removed but has malted grains of wheat and rye added.

A stoneground loaf is made from flour that has been slowly ground between millstones. Other types are most probably made from roller-ground flour.

Wheatgerm The germ of the wheat, which takes up only a small part of the whole grain, contains all the vitamins and minerals. This can be separated into tiny, flaky brown particles known as wheatgerm. It can be added to bread mixes and sprinkled over cereals and fruit and some cooked dishes. It is highly nutritious and a little goes a long way.

Bran This must be one of the most talked about commodities in the past few years. It is the outer coating of the wheat grain and when separated from the rest forms flaky, brown particles, slightly larger than wheatgerm and coarser and drier. Bran provides insoluble dietary fibre which helps to prevent constipation. However, excessive sprinkling of bran over and into everything can inhibit the absorption by the body of certain minerals, particularly calcium, zinc and iron. The best way to get fibre in your diet is from wholegrains (wheat, oats, rice) and from fruits and vegetables.

Wholewheat semolina is produced by coarsely grinding the whole grains of a special hard type of wheat called durum wheat, also used to make pasta. It can be used to make puddings (pages 55 and 80–1) in exactly the same way as white semolina.

Wholewheat pasta There is a wide range of wholewheat pastas on the market and even some types of spinach pasta are made with wholewheat flour. It is just as easy to use as the white varieties and tastes delicious. Buckwheat pasta is made with a mixture of wholewheat and buckwheat flours. Some brands are 100 per cent buckwheat and these are suitable for a gluten-free diet.

Burghul wheat consists of wheat grains that have been soaked and then heated to such a high temperature that they crack, to produce tiny, translucent yellow grains. The grains make delicious salads and you don't even have to cook them: simply soak them in warm water for twenty minutes, then drain and squeeze dry.

Brown rice consists of rice grains that have not had their outer coating removed. The grains are a browny-green colour and have a nutty flavour when cooked. Brown rice takes longer to cook than white (40–45 minutes instead of 15–20), but you will probably have more success with it since the grains don't stick together.

Oats This cereal is rich in soluble dietary fibre. Most of the recipes in this book require porridge oats, which are easy to come by. Oats can also be bought in the form of jumbo oats, which are longer and are therefore good for muesli; varying grades of oatmeal; and oat groats, which are whole oat grains. They can be cooked exactly like rice.

Pot barley consists of whole barley grains, whereas the pearl barley that is most commonly used in stews has had the outer fibrous layer removed. Pot barley is used in exactly the same way as pearl barley.

Millet consists of tiny, yellow grains which cook to a fluffy texture with a light, bland flavour. It is a suitable early food for young children, and provides B vitamins, minerals and vegetable protein (page 20).

Cornmeal The ground kernels of sweetcorn produce cornmeal in the form of a coarse, yellow flour. It can be used in baking and features mainly in the gluten-free recipes.

Arrowroot is a fine powder produced from the root of a plant which grows mainly in the Caribbean. It is a useful thickening agent. I prefer it to cornflour since it has no flavour and gives thickened liquids a clear appearance and smooth texture.

Milk

Milk is often referred to as the perfect food; it provides large amounts of calcium plus other minerals, vitamins A and D and some B vitamins. If members of your family don't like it, or are allergic to dairy foods (pages 148–9), don't worry, the nutrients that it provides can be obtained from other foods. However, a glass of milk does provide a quick and easy daily intake of the essential nutrients, so makes a nourishing snack. Milk shakes (page 73) make good cold desserts.

Skimmed milk has had the cream skimmed off it to reduce its calorific value. However, the fat-soluble vitamins A and D are also removed with the cream, so skimmed milk is not a suitable food for young children, who need the calories anyway (pages 20–1), unless they are overweight.

Yoghurt is a more important food for a young child than milk. It contains the same nutrients as milk besides having other advantages. If a little is eaten every day, it can help the body to manufacture some B vitamins.

There are many different types of yoghurt on the market. Many children prefer the flavoured types, but these contain sugar and sometimes colourings and preservative. It is better to buy natural yoghurt and flavour it yourself (page 72).

If your family eats a lot of yoghurt, you may find it more economical to make it yourself. All you need is some milk and natural live yoghurt. Bring the milk gently to the boil and remove it from the heat when it begins to rise up the sides of the pan. Cool the milk to 45°C/113°F. (If you are using long-life or sterilized milk, simply bring it up to this temperature.) Put the yoghurt into a bowl, 1 tablespoon of yoghurt to every 575 ml (1 pint) of milk, and gradually mix in about 150 ml (5 fl oz) of the milk. Stir until the mixture is smooth and then stir in the remaining milk. Pour the mixture into a wide-necked vacuum flask, cover lightly and leave for 8–9 hours. Put the yoghurt into small pots and store them in the refrigerator. If you want thicker yoghurt, try adding 2 tablespoonfuls of skimmed milk powder to the mixture.

Cheese

It is unusual for a child to dislike all the different cheeses available. All cheeses are excellent sources of calcium, phosphorus, some B vitamins and vitamin A – of which the full-fat types contain the largest amount. Cheese is also high in protein.

Cheeses such as Cheddar, Cheshire and Double Gloucester are known as hard cheeses. Edam is also a hard cheese, but lower in fat. Store hard cheeses covered in the refrigerator: they should keep fresh for up to one month. If possible, bring them up to room temperature one hour before serving.

Cheeses such as Camembert and Brie are soft in texture and generally bland tasting. They may not sound like ideal baby foods, but when eaten fresh many young children love them.

Those cheeses classed as 'soft' – curd, cottage, quark – are usually medium or low fat and are ideal for mixing into baby foods. Avoid the use of full-fat cream cheese which will be far too rich for a baby. Cottage cheese is the lowest in fat, but some brands now contain preservative so you need to read the label before you buy it.

Fats and Oils

A small amount of fat in the diet is necessary (pages 20–1). Fats are classified according to their chemical make-up and have a different effect on our bodies. For example, saturated fats such as those found in many animal sources (butter, meat) are thought to have the effect of encouraging the production of higher levels of cholesterol in the blood. This has been associated with coronary heart disease. Polyunsaturated fats such as soya and sunflower oils can help to reduce the blood cholesterol level by discouraging the body from producing cholesterol. They contain the same number of calories as saturated fats.

Butter is made simply by churning cream and then perhaps adding a little salt: this makes it the most natural fat available. Provided that the diet you are giving your family is not too high in fat – you don't eat meat every day, you don't fry foods often and your diet has plenty of fibre – a little butter will do no harm.

Many people now prefer to use margarine. If this is your choice, buy a soft margarine that is made only from vegetable oils and is consequently high in the more desirable polyunsaturated fats.

My choice for cooking is a pure vegetable oil such as sunflower, which is high in polyunsaturated fats but has not been as heavily processed as margarine. It is quite possible to use oils for baking as well as frying,

softening and salad dressings. Keep oils in a cool, dark place and use them within three or four weeks if possible.

Eggs

These are a high-protein food. They contain vitamin A, most of the B vitamins and vitamin E, plus fats and important minerals. A lot of goodness is packed into a tiny egg shell and it is the perfect food for babies' appetites. It is digested slowly and will keep hunger away for some time. Keep eggs in a cool larder and use them within a week.

Sugar

I have avoided the use of refined sugar in the recipes in this book as I do not think it is necessary. In fact we don't need to add sugar to our diet at all. Sweetness can be obtained from the natural sugars present in, for example, fruit or nuts, ingredients which supply several nutrients at the same time. White sugar is almost pure carbohydrate, containing no other nutrients and no fibre. In order to digest it, valuable B vitamins are used up. Sugar is digested very quickly and the energy that it provides soon runs out, leaving a craving for yet more. Sugar in any form is also one of the main causes of tooth decay. Try to avoid buying any commercial products that list sugar as an ingredient. Commercial peanut butter, tomato ketchup, breakfast cereals and tinned baked beans – all favourites with children – have high levels of sugar and should be avoided in your child's diet.

If, however, you do choose to use sugar, buy the stronger-tasting types such as Barbados or Muscovado: you will find you use less to achieve sweetness and flavour.

Honey is made up of 75 per cent sugar, mainly in the form of fructose, and water. It is sweeter than sugar and you therefore need to use less of it; it also contains two-thirds of the calories of sugar.

Molasses The nutritious substances of the sugar cane that are thrown out during the manufacture of white sugar go to make up molasses. It contains ten different minerals and large amounts of B vitamins and, like honey, two-thirds of the calories of sugar. It has a strong flavour so few people can take more than one spoonful neat. Like honey, it is good blended with milk.

Sugar-free jam Technically there is no such thing as sugar-free jam. What I have described as 'sugar-free' is actually jam made without added sugar but which still contains natural sugars in the fruit juices and natural pectin that are used as setting agents. These sugars are just as harmful to teeth as refined sugar. However, 'sugar-free' jam is an invaluable product if you believe that children should not be given foods with added unnecessary sugar. It has a similar texture to ordinary jam and is an effective sweetening ingredient in recipes; you can buy it in most varieties, including marmalade.

When buying 'sugar-free' jam, look for labels that say 'no added sugar'; there are many jams on the market described as 'reduced' or 'low' sugar, but these offer no real advantage over ordinary jam. Many chemists and healthfood shops stock jams with no added sugar, but if you have difficulty you could write to the manufacturer for the nearest stockist.

Apple and pear spread (or pear and apple spread, as it is called when a higher proportion of pears is used) is made by concentrating the juices of apples and pears to make a thick, sticky, dark-brown syrup. It can be used as a spread on bread or as a sweetener for desserts and baked goods. It should be used sparingly.

Carob powder or flour is a cocoa substitute. It is a mid-brown colour, but once added to cake and pudding mixtures it will colour them very dark. Carob powder is produced from the pod of the carob tree. It contains protein, vitamins A and D, some B vitamins and important minerals. Unlike cocoa, it is naturally sweet and so will help you to cut down on other sweeteners in recipes. It also contains less fat and salt than cocoa, fewer calories and no caffeine.

Carob bars are similar to chocolate bars and are made from carob instead of cocoa. Some carob bars contain Barbados sugar; others have no added sugar. Flavoured bars are available.

—Fruit Juices and Drinks—

There is a wide variety of fruit juices on the market and they all make suitable drinks for children when diluted with water to reduce the sugar and acid content. Make sure that the label actually says 'juice': if it says 'fruit drink' then you are buying a product that has added sugar and possibly other additives, so read the labels.

Concentrated apple juice This is made by processing natural apple juice to remove a proportion of the water content. This leaves a sticky, dark-brown syrup which can be used as a sweetener in cooking or for drinking diluted with water. Mixed with hot water it makes a warming winter drink.

Vegetable juices If possible buy the natural tomato or tomato and vegetable juice made without any added ingredients except salt. It can be used as an appetizer drink or as the liquid ingredient in soups and stews. The type used in the recipes in this book is Campbell's V8.

Water I would always choose a natural mineral water for a baby or a young child in preference to tap water, since it does not contain added chemicals such as fluoride, lead and chlorine. However, it is wise to boil mineral water for young babies as some brands have a high sodium content. Tap water should always be boiled for babies under one year old. Water purifiers are now also available: information can be obtained from the organization listed on page 156. If you are worried about your child's fluoride intake, buy toothpaste with fluoride or fluoride tablets and ask your dentist's advice.

Herbs

Herbs provide flavour and valuable minerals, and introducing small amounts to your baby's food will accustom him to the flavours and ease the adaptation to adult food. Bombarding young and delicate taste buds, however, is not the way to introduce your baby to subtle flavours. Use small amounts of fresh herbs – they have a gentler flavour – and remove every trace of woody stem. Introduce just one or two tiny leaves at first. In most of the recipes I have given quantities for fresh herbs only, but you may sometimes find that dried herbs are all that is available; if that is the case, remember that drying concentrates the flavour of herbs and you should reduce the amounts you use by about three-quarters.

Salt

A very young child should not be given salt since the sodium it contains will put unnecessary strain on immature kidneys. Having a baby in the house may help all the family to become accustomed to less salt. If you use plenty of vegetables with some herbs in casserole-type dishes, you will find that you do not really need to add salt at all.

Salt, however, significantly improves the flavour of bread, scones and pastry. If possible, use a sea salt or natural rock salt that is free from chemical additives.

Spices

If your family eat spiced foods, don't isolate your baby from these flavours. From about ten to twelve months your baby should enjoy both the savoury and sweet spices in his food. The strong peppers – chilli and cayenne – should be avoided as they may inflame a baby's mouth and stomach even in tiny amounts, but as long as you introduce the flavours gently, your child will more quickly accept the family diet without complaint. You will soon know by his reaction if he likes it or if it upsets his digestion.

Stock

It is a good idea to keep a covered container of stock in the refrigerator at all times. Use it for cooking your baby's foods, casseroles and soups. You will be able to prepare a tiny meal quickly.

Kitchen Equipment

You need very little special kitchen equipment to prepare foods for babies and children. In the early stages, the

MEAT STOCK

giblets from one chicken, or
1 chicken portion, or
1 small piece beef marrowbone
1 onion
1 carrot
1 celery stick
1 teaspoon black peppercorns
bunch fresh herbs, or 2 teaspoons mixed
dried herbs

Halve but do not peel the onion. Split the carrot lengthways and break up the celery. Put the meat and vegetables into a large saucepan and set them on a low heat. Cook them gently in their own juices until they brown, turning several times. Pour in water to within 5 cm (2 in) of the top of the pan and add the peppercorns and herbs. Bring to the boil and simmer, uncovered, for 1½ hours. Cool. Strain and pour into a sealable plastic container. Store in the refrigerator for up to 1 week.

VEGETABLE STOCK

1 onion
2 carrots
2 celery sticks
any other vegetable trimmings such as
pieces of root vegetable or potato, outer
leaves of cabbages
2 teaspoons Vecon (a vegetable
concentrate: do not use until the baby is
about 12 months old)
1 teaspoon black peppercorns
bunch fresh herbs, or
2 teaspoons mixed dried herbs

Halve but do not peel the onion. Split the carrots lengthways and break up the celery. Put all the ingredients into a large saucepan. Pour in water to within 5 cm (2 in) of the top of the pan. Bring to the boil. Simmer, uncovered, for 1 hour. Cool, strain and store as for meat stock.

two invaluable gadgets are a baby food mill and a coffee grinder with small blender attachment. Baby food mills can be bought from babycare shops, kitchenware shops and hardware stores; the grinder/blender can be bought from any electrical supplier.

If you are lucky enough to have a microwave oven, it is ideal for cooking baby-sized portions of food at times when you are not cooking for the rest of the family. If you do not own a vegetable steamer, buy one now. Use it not only for the baby but for the whole family.

Labels

When buying foodstuffs that have been packed or processed commercially, always take a careful look at the labels. The ingredients are listed in order of concentration; so if sugar appears high on the list, beware! With commercial children's foods, don't buy anything that contains salt, sugar or chemicals. Reading labels is particularly important if a member of your family suffers from a food intolerance such as gluten sensitivity (page 149).

Some of the ingredients on the label may be in the form of an E serial number. These are classifications of colour, flavouring and preservatives. They are not all chemicals: companies that pride themselves on their natural ingredients will usually name the E ingredients, though they don't give quantities. For example, E 160 (B) is annatto, an orange-red dye from the pulp of a fruit. It is a common colouring in cheese and margarine.

THE ESSENTIAL NUTRIENTS

NUTRIENT

SOURCE

PROTEIN
The body needs protein for the growth and repair of tissue, but cannot store it. Animal sources of protein contain all the necessary amino acids in the correct proportions. Vegetable sources must be eaten in combination to give the same balance.

Meat, offal, fish, soya beans, yeast, wheatgerm, cheese and eggs are sources of complete protein. Pulses, seeds and nuts eaten in combination with grains such as wholewheat bread, pasta or oatmeal produce complete protein.

CALORIES
These are units of heat used to measure the energy value of food.

Found in all foods. Fats have calories in the highest concentration, fruit and vegetables in the lowest.

CARBOHYDRATES
These supply energy. There are good and bad sources. The bad sources are foods such as sugars (page 16), which are easily overeaten. The good sources are the unrefined grain products. The means of converting carbohydrates into energy and the time it takes depends on the carbohydrate. Refined sugar gets into the blood more quickly than whole grains, for example.

Cereals and cereal products, potatoes, sugar, milk, root vegetables, fresh and dried fruits, nuts and seeds.

FATS
Our bodies need traces of certain fatty acids to carry the fat-soluble vitamins around the body. These are found in animal and vegetable fats. Fats are the most concentrated form of calories, and they give flavour to food.

Butter, margarine, cream, milk, egg yolk, nuts and seeds, meat, cooking fats and oils.

VITAMINS
These are needed in small amounts to maintain good health. The fat-soluble vitamins (A, D, E and K) can be stored by the body, but the rest need to be taken daily in the diet.

A diet containing a wide range of foods will generally supply all the vitamins necessary for health.

VITAMIN A (retinol) helps to maintain the health and growth of bones, teeth and skin and to resist infection. Needed for the health of mucous membranes and for good vision.

Fish liver oils, butter, margarine, cheese, liver, milk, egg yolk, yellow vegetables and fruits, green leafy vegetables.

B VITAMINS help the body to convert carbohydrates into energy, to metabolize proteins and fats, and to maintain a healthy nervous system.

Found together in a wide range of foods in their natural state, except for B12 which is found only in animal sources. Folic acid is found in green leafy vegetables, liver and walnuts.

NEEDS DURING PREGNANCY

NEEDS FOR A BABY AND CHILD

Twice as much as in your non-pregnant state. Don't bother to calculate the protein intake; just become more aware of foods rich in protein and eat more of them.

Children need at least twice as much protein for their growing bodies. Protein also provides energy and warmth if calorie intake from carbohydrates and fats is not sufficient.

2300–2600 per day during pregnancy and when breastfeeding (page 27).

Your child will use vast amounts of energy growing, learning and playing and his needs will increase. At four years old he will need about 1600 calories per day. As long as the diet is not too full of concentrated calories such as fats and sugar, calorie intake will be satisfied by hunger.

Carbohydrates supply bulk in your diet as well as energy. The bowel tends to slow down during pregnancy so eat plenty of fresh fruit, vegetables and unrefined cereals to ensure a supply of dietary fibre and avoid constipation.

Unrefined carbohydrates help your child feel full after a meal, aid digestion, prevent constipation and save the body from burning proteins for energy.

Unwise to eat fatty meats and fried foods all the time. Use butter or margarine sparingly to prevent excess weight gain and choose polyunsaturated oils for salad dressings and cooking (page 16).

Better for all the family if fat intake is reduced. Enough fat for good health can be obtained from a balanced, normal diet.

If you are eating good food, vitamins will be provided without having to take supplements.

Certain vitamin supplements are recommended for babies and growing children (page 38).

Necessary for a healthy lining of the womb.

Even if your child doesn't like milk or carrots, he will get adequate supplies from other sources.

These are the most important during pregnancy. It is believed they may help in relieving nausea. Folic acid is vital for the growth of the fetus.

As cooking can destroy the B vitamins, raw foods in your child's diet can ensure a good supply.

NUTRIENT	SOURCE
VITAMIN C (ascorbic acid) is important for healing. It must be taken every day. Our needs for this vitamin vary; for example, at times of stress, infection or illness, it is used more rapidly. Needed for the efficient absorption of iron.	Fruit and vegetables, particularly citrus and berry fruits and watercress, potatoes and broccoli. Vitamin C can be destroyed by contact with air and overcooking.
VITAMIN D (calciferol) enables the body to make use of calcium and phosphorus and therefore is essential for health and the formation of bones and teeth.	Produced by the body and stored after exposure of the skin to sunlight. Not much needed. Also found in fish liver oils, eggs and margarine.
VITAMIN E protects membranes of body cells.	Oils, especially fish liver oils, nuts, seeds, wheatgerm, green leafy vegetables.
VITAMIN K aids in blood clotting.	Kelp, green leafy vegetables, yoghurt, peas, cauliflower and cereals.
CALCIUM Essential for healthy bones and teeth, and to maintain muscle tone.	Cheese, milk, yoghurt, fish with edible bones such as sardines and anchovies, watercress, figs, sesame seeds, sunflower seeds, lentils, haricot beans.
IRON Essential for the formation of red blood cells. It is stored in the liver, but a deficiency can cause anaemia when the muscles do not receive enough oxygen from the blood. Iron is fairly difficult for the body to absorb and needs vitamin C to help.	Liver, sardines, raisins, brewer's yeast, prunes, dried fruits, rice, nuts, carob. Cooking in iron pots increases the iron content of foods. Iron from supplements is not as readily available to the body as that taken from natural sources.
ZINC This is important in the healing process.	Wheatgerm, brewer's yeast, pumpkin and sunflower seeds, eggs, seafood.
PHOSPHORUS This is vital for healthy teeth and bones.	Present in nearly all foods.
IODINE This is necessary for the proper functioning of the thyroid gland.	Kelp, onions, seafood, iodized salt.
SODIUM Sodium is found in most vegetables and so we need not add it to our food. It is important to help maintain the balance of fluid in our bodies.	Salt, traces in seafood, and plants, depending on the soil they were grown in.

NEEDS DURING PREGNANCY

NEEDS FOR A BABY AND A CHILD

Essential to help the body make use of iron.	Must be taken daily.
As it helps the body to make use of calcium and phosphorus, it is essential for the baby in the womb too (see below). Supplements necessary for vegans and Asian women who live in wintry climates.	This vitamin can be easily made and stored by the body if your child plays in the sunlight. As there are only traces of vitamin D in breast milk, it is present in the vitamin supplements recommended for breastfed babies (page 38). Deficiency causes rickets, resulting in bone abnormalities.
Adequate supplies are thought to be important in establishing pregnancy and avoiding miscarriage.	Colostrum is rich in this vitamin and it may be important for premature babies.
Good supplies may help to prevent postpartum haemorrhage.	Antibiotics kill the bacteria that produces vitamin K in the intestine, so if your child has a course of antibiotics, increase sources of this vitamin.
Needs double during pregnancy – the body excretes calcium, the baby needs it and some is stored for lactation. Essential for the healthy bones and teeth of your baby and most important during the early months.	Vital for healthy bones and teeth. Milk and cheese are the best sources. If enough calcium is not provided at an early age the damage cannot be reversed; your child's teeth will suffer.
One of the most important nutrients. The demands of the placenta and your increased blood volume could result in anaemia if not enough iron is taken. The baby will take iron to store in its liver for after the birth and, provided the baby is born at term, these iron supplies should last six months. Iron supplements have not been found to have any benefit for healthy pregnant women and their babies.	No problem for babies born at term as they will have sufficient stores of iron in the liver. Iron-rich foods are essential from six months. If given with vitamin C, the iron will be more efficiently absorbed (page 38).
Without zinc, muscle contraction may not be as efficient.	Helps to avoid anaemia.
As for calcium.	If you monitor calcium intake, phosphorus will be supplied too.
Important for the health of your baby's hair, nails, skin and teeth.	The thyroid gland regulates growth and development, therefore iodine is important during your child's growing years.
More important during pregnancy than before. A certain amount helps to maintain healthy bone, brain and body tissue. Sodium is found naturally so there is no need to be heavy-handed with it.	None for children under two years. Restrict intake for children generally as sodium is present in so many foods, particularly processed foods.

CHAPTER TWO

EATING FOR TWO

Diet and Nutrition for the Pregnant and Nursing Mother

Pregnancy should be a happy and exciting
nine months that is not marred by ill-health, tiredness
or worry. Be positive and look on your pregnancy as a challenge
to provide the best possible health for you and your growing
baby. Diet takes on a special significance during pregnancy
and breastfeeding, so pay special attention to it.

Why do I need a good eating plan?
Think about what is happening to
you. As soon as you conceive, your
body is placed under considerable
stress and great changes take place
within it. In order to maintain and
support the pregnancy there is an
immediate change in hormonal
patterns and this has an effect on
your physical and emotional
condition. The volume of blood in
your body increases by almost half as
much again, and this puts additional
strain on your heart. In the womb, the
placenta develops to take over the life
support of the fetus. It is through the
placenta that nutrients cross from the
mother to the baby, and the baby
sends back waste products to the
mother. This places a higher than
normal strain on the liver and
kidneys.

All this adds up to hard work, and
for it to be carried out efficiently and
for your vital organs, bones and
muscles to be maintained in top
condition, fuel and nutrients are
required in greater amounts than in
your non-pregnant state. Therefore
you have to eat more good food. If
your body does not get enough fuel,
for example, it will not work to its full
potential and you may feel lethargic,
tired and irritable. You will also be
more prone to suffer from the minor
complaints of pregnancy (pages 28–9).

If you take care of yourself and
watch your diet, you will enjoy better
health, your baby will be given the
best possible environment in the
womb that you can provide, and you
may even be helping your emotional
state, enabling you to stay calm and
prepare yourself for the strains of
feeding and caring for a tiny baby.

Your specific dietary requirements
during pregnancy are given on pages
20–3. For advice on using diet to make
pregnancy a more comfortable time
for you, see pages 28–9.

**When should you and your partner
start a wholefood diet?**
If you are able to plan your
pregnancy, try to start your
wholefood eating plan as soon as you

decide that you would like to have a baby. Your body will then be better able to cope with the initial stresses of the pregnancy.

The nutritional state of the potential father has also to be considered. Although research is patchy as to how drugs and environmental factors may affect the male reproductive system, certain chemicals and drugs have been implicated in male infertility studies. Diet too might play its part in successful reproduction. If you are planning a baby, both would-be parents should change to a wholefood diet and this will help to lay a foundation for sensible eating habits for your family to imitate.

If you already have other children and are planning another, good nutrition prior to conception is even more important for you since your reserves may have run low through pregnancy and breastfeeding. If, however, you find that you have an unplanned pregnancy and have not so far paid special attention to your diet, don't worry; it is never too late to start. Your baby is growing and developing and will benefit from any extra nutrients that you can provide.

Substances to avoid
The placenta sends essential nutrients to the baby from the mother, but it is not an effective barrier against dangerous substances that may be in the mother's bloodstream. Many drugs, for example, can cross the placenta and harm the baby. Chemicals in food can also cross the placenta to the baby. If you drink more than six cups of tea or coffee a day, for example, you would be wise to cut down. Caffeine in coffee and tannic acid in tea, if taken in large

amounts, may harm the baby. Caffeine is also to be found in cola drinks, so avoid these too.

If you drink alcohol, whether you take small amounts regularly or have the occasional binge, this could harm the development of the fetus. There is no proven safe level of alcohol consumption during pregnancy, so if you are intending to become pregnant, giving up alcohol should be the first step you take. The baby's brain develops rapidly during the first weeks, often before you know you are pregnant.

Something not directly related to diet that must be mentioned here is smoking. Nicotine restricts the blood vessels in the placenta, preventing nutrients and oxygen from passing through to the baby. The level of carbon monoxide in a smoker's blood is higher and this also reduces the amount of oxygen carried in the blood to the baby. This may lead to prematurity, low birthweight, birth defects and later learning difficulties. Smoking may also curb your appetite. It is important that you try very hard to stop smoking before you conceive and particularly during pregnancy.

The body's needs during pregnancy
As soon as you become pregnant, you are eating for two. This doesn't mean double quantities of everything, but rather that you should consume enough protein, carbohydrate, fat, vitamins and minerals to keep your body and your baby healthy (pages 20–3). The amount of calories should also increase, but not as much as you might think. The healthy eating plan should be accompanied by gentle exercise, such as swimming, yoga or dancing; walking for twenty minutes a day is a good idea.

There are around fifty essential nutrients that the body cannot make itself, or not in sufficient quantities, so you must be more aware of what your diet contains. Your body needs to be fit as well as healthy for labour and childbirth.

Supplements
With all this good food around, is it necessary to take supplements at all if you are healthy and fit? Pregnancy is a special time when your body's needs increase, but if you are eating a healthy, well-balanced diet and are not allergic to certain key foods, you should not need to take any extra supplements. Some women are particularly vulnerable, however, and need supplements, but never take any without consulting your doctor first. The women in this group are those who suffer from food-related allergies, chronic ill health requiring constant medication, those who are underweight or have a multiple pregnancy, or women who have just finished feeding a child.

Vegetarians in pregnancy
You will have just as healthy a pregnancy if you are a vegetarian, though you should watch your intake of certain vitamins and minerals as well as making sure you get enough complete protein (pages 20–1). If you don't include dairy foods in your diet, you may need to consult your doctor about calcium supplements. Watch out for iron too: vegetables don't contain large amounts. The one supplement recommended for vegetarians is vitamin B12 (pages 20–1). It is only found naturally in any quantity in animal sources and its absence can lead to anaemia. Consult your doctor about this.

Putting on weight
You are inevitably going to put on weight during pregnancy, so don't be

vain and try to slim, it will only be to your detriment and to the baby's. The average weight gain of 11–13 kg (25–30 lb) will be made up of:

baby	3.4 kg (7½lb)
placenta	680 g (1½lb)
amniotic fluid	900 g (2 lb)
uterus	900 g (2 lb)
breasts	450 g (1 lb)
blood volume increase	1.82 kg (4 lb)
increase in body fluid	1.14 kg (2½lb)
fat stores in preparation	
for lactation	2.25–4.5 kg (5–10lb)

Medical staff in antenatal clinics can place a lot of emphasis on weight gain. This is worrying for pregnant women, so try to wear the same clothes at your regular check-up and don't eat a large meal before going to the clinic. Arbitrary weight gains are no longer rigidly adhered to. If you find that you have put on 11 kg (25 lb) plus by week 32, say, don't suddenly try to slim. Just make sure that the foods you are eating aren't too high in calories and are as nutritious as possible.

Maintaining the milk supply
If you decide to breastfeed your baby, attention to diet should not stop after the birth. For as long as you breastfeed, you will still have to eat enough nourishing food to maintain two people and to give yourself the strength and energy to cope with the baby's demands.

If you thought that the nutritional demands of pregnancy were great, then you might be surprised at the amount of energy you need to breastfeed your baby – 600–800 extra calories a day. Some of these calories are used in milk production, the others go into the breast milk itself. Your body will find some calories in the fat which was stored during

pregnancy, but the rest must come from nutritious foods, which should supply 2300–2600 calories per day.

Does your diet affect the quality of your milk?
Vitamins, minerals and protein will all be present in your breast milk, though if you are consuming insufficient calories the amount of milk produced could be reduced. This has been shown in research comparing the components in the breast milk of mothers in the rich and less well-nourished countries. The differences in nutrients were less significant, though the quantity was affected.

When should I eat?
When you are breastfeeding it is wise to eat whenever you are hungry. The increased calories should be distributed throughout the day so that you aren't exhausted by the evening. The additional requirements of your diet can easily be made up with snacks (pages 30–1). You will also find that you are thirstier than usual, so drink whenever you are thirsty. Fruit juices and mineral waters are the most thirst-quenching. Milk is nourishing and you can add flavourings such as fruit, molasses or honey to it.

Watching the baby's reactions
Eat your normal diet when breastfeeding – though certain harmless substances may, in rare instances, result in allergic reactions in your baby. Each baby's preferences are different so there is no list of foods which you must avoid. Just observe any differences in your baby. Consult your doctor if you are at all worried, but don't cut out good foods from your diet: you could do yourself more harm than good.

COPING WITH PROBLEMS IN PREGNANCY

There are many physical problems that can occur during pregnancy and you may suffer from one or more of them at some time. However, if you follow a healthy eating plan, keep yourself fit, pay attention to good posture and get plenty of rest, many of these problems may never occur at all. Some can be alleviated by attention to diet.

Anaemia

Anaemia due to iron or folic acid deficiency can develop in a pregnant woman, when her blood volume is increased by almost 50 per cent. The blood can't carry enough oxygen to the muscles resulting in tiredness, listlessness and irritability.

Increase iron-rich foods and vegetables in your diet; if your routine blood tests show that you are not anaemic, there should be no need to take iron supplements. Another type of anaemia is caused by folic acid deficiency (megaloblastic anaemia). This is found sometimes in pregnant women, so supplements of folic acid are often prescribed.

Constipation

High levels of the hormone progesterone cause the muscles to relax in preparation for childbirth. As a result the bowel may be more sluggish, leading to hard stools and constipation.

Provided you are eating whole grain cereals, you should have a rich source of fibre in your diet. It is not wise to add bran to foods to combat constipation since this could inhibit the absorption of some minerals. Drink plenty of liquids; natural yoghurt with every meal will help to soften your stools. Chemical laxatives should not be taken as they dehydrate body tissues and cause mineral deficiencies besides irritating the lining of the intestines. Some iron tablets can cause constipation.

Cramps

Muscles stiffen suddenly causing intense pain, most often in the thigh, calf and foot. The cramps are usually worse at night as your blood has pooled in slack blood vessels while you are asleep.

These may be cured by extra calcium, though it is not known why. Make sure that you are eating foods that contain this nutrient (pages 22–3). If you take a drink of hot milk, perhaps fortified with brewer's yeast or molasses, before going to sleep, this may help. In case of an attack, massage the muscle vigorously.

Flatulence

Certain foods, such as fried foods and pulses, encourage excessive wind. Because the intestine is sluggish during pregnancy, the wind may be difficult to expel, causing discomfort.

Avoid the foods that you find give you wind. If you're worried about your digestion generally, increase foods rich in vitamin B in your diet.

Haemorrhoids

These are varicose veins around the anus. If you strain with constipation, the veins swell and irritate the anal area. You may suffer from haemorrhoids after your baby is born because of the pressure on the back passage during childbirth.

Eat plenty of whole grains to increase fibre in your diet and prevent constipation. Don't strain when you open your bowels but don't delay should you feel like going. Keep the area clean to avoid irritation. Ice packs may help.

Heartburn

If small amounts of the acid contents of the stomach get into the oesophagus (the tube running from the mouth to the stomach), you will feel an intense burning in the lower chest. The condition is common in the last months of pregnancy when the enlarged uterus crowds out the stomach.

Heartburn and indigestion may result if you are tense while eating, so try to make meals a relaxed occasion. Cut out foods that make the condition worse and avoid eating large meals; instead eat little and often. Sleep in a more upright position so that the offending acids don't flow back into your oesophagus.

Nausea

Morning sickness, involving vomiting or just a feeling of nausea, can occur at any time of the day and, for some unfortunate women, throughout pregnancy. It is the most common problem of pregnancy, and may be caused by a massive increase in the hormones in your body as they establish the pregnancy. By week 12, the sickness usually subsides.

Low levels of blood sugar in the morning can make the nausea worse. It will probably help to drink a glass of milk or a fortified milk drink (page 35) or eat a piece of cheese and fruit before you go to bed. Have a hot drink and dry wholewheat toast before getting out of bed in the morning. Never let yourself get too hungry and eat plenty of high-protein foods. A diet high in protein will help to stabilize the blood sugar level. Your supplies of B vitamins, especially vitamin B6, can also be a factor in the severity of the nausea. Eat foods rich in these vitamins or if the sickness persists take a vitamin B6 supplement, but consult your doctor first. Tiredness makes the nausea worse, so get plenty of rest. Nibbling dried fruits or crackers may help to stop the feeling of nausea.

Oedema

The increase in body fluid can result in a pooling of this fluid in the ankles and hands. Rings become tight on your fingers and shoes may cut into your feet.

Watch your diet if you are gaining too much weight, and don't restrict your fluid intake. Rest with your feet up as much as possible.

Tiredness

The hormonal and physical changes in your body and the increase in weight that you have to carry result in fatigue and emotional upsets. Rest is essential during pregnancy.

Don't go without food for several hours at a time. Try to keep your blood sugar levels high by eating nutritional energy-giving foods such as whole grains. Don't rely on sugary foods to give you energy and rest often during the day as well as for at least eight hours at night. Intense tiredness could be the result of too little iron, leading to iron deficiency anaemia.

SPECIAL MUESLI BREAKFAST
E W Serves 1

2 prunes
4 dried whole apricots
25 g (1 oz) dates
25 g (1 oz) raisins
3 tablespoons jumbo oats
2 teaspoons sesame seeds
110 ml (4 fl oz) water, or unsweetened
orange or apple juice
fresh fruit such as 1 dessert apple,
or 1 small pear, or 1 orange,
or up to 50 g (2 oz) grapes
4 tablespoons natural yoghurt (optional)

Stone and chop the prunes. Chop the apricots and dates, and mix all the dried fruits with the oats and sesame seeds. Pour on the water or juice and leave to soak overnight.

The following morning, chop the unpeeled apple or pear; or peel the orange, leaving on some of the pith, and chop; or halve and seed the grapes. Mix them into the muesli and top with the yoghurt.

WHEATY FRUIT PORRIDGE
E Serves 1

2 dried whole apricots
1 dried fig
25 g (1 oz) porridge oats
2 tablespoons wheatgerm
225 ml (8 fl oz) water, or milk,
or milk and water mixed
4 tablespoons natural yoghurt
1 teaspoon honey

Finely chop the apricots and the fig, and mix with the porridge oats and wheatgerm. Put the water or milk into a saucepan and bring it to the boil. Scatter in the oat mixture. Cook, stirring, for 3 minutes, then take the pan from the heat and leave to stand for 5 minutes.

Mix the yoghurt with the honey and spoon the mixture over the porridge just before serving.

HERB CHEESE AND WALNUT OPEN SANDWICH
E Serves 1

1 large slice wholewheat bread
25 g (1 oz) herb-flavoured cream cheese,
such as Boursin
few sprigs watercress
1 tablespoon walnuts
1 celery stick

Spread the bread with the cheese. Chop the watercress if preferred, and press it on top. Chop the walnuts roughly and put them in the centre, then finely chop the celery and put it round the walnuts.

TUNA OPEN SANDWICH
D Serves 1

1 large slice wholewheat bread
$\frac{1}{2}$–1 × 100 g (3$\frac{1}{2}$ oz) tin tuna
2 tablespoons tinned sweetcorn
4 slices cucumber
2 teaspoons mayonnaise

Spread the tuna straight from the tin on the bread. Press the sweetcorn on top. Put a slice of cucumber in each corner of the sandwich, and the mayonnaise in the centre.

OPEN SANDWICHES · SNACKS

PEANUT AND AVOCADO OPEN SANDWICH
D E Serves 1

1 large slice wholewheat bread
1 tablespoon crunchy Peanut
Butter (page 120)
½ ripe avocado
1 tomato
2 teaspoons currants

Spread the bread with the peanut butter. Peel and mash the avocado and spread it over the peanut butter. Cut the tomato into four slices and arrange them on the bread with a pile of currants in the centre.

BANANA OPEN SANDWICH
E Serves 1

1 large slice wholewheat bread
butter
sugar-free jam,
or pear and apple spread,
or honey
1 banana
1 tablespoon sunflower seeds
2 teaspoons curd cheese, or cottage cheese

Lightly butter the bread. Spread it with the jam, spread or honey. Mash the banana, reserving 4 slices, and spread it over the bread. Scatter the sunflower seeds over the top, put a banana slice in each corner and the cheese in the centre.

WHEATGERM SODA BREAD
E

350 g (12 oz) wholewheat flour
50 g (2 oz) wheatgerm
½ teaspoon fine sea salt
75 g (3 oz) margarine
225 ml (8 fl oz) natural yoghurt, or
buttermilk, or sour milk, or fresh milk with
1 teaspoon cream of tartar dissolved in it
2 teaspoons molasses

Heat the oven to 200°C/400°F/Gas Mark 6. Put the flour, wheatgerm and salt into a bowl and rub in the margarine. Make a well in the centre and put in the yoghurt or other liquid and the molasses. Mix everything to a dough, turn it on to a floured board and knead until it is smooth. Form the dough into a flat round and put it on to a floured baking sheet. Bake the bread for 30 minutes or until it is firm and risen. Lift it on to a wire rack to cool.

This is a semi-sweet, moist bread which can be eaten plain or topped with sweet or savoury ingredients.

OAT CRUNCH
D E W

125 g (4 oz) jumbo oats
50 g (2 oz) sunflower seeds
25 g (1 oz) hazelnuts
25 g (1 oz) roughly chopped brazil nuts
4 tablespoons oil
1 tablespoon honey
50 g (2 oz) dried banana chips
50 g (2 oz) raisins

Heat the oven to 180°C/350°F/Gas Mark 4. Mix together the oats, sunflower seeds and nuts. Put the oil and honey into a saucepan and set over a low heat for the honey to melt. Mix into the oats and nuts. Line a baking sheet or Swiss roll tin with greaseproof paper and spread the mixture out on top. Put it into the oven for 20 minutes, stirring after each 5 minutes, until it becomes an even golden brown. Turn it into a bowl and leave to cool completely. Mix in the banana chips and raisins.

Store in an airtight container.

HEALTHY LUNCHTIME SALAD

D E G W Serves I

4–5 sprigs watercress
2 tomatoes
2 celery sticks
I spring onion
2.5 cm (I in) piece cucumber
I medium carrot
I very small beetroot
I tablespoon sunflower seeds

Dressing
I tablespoon tahini
2 tablespoons sunflower oil
small piece garlic
freshly ground black pepper
2 tablespoons cider vinegar

Chop the watercress, tomatoes, celery, onion and cucumber. Mix them in a bowl and grate in the carrot and beetroot.

Put the tahini into a small bowl and mix in the oil, crushed garlic and pepper. Add the vinegar and mix well: the dressing will be very thick. Mix it into the salad and scatter the sunflower seeds over the top.

Eat the salad straight from the bowl with fresh unbuttered wholewheat bread.

EGG AND AVOCADO SALAD

D G W Serves I

I ripe avocado
I egg, hard-boiled
I tablespoon mayonnaise
I tablespoon chopped parsley
I teaspoon chopped chives
4 lettuce leaves
4 sprigs watercress
handful of mustard and cress
½ small red pepper

Dressing
I tablespoon oil
2 teaspoons lemon juice
fine sea salt and freshly ground black pepper

Halve, stone and peel the avocado. Mash the egg with the mayonnaise and herbs. Fill the avocado halves with the egg mixture.

Make a bed of lettuce, watercress and mustard and cress on a plate. Cut the pepper into strips and arrange them round the edge. Beat together the oil, lemon juice and seasonings and sprinkle them over the salad. Put the avocado halves on top.

Instead of egg and mayonnaise, fill the avocado halves with a mixture of 3 tablespoons natural yoghurt and 1 tablespoon tahini, plus a little crushed garlic if wished. Scatter sunflower seeds or chopped nuts over the salad base.

COURGETTES AU GRATIN
E Serves 1

175 g (6 oz) small courgettes
15 g (½ oz) butter
1½ tablespoons wholewheat flour
150 ml (5 fl oz) milk
40 g (1½ oz) mature Cheddar cheese, grated
fine sea salt and freshly ground black pepper
2 tablespoons wheatgerm

Heat the oven to 200°C/400°F/Gas Mark 6. Cut the courgettes into 6 mm (¼ in) slices and put them into an ovenproof dish.

Melt the butter in a saucepan over a medium heat. Blend in the flour and cook it gently for 2–3 minutes, then gradually add the milk and bring to the boil, stirring continuously. Simmer the sauce for 1 minute. Take the pan from the heat, beat in about two-thirds of the cheese and season. Pour the sauce over the courgettes. Scatter half the wheatgerm over the top, then the remaining cheese and finally the rest of the wheatgerm. Bake the courgettes for about 30 minutes so the cheese sauce has risen and is browned on top.

Serve with a mixed salad.

YEASTY LENTIL SOUP
D E G W Serves 2 as a main meal, 4 as a light meal or snack

1 large onion
1 garlic clove
225 g (8 oz) carrots
3 tablespoons oil
75 g (3 oz) split red lentils
75 g (3 oz) brown rice
1 tablespoon brewer's yeast powder
2 teaspoons mild curry powder
1.15 litres (2 pints) stock
2 teaspoons yeast extract
1 bayleaf

Finely chop the onion, garlic and carrots and soften them in the oil over a low heat. Stir in the lentils, rice, brewer's yeast and curry powder. Cook them, stirring, for 2 minutes. Pour in the stock and bring it to the boil. Add the yeast extract and bayleaf, cover and simmer gently for 1 hour or until the lentils and rice are very soft. Remove the bayleaf before serving.

This makes a meal in itself which is easy to cook when you may not feel like coping with a large meal. Always try to follow it with a mixed salad. Any leftover soup can be served as a light meal or snack on the following day.

HERBED GRILLED MACKEREL
D E G W Serves 2

2 small to medium mackerel
2 tablespoons olive oil
juice ½ lemon
freshly ground black pepper
⅛ nutmeg, grated, or ¼ teaspoon
ground nutmeg
2 tablespoons chopped parsley
2 tablespoons chopped lemon thyme, or
ordinary thyme

Clean the mackerel or ask the fishmonger to do it for you. Cut off the heads and fins and trim the tails into V-shapes. Make 3 diagonal slits on each side, running backwards and downwards from head to tail.

Beat together the oil, lemon juice, pepper and nutmeg. Brush the mackerel inside and out with the mixture, getting it well into the slits. Mix the herbs together and stuff them into the slits. Leave the mackerel for 4 hours at room temperature.

When you are ready to cook, heat the grill to high, and if you have an open wire rack, cover it with foil. Lay the mackerel on the hot rack and grill them for about 4 minutes on each side, so the skin browns and they are cooked through.

LAMB'S LIVER WITH SPICED BREADCRUMB SAUCE

The crumbs used here help to make a light but thick spicy sauce for the liver.
D E Serves 2

350 g (12 oz) lamb's liver
1 medium onion
1 garlic clove
3 tablespoons oil
2 tablespoons sherry vinegar,
or white wine vinegar
2 tablespoons Worcestershire sauce
1 tablespoon tomato purée
25 g (1 oz) fresh wholewheat breadcrumbs
1 teaspoon chopped rosemary
1 tablespoon chopped thyme

Cut the liver into small, very thin slices. Finely chop the onion and garlic and soften them in the oil over a low heat. Meanwhile, mix the vinegar, Worcestershire sauce and tomato purée together. When the onions are done, put the breadcrumbs into the pan and move them around until they are brown. Pour in the vinegar mixture and bring to the boil, then add the slices of liver and the herbs. Turn them in the sauce and cook gently for 10 minutes.

Serve with brown rice or jacket potatoes.

SUPERCHARGED MILKSHAKE
E G W

425 ml (15 fl oz) milk
2 tablespoons skimmed milk powder
2 teaspoons dried brewer's yeast
few drops vanilla essence
1 tablespoon sunflower oil
one of the following:
1 banana
75 g (3 oz) strawberries or any soft fruit
1 thick slice fresh pineapple
2 slices pineapple tinned in natural juice
4 tablespoons undiluted frozen orange juice

Put all the ingredients into a blender or food processor and work until well blended and frothy. Keep the drink in the refrigerator and sip it at regular intervals throughout the day, stirring before you do so to distribute the yeast powder evenly.

APRICOT AND APPLE WHIP
E G W

4 dried whole apricots
6 dried apple rings
150 ml (5 fl oz) milk
150 ml (5 fl oz) natural yoghurt
1 tablespoon tahini

Soak and drain the fruits. Work them to a rough purée in a blender or food processor, then add the milk, yoghurt and tahini and blend again until the mixture becomes smooth.

ORANGE, LEMON AND BANANA DRINK
D E G W

225 ml (8 fl oz) unsweetened orange juice
juice ½ lemon
½ banana
1 teaspoon honey

Put all the ingredients into a blender or food processor and work until you have a frothy liquid.

FRUIT AND ALMOND WHIP
E G W

150 ml (5 fl oz) natural yoghurt
150 ml (5 fl oz) milk
50 g (2 oz) fresh soft fruits,
or any fruit tinned in natural juice
2 tablespoons ground almonds

Put all the ingredients into a blender or food processor and work them until you have a thick frothy liquid. Honey to taste can be added if wished.

PINEAPPLE CRUSH
D E G W

1 thick slice fresh pineapple, cored,
or 2 slices pineapple tinned in natural juice
150 ml (5 fl oz) unsweetened orange juice
150 ml (5 fl oz) unsweetened pineapple juice
100 ml (3½ fl oz) sparkling mineral water

Chop the pineapple. Put it into a blender or food processor with the juices and mineral water and work to a frothy liquid.

CHAPTER THREE

FIRST FOODS
Weaning the Six to Eight-Month-Old Baby

The solid foods that you first
give to your baby will be the raw materials
from which she has to grow, and the more nutritious
they are the better are her chances of a normal, happy
development and of resisting infection. Many babies are quite
happy with the breast or bottle for the first six months of life;
others, who grow faster or are just hungrier, may be ready for
other foods by four and a half months. A baby's digestive
system is not able to cope with foods other than breast
milk or specially processed cow's milk, so don't be
tempted to introduce solid foods before four
months unless your doctor advises.

First drinks
Breast or formula milk is made up of
a large proportion of water, but some
babies are thirstier than others,
particularly during hot weather. After
about six weeks you can give a thirsty
baby cooled, boiled water from a
teaspoon – just enough to refresh her
mouth. From about three months you
can give freshly squeezed and strained
orange juice, diluted with boiled,
cooled water. Don't introduce your
baby to sweet blackcurrant or sugar-
based drinks.

First tastes
Any solid foods you give to your baby
at first should only be for taste and
getting her used to new textures and
flavours. They should not replace any
of the milk feeds. The milk provides
the essential fluids and nutrients and
too much solid food may deplete her
desire for milk.

When and how to wean
You know your baby best. Choose a
time of day either when your family
would normally be in the kitchen

eating or preparing food, or, if this proves too distracting, when you are alone together and relaxed. If she is introduced to food tastes at the same time as the rest of the household, she will begin to feel that eating is a pleasant social occasion and food is associated with fun and company. If the taste of solid food is offered directly after the milk feed, she may be too sleepy. If it is offered before, she may be too hungry. So offer these first tastes in between milk feeds when she's happy and contented.

Introduce the food on a tiny spoon (salt or mustard size) and put it just between her lips. She should instinctively suck the food off the spoon. If she spits it out, grimaces or cries, try not to get angry and frustrated. She might not like the taste, she may not feel like more food or she may not be ready yet. Try again a few days later.

Special equipment
While your baby is young her food must be sieved. You can use an ordinary nylon sieve or a baby food mill, which is less time consuming. It is not sufficient to blend a tiny baby's

first solids in a blender or food processor without also sieving it. Babies cannot chew their food yet and they will not be able to digest lumps, skin or pips.

At this early stage, bibs and wipers are essential. Perhaps the only dish needed is something as small as a ramekin or even an egg cup. As long as you keep the baby's feeding equipment clean and put away, there should be no need to sterilize it after the baby is six months old.

How to introduce new foods
Remember that the eating experience is a totally new one for your baby, so try not to overwhelm her. She is used to bland-tasting food, so she must have time to learn and to develop her taste buds. For the first days, just feed her a teaspoonful of one food at a time. If your family has a history of allergy (pages 148–9) or if your baby

has shown some signs of allergy, for example if she has had infantile eczema, seek your doctor's advice before you begin mixed feeding.

Which foods first?

First foods should be nutritious without supplying too many calories or your baby might become overweight – what used to be regarded as a charming 'chubby' baby. Avoid cereals, except for rice, until mixed feeding is established; concentrate instead on introducing a wide range of fruit and vegetables and the lean iron-rich foods such as liver. The ideal first tastes are sweet fruits that are easy to prepare in tiny amounts – mashed banana, puréed apple and ripe pears. If you think the taste is sharp, don't be tempted to sweeten; though if they taste acidic even to you, don't give them to your baby. Vegetables such as sieved tomato and avocado are also easy to prepare and perfect for a baby's palate. Wait until some sort of mealtime is established before you introduce combinations of foods.

By about eight months, you may want to phase out all breastfeeds, particularly if you are going back to work. You can wean your baby on to formula milk, but as long as she is getting plenty of nutritious foods and liquids, there is no need for a baby to continue having milk every day. Introduce yoghurt at around eight months, or goat's milk, which is more easily digested than cow's milk, at around ten months. It is generally believed that doorstep cow's milk should not be given to a baby under twelve months. The protein in cow's milk is difficult for a young baby's immature digestive system to cope with and an allergic reaction may result (page 148). Specially formulated soya milk is a more easily digested

substitute for cow's milk.

If you do give your baby doorstep cow's milk, you should boil it and simmer for ten minutes, then leave it to cool. This modifies the protein in the milk.

When preparing cooked meals for your baby, remember to use no salt, sugar, chemicals of any sort (for example, stock cubes contain salt and sometimes monosodium glutamate), or fruit with pips which have not been sieved.

Introducing the nutrients

From about one month your doctor may advise you to give your baby vitamin drops, particularly if you are breastfeeding. Formula milk has all the necessary vitamins added.

By six months, the reserves of iron built up in the baby's liver during pregnancy will have been depleted. If your baby was premature or if you were anaemic during pregnancy, you will have been advised to introduce iron to your baby earlier. Egg yolk is an ideal source of iron, but leave out the egg white until about eight months in case of an allergic reaction. Good iron absorption is aided by vitamin C, so orange juice and cooked egg yolk is a good combination for a baby's meal from about eight months.

Are commercial baby foods necessary?

As soon as your baby is having small mixed meals several times a day you may wonder whether bought baby foods are a good idea. There are many excellent brands on the market at the moment, though they are expensive. No food is as nutritious, however, as freshly prepared food. The processing and reheating of baby foods, no matter how good the ingredients, will inevitably destroy vitamins. Also, freshly prepared foods tend to taste different and if you want your baby to prefer the fresh, natural flavours of wholefoods, it is best to start her off on the right lines.

Should you need to use commercial baby foods, read the labels before you buy. Make sure that whatever you choose contains no salt or sugar and that the proportion of cereal is not higher than that of the other ingredients (page 19).

Phasing out milk feeds
The weaning process depends very much on individual circumstances. If you are breastfeeding and are returning to work when your baby is six months old, you will want to wean her on to drinks from a cup and solid foods, and perhaps feed her yourself morning and night. If you have the opportunity to wean more slowly, you can let the baby and your inclinations guide you. By about seven months, your baby should have dropped at least one breast or bottle feed entirely and be taking solid food and water or juice at that time. The other two family meals may still be organized around a breast or bottle feed, depending on your daily routine and whether your baby is prepared to give up the breast. If she is tired, ill or fretful, you can forget the solid food for that particular day and offer just milk. This is not a step backwards, it is simply a part of the gradual process of weaning.

By eight months your baby should be ready for three small meals a day. Her appetite will probably not be the same every day, but as it increases gradually give her larger amounts. Give her a meal first and while you

FRUIT PREPARATION AND SERVING

Fruit	Age to Introduce	Type	Preparation
Apple, dessert	4½–6 months	Small and sweet	Core, put into ovenproof dish with water, bake in hot oven 20 minutes, peel, sieve
Apricot	4½–6 months	Very ripe	Skin, stone and sieve
Banana	4½–6 months	Ripe and speckly	Sieve
Blackberries	6 months	Ripe and soft	Sieve
Kiwi fruits	6 months	Ripe and soft	Skin and sieve
Mango	5–6 months	Ripe and soft	Sieve flesh only
Melon	6 months	Cantaloupe, ripe and soft	Sieve
Pear	4½–6 months	Ripe and soft	Skin, core and sieve
Raspberries	6 months	Sweet and soft	Sieve
Strawberries	6 months	Ripe, not overripe	Sieve

VEGETABLE PREPARATION AND SERVING

Vegetable	Age to Introduce	Preparation
Artichoke, Jerusalem	7–8 months	Peel, slice, steam 20 minutes or until soft, sieve
Aubergine	7–8 months	Slice, steam 25 minutes, sieve without peel
Avocado	6–7 months	Peel, stone, sieve or mash, serve raw
Beans, broad	5–6 months	Steam 15 minutes or until soft, skin, sieve
Beans, green	5–6 months	Steam 20–30 minutes or until soft, sieve
Beetroot	5–6 months	Boil whole 40 minutes or until soft, skin, sieve
Brussels sprouts	6–7 months	Steam whole 20 minutes, sieve
Cabbage	6 months	Shred, steam 20 minutes, sieve
Cauliflower	5–6 months	Chop, steam 20 minutes, sieve
Carrots	5–6 months	Slice, steam 25 minutes, sieve
Celery	5–6 months	Chop, steam 30 minutes, sieve
Courgettes	5–6 months	Wash, thinly slice, steam 15 minutes, sieve with skin
Cucumber	6–7 months	Peel, remove seeds, chop, sieve raw
Curly kale	6–7 months	Remove stems, boil 20 minutes, sieve
Leeks	6–7 months	Slice, wash well, steam 20 minutes, sieve
Marrow	6–7 months	Peel, remove seeds, cut into chunks, steam 15 minutes, sieve
Mushrooms	8 months	Use buttons, thinly slice, steam 15 minutes, sieve
Peas, fresh	5–6 months	Steam 20 minutes or boil 15 minutes, sieve
Peppers, red and green	7–8 months	Core, seed, slice or chop, steam 15 minutes, sieve
Potatoes	5–6 months	Scrub, slice, steam 20 minutes, skin, sieve
Spinach	5–6 months	Remove stems, chop leaves, steam 15 minutes, sieve
Spring greens	6–7 months	Remove stems, chop leaves, steam 20 minutes, sieve
Swede	7–8 months	Peel, chop, steam 20–25 minutes, sieve
Tomato	6 months	Scald, skin, deseed, sieve

COOKING VEGETABLES

Steaming preserves more goodness than boiling, so try to use this method whenever possible. First, prepare the vegetables and put them into a steamer. Bring some water to the boil in a saucepan. There must not be so much that the water will bubble through the holes of the steamer once it is boiling. Lower in the steamer and vegetables, turn down the heat and cover the pan. Cook the vegetables until they are tender enough to be put through a sieve or baby food mill, but are not so soft that their flavour is impaired and all their goodness has gone.

Once the vegetables have been put through a sieve or food mill, they will probably have cooled down considerably. If they are still too hot, wait before giving them to the baby.

and the family eat your own meal, she can be sucking on finger foods – such as sticks of carrot or celery – though if she already has teeth, watch her carefully in case she bites off a chunk and chokes.

Introducing cereals

From about six and a half months, depending on when you first gave your baby vegetables and fruits, the first baby cereals can be introduced. There are many different types on the market. The first priority is to choose one that does not contain salt or sugar-related substances. Secondly, it should be made up of mixed cereals. If wheat is given before a baby is four months old, you could in extreme circumstances cause a gluten allergy which will be a problem in years to come (page 149). Adult cereals are not suitable until your baby is eight or nine months old; even then, avoid those with added sugar or salt.

Make up cereals with boiled water or boiled mineral water (page 18). They will probably taste bland to you, but don't be tempted to add sweeteners or salt. Porridge, again made up with water, is also suitable. Make up a small amount and sieve it before offering it to your baby.

Vary the food that you give your baby every day. The wider the range of foods, the wider the range of vitamins and minerals she will be getting, and this is more and more important as she begins to rely on solid foods and less on milk feeds. Here are some suggestions:

Breakfast
Puréed baked apple with cereal
or
Puréed dried fruits with porridge
or
Sieved soft fruits with porridge
or
Mashed banana

Lunch
Mixed vegetable purée with a protein food such as egg yolk or white beans
or
Soup with cheese added

Sieved fresh fruits

Dinner
Cereal food, either sweet or savoury, provided cereal was not eaten at breakfast
or
Soup
or
Fruit puréed with soft cheese
(if cheese was not eaten at lunch).

VEGETABLE DISHES

RAW VEGETABLE PURÉES
D E G W

Try these from six months onwards:

Tomato and Cucumber Scald, skin and seed one small ripe tomato. Remove the skin and seeds from a 6 mm ($\frac{1}{4}$ in) thick slice cucumber. Finely chop them both and work them in a blender or food processor.

Tomato and Celery Scald, skin and seed one small ripe tomato. Chop it finely with a 5 cm (2 in) piece celery. Work the tomato and celery in a blender or food processor and then put through a baby food mill.

Celery and Cucumber Finely chop a 5 cm (2 in) piece celery. Remove the skin and seeds from a 6 mm ($\frac{1}{4}$ in) thick slice cucumber, and finely chop it. Put through a blender or food processor, then sieve.

Tomato and Carrot Scald, skin, seed and chop one small ripe tomato. Grate a 2.5 cm (1 in) cube of carrot. Put both through a blender or food processor, then sieve.

EGG AND VEGETABLES
D G W Serves 1

1 hard-boiled egg yolk
1 small potato
one of the following:
6 spinach or Swiss chard leaves
1 leek
1 small courgette
1 leaf curly kale
1 leaf spring greens
1 small parsnip
2 tablespoons fresh peas
2 tablespoons young broad beans

Scrub and halve the potato. Chop or slice the other vegetable. Put them into a vegetable steamer, lower over simmering water, cover and steam for 20 minutes or until tender. Skin the potato. Put the vegetables and egg yolk through a baby food mill. If the mixture is too stiff it can be moistened with a small amount of very weak gravy or stock (page 19).

AVOCADO WITH CASHEW NUTS
E G W Serves 1

$\frac{1}{2}$ ripe avocado
15 g ($\frac{1}{2}$ oz) cashew nuts
juice $\frac{1}{2}$ small orange
1 tablespoon natural yoghurt

Sieve or mash the avocado. Grind the nuts very finely, making sure that there are no large pieces left. Mix them with the avocado, orange juice and yoghurt.

WATERCRESS AND POTATO SOUP
D E G W Serves 1

1 small potato
1 small slice onion
4–5 sprigs watercress
225 ml (8 fl oz) stock (page 19), or water
1 tablespoon chopped parsley

Peel and chop the potato. Chop the onion. Remove the leaves from the watercress and chop them. Bring the stock to the boil in a saucepan and put in the potato, onion, watercress and parsley. Cover and simmer for 20 minutes. Put the soup through a baby food mill. Reheat very slightly if necessary.

TOMATO AND CARROT SOUP
D E Serves 1

2 small ripe tomatoes
1 small carrot
$\frac{1}{4}$ small onion
150 ml (5 fl oz) stock (page 19), or water
2 teaspoons sugar-free baby cereal

Scald, skin and finely chop the tomatoes. Finely chop the carrot and onion. Put them into a saucepan with the stock, bring to the boil and simmer for 15 minutes or until the carrots are soft. Sprinkle in the cereal and stir until the soup thickens. Put the soup through a baby food mill.

VEGETABLE · FRUIT DISHES

POTATO AND LEEK SOUP
D E G W Serves I

I small potato
50 g (2 oz) leek
225 ml (8 fl oz) stock (page 19), or water
I tablespoon chopped parsley

Peel and chop the potato and chop the leek. Put them in a saucepan with the stock, bring to the boil and simmer for 20 minutes. Add the parsley and put the soup through a baby food mill.

CAULIFLOWER SOUP
E G W Serves I

2 medium cauliflower florettes
I small slice onion
5 cm (2 in) piece celery
225 ml (8 fl oz) stock (page 19), or water
I tablespoon chopped parsley
I teaspoon low fat soft cheese (optional)

Chop the cauliflower, onion and celery and put them into a saucepan with the stock. Bring to the boil and simmer for 15 minutes. Add the parsley and the cheese if using, and put the soup through a baby food mill.

BUTTERBEAN MASH
D E G W Serves I

I small potato
I small carrot
½ celery stick
I slice onion
6 cooked butterbeans (page 19), plus
about 2 tablespoons of the cooking liquid
I teaspoon chopped parsley

Scrub the potato and cut it in half. Slice the carrot and chop the celery. Put them all into a vegetable steamer with the onion, lower over simmering water and steam for 20 minutes or until tender. Skin the potato. Put the vegetables through a baby food mill with the beans and parsley. Moisten with the butterbean cooking liquid if necessary.

BANANA WITH APPLE AND ORANGE
D E G W Serves I

½ banana
¼ small sweet dessert apple
juice ½ small orange

Mash the banana and finely grate the apple. Sieve them together. Mix in the orange juice.

PURÉED FRUITS

Tinned blackcurrants or blackberries in apple juice, and peaches in grape or peach juice can be used instead of fresh fruits to mix with cereal or bananas and yoghurt. Drain them and put through a baby food mill, adding a little of the juice to thin the purée down slightly if wished. Any remaining juice can be diluted with mineral water or cooled boiled water and used as a drink.

BANANA, PEAR AND YOGHURT
E G W Serves I

½ banana
¼ ripe pear
I tablespoon natural yoghurt

Mash the banana. Peel, core and mash the piece of pear. Mix them together and sieve them, then mix in the yoghurt.

CHEESE · CEREAL DISHES

CAULIFLOWER AND POTATO CHEESE
E G M Serves 1

3 cauliflower florettes
1 small potato
¼ small onion, or small piece leek
1 parsley sprig
25 g (1 oz) curd cheese,
or other low fat soft cheese

Scrub and halve the potato, and slice the onion or leek thinly. Put the vegetables and parsley sprig into a steamer, lower over simmering water, cover and steam for 20 minutes or until tender. Skin the potato. Put the vegetables through a sieve or baby food mill, then mix in the cheese.

Other Vegetable Cheeses
Use one of the following instead of the cauliflower:
● 1 small carrot
● 1 small parsnip
● 1 leaf curly kale
● 15 g (½ oz) spinach or Swiss chard leaves
● 3 small broccoli spears
● 1 small courgette
● 1 celery stick
● 2 tablespoons fresh peas, or young broad beans.

AVOCADO AND CHEESE
E G M Serves 1

½ ripe avocado
25 g (1 oz) curd cheese,
or other low fat soft cheese
juice ½ small orange

Sieve or mash the avocado. Mix it with the cheese and orange juice.

CARROT AND CHEESE SOUP
E G M Serves 1

1 small carrot
¼ small onion
tiny piece garlic (optional)
150 ml (5 fl oz) stock (page 19), or water
1 teaspoon curd cheese,
or other low fat soft cheese
150 ml (5 fl oz) milk

Finely chop the carrot, onion and garlic if using, and put them with the stock into a saucepan. Bring to the boil, cover and simmer for 20 minutes or until the carrot is tender and the stock has reduced by about three-quarters. Put the contents of the pan into a blender or food processor and work until you have a smooth purée. Add the cheese and blend again, adding as much milk as is necessary to make a thick soup. Blend again. Reheat the soup if necessary before serving – it should be just warm.

VEGETABLE OATIE
D E M Serves 1

small piece celery
½ small carrot
1 slice onion
15 g (½ oz) green cabbage,
or broccoli, or spinach
110 ml (4 fl oz) stock (page 19), or mineral
or tap water
1 teaspoon chopped parsley
1 tablespoon porridge oats

Finely chop the vegetables. Put the water into a saucepan, bring to the boil and put in the vegetables, parsley and oats. Cover and simmer for 15 minutes or until the vegetables are tender. Put everything through a baby food mill.

CEREAL DISHES

BABY CEREAL WITH APPLE
E Serves I

I small dessert apple
mineral or tap water
3 teaspoons baby cereal
6 tablespoons unsweetened apple juice
2 teaspoons natural yoghurt

Heat the oven to 200°C/400°F/Gas Mark 6. Core the apple and score it round with a sharp knife. Put it into an ovenproof dish and add water to come halfway up the side. Put it into the oven for 20 minutes or until the apple is soft. Skin it and put the flesh through a sieve or baby food mill.

Put the cereal into a bowl. Bring the apple juice or cooking water to the boil and mix it into the cereal to the required consistency. Mix in the sieved apple and the yoghurt.

BABY CEREAL AND VEGETABLES
D E Serves I

25 g (I oz) leek or ¼ small onion
110 ml (4 fl oz) stock (page 19), or water
2 tablespoons sugar-free baby cereal
25 g (I oz) *one of the following:*
green cabbage
broccoli
spring greens
spinach or Swiss chard
curly kale
courgette
fresh peas
broad beans

Finely chop the vegetables. Bring the stock to the boil in a small saucepan, put in the vegetables, cover and simmer for 15 minutes. Sprinkle in the cereal and stir until the mixture thickens. Take the pan from the heat. Put the vegetables and cereal through a baby food mill.

BABY CEREAL WITH RAISINS
E Serves I

10 raisins
110 ml (4 fl oz) mineral or tap water
3 teaspoons baby cereal
¼ teaspoon tahini (optional)
2 teaspoons natural yoghurt

Put the raisins into a saucepan with the water. Bring them to the boil and simmer for 3 minutes, then drain, reserving the water. Put the cereal into a bowl and mix in the water, tahini and yoghurt. Sieve the raisins or put them through a baby food mill, and add them to the cereal.

BABY CEREAL WITH EXOTIC FRUIT
E Serves I

3 teaspoons baby cereal
3 tablespoons boiling water
I ripe kiwi fruit, or ½ ripe mango,
or ½ soft peach
2 teaspoons natural yoghurt

Mix the cereal with the boiling water to the required consistency. Peel and sieve the fruit. Mix it with the cereal and mix in the yoghurt.

BABY CEREAL WITH PRUNES
E Serves I

2 prunes
110 ml (4 fl oz) mineral or tap water
3 teaspoons baby cereal
juice ½ small orange
2 teaspoons natural yoghurt

Put the prunes and water in a saucepan and leave to soak for 2 hours. Bring them to the boil, cover and simmer for 20 minutes or until they are tender. Drain, and mix the hot water into the cereal until it is the required consistency. Rub the prunes through a sieve and add them to the cereal with the juice and yoghurt.

Four dried whole apricots can be used instead of prunes, but they will need to be puréed in a baby food mill.

CHAPTER FOUR

TOWARDS A COMPLETE DIET

Foods for Children up to Eighteen Months Old

By the time your baby is eight months old, he will be partly relying on the solid food that you give him for growth and energy. His digestive system is becoming more sophisticated and by one year his growth rate has slowed down. He should, as far as possible, be eating at the same time as the rest of the family. As he matures, he will start to imitate you and try to feed himself. Teeth will appear during this time too and so the consistency of his food can change.

Fitting in with the family

If all the family are eating their main meal together and the food is plainly cooked without additional fat, rich sauces or strong spices, there is no reason why your baby cannot eat the family's food from eight months. Cook without salt and if you are thickening sauces or adding butter to dishes, take the baby's portion out first.

You will find that your baby will more quickly learn to feed himself if you leave a spoon by his plate for him to use as and when he wants to, and if you allow him to put his fingers in his food. You will still need to feed him yourself until at least one year, but fingers will find their way into food for a long time after that. Don't worry; he is learning about the texture of food as well as experiencing the taste.

From about nine months onwards, with the arrival of teeth, foods can be mashed rather than sieved or blended. One food at a time can be diced finely and either mixed into the purées or left on the plate so that he can pick it up in his fingers and begin to chew. Don't change textures all at once. Keep the other foods in the familiar mashed state so that only one new texture appears on the plate at a time.

Finger foods

As soon as your baby is able to pick up small objects with his finger and thumb he is ready to start eating with his fingers. Try pieces of ripe fruits, small pieces of cheese, slices of raw vegetables, wholewheat bread 'soldiers', oatcakes, plain wholewheat crispbreads and puffed rice cakes.

All these can be given as part of a main meal or as snacks between meals. Finger foods are not, however, a major part of your baby's nutritional intake. Most of them are spat out and end up on the floor or in the bib. Always make sure that your baby is in his high chair when eating and always stay in the room with him.

What should he have to drink?

Milk should be treated more as a food than as a drink (page 48). To quench your baby's thirst choose water or natural fruit juices diluted with cooled boiled water.

If your baby has been bottlefed, save the bottle for the night and morning milk feeds. If you have breastfed your baby and are still doing so, there is no need for you ever to use a bottle. From the age of six months, encourage your baby to drink from a cup. Whichever design of cup you use, guide it into your baby's mouth so that he understands how far to tip it to get the drink.

What if the food is rejected?

Food is rejected at this time for the same reasons as when your baby was younger: he may not like it or fancy it today, he may not be hungry, or he may be teething or ill. There is still no need to scold, wheedle or coax. Take the food away and offer something else. Make it simple so you don't have to give yourself extra work. Fingers of cheese or wholewheat bread will do quite well. Your attitude to the rejection is also important. You will be upset in proportion to the amount of effort you have put into preparing the food or by how important you feel this food is in your child's diet. There are always alternative sources of vital nutrients and you can reintroduce the rejected food days or weeks later.

If you offer a wide range of foods, your baby is less likely to develop fads. Try to vary foods from meal to meal and from day to day. It does not matter if for one day he pushes away all savoury foods and only eats the sweet. If the meal is missed completely, don't worry or make an issue of it. Just try again next time. One missed meal will do no harm. If he is just playing up, he will be hungrier than ever at the next mealtime. If there is something wrong, you will soon notice other signs of illness and can call the doctor.

SUITABLE FOODS FOR CHILDREN OVER EIGHT MONTHS OLD

Fresh Fruit and Vegetables

All the fruits and vegetables that are recommended for giving to the younger baby (pages 38–41) are suitable for the older child. They need no longer be sieved but can be puréed in a blender or food processor or simply mashed. Aim to vary both the textures and the types of fruit and vegetables that you give your child. Introduce a small salad meal on some days and continue to provide raw fruits.

Pulses

White beans, split peas and lentils are still the best pulse foods. Cook them thoroughly (page 12) and sieve them up to about ten months. After this they can be mashed.

Dried Fruits

All types of dried fruits can be soaked and cooked, or cooked with fresh fruits as a substitute for sugar. From one year they can be eaten as snack foods, though any stones must be removed first.

Nuts and Seeds

These are not safe for small children in their natural form. Finely grind nuts and add them to desserts and raw vegetable purées. Nut butters can be spread on wholewheat bread from about one year. Do not give whole nuts or seeds yet: they may cause your baby to choke.

Eggs

From eight months you can give your child whole egg. Wait for several days to make sure that there is no allergic reaction to the egg white. Eggs can be boiled, baked or poached and mashed before serving, or they can be scrambled with a little butter or margarine or made into an egg custard (page 85). Small amounts of grated cheese or chopped tomato can be added to scrambled eggs.

Cheese

Cottage and curd cheeses can be mixed with cooked vegetable purées, raw mashed tomatoes and puréed fruits, or served separately on the same plate. Small amounts of grated hard cheese can be sprinkled over vegetables or mixed into sauces for toppings.

Milk

Treat milk more as a food than a drink. Use it for cooking sauces, junkets and custards. Use milk drinks as desserts rather than thirst quenchers, blending the milk with small amounts of fruit purée. Provided that he is still having a breast or bottle feed twice a day and is getting a good balanced diet, an eight-month-old baby will not need milk drinks. Cow's milk is not easily digestible, and even after he is weaned milk drinks are not an essential item in your child's diet.

Yoghurt

From eight months, start introducing a little natural yoghurt (page 15) into your child's diet. Use it in both sweet and savoury dishes. Mix it into cereals or puréed fruits or use it as a dressing for first salads. Yoghurt is easily digested by a baby and with fresh fruits can be an easy stand-by.

Fish

White fish is an excellent food for the weaned child over nine months old since it is high in protein but low in fat. Flat fish are soft textured and mild flavoured. Later introduce other varieties such as cod or haddock. Steam fish or bake it in a little milk or stock. Oily fish such as herring, mackerel and trout can be introduced at around one year. Fish tinned in oil or brine such as sardines and tuna, can be brought into the diet at the same time, but drain the oil or brine off first.

Meat

Liver is the ideal first meat to introduce as it is high in iron and soft in texture. Always choose lean, not marbled, meats and leave pork out altogether until around ten months. Trim off excess fat, and casserole, steam or grill the meat rather than fry. You don't have to give your child meat every day. Chicken is ideal for young children as it is easily digested, but remove all the skin.

Cereals and Grains

Baby cereals are useful until your child is a year old, but from the age of eight months you can give him whole grain products. Porridge is the ideal breakfast, whether made with milk, water, or milk and water mixed. Make your own baby muesli by finely grinding sugar-free muesli in a blender or food processor. Soak it overnight in boiled milk, yoghurt or boiled water.

Wholewheat semolina makes a nutritious bland dessert that can be mixed with a variety of fruits.

Brown rice can be introduced at eight to nine months. Cook it until it is tender and sieve it with vegetables and pulses. Make rice puddings with the short grain variety.

Millet Cooked and mixed with pulses and vegetables this is a perfect food for a young child.

Wholewheat pasta is also suitable. Sieve it with vegetables or pulses at first. Later on you can mash it.

Bread Now is the time to introduce wholewheat bread. Cut it into thin fingers. Lightly spread it with a small amount of butter, margarine or yeast extract. This makes a good accompaniment to boiled eggs or salad, or even for breakfast.

FISH DISHES

PLAICE WITH TOMATOES
E G W Serves 1

1 small plaice fillet
150 ml (5 fl oz) milk
2 tomatoes
2 parsley sprigs
1 small potato
¼ small onion

Heat the oven to 180°C/350°F/Gas Mark 4. Put the plaice fillet into a dish and pour in the milk. Halve the tomatoes and put them round the plaice. Break the parsley sprigs into small pieces and put them into the dish. Cover the dish with a lid or aluminium foil, and put it into the oven for 20 minutes or until the plaice is cooked through.

Scrub and halve the potato; thinly slice the onion. Put them into a vegetable steamer, lower over gently simmering water, cover and steam for 20 minutes or until the potato is tender.

Skin the fish, the tomatoes and the potato. Put all the ingredients through a sieve or a baby food mill, moistening with a little milk from the dish if necessary. For older babies, the fish, tomatoes and parsley can be mashed together, leaving the potatoes and onions as a separate mashed accompaniment.

PLAICE WITH VEGETABLES
E G W Serves 1

1 small plaice fillet
150 ml (5 fl oz) milk
2 parsley sprigs
1 tomato
1 small potato
¼ small onion
2 cauliflower florettes,
or 4 broccoli spears,
or 6 spinach leaves

Heat the oven to 180°C/350°F/Gas Mark 4. Put the plaice into a dish, pour in the milk and put in the parsley and tomato, cut in half. Cover with a lid or aluminium foil and put into the oven for 20 minutes or until the plaice is tender.

Scrub and halve the potato. Thinly slice the onion. Put them into a vegetable steamer with one of the other vegetables, lower over lightly simmering water and steam, covered, for 20 minutes or until the potato is tender.

Skin the fish, tomato and potato. Put all the ingredients through a sieve or a baby food mill, moistening with a little milk from the dish if required. For older babies, mash the plaice with the parsley and a little milk if necessary. Mash the potato with the tomato and onion, and mash the other vegetable separately.

CHICKEN WITH COURGETTES
D E G W Serves I

½ chicken breast
I slice onion
I slice carrot
small piece celery
I parsley sprig
I small courgette
I small potato

Put the chicken breast into a saucepan with the onion, carrot, celery and parsley sprig, and cover it with water. Bring to a gentle boil, skim and simmer for 45 minutes or until the chicken is completely tender. Lift it out, discard the vegetables and strain and reserve the stock.

Wipe and thinly slice the courgette. Scrub and halve the potato. Put them into a vegetable steamer, lower over simmering water and steam, covered, for 20 minutes or until both vegetables are tender. Skin the potato.

For young babies, put about 15 g (½ oz) of the cooked chicken through a baby food mill with the courgette and potato, moistening with a little of the stock to the required consistency.

Use about twice as much chicken for older babies, finely minced or very finely chopped. Mash the courgette and potato together or separately, moistening with the stock.

Instead of courgettes in this recipe you could use 6 spinach leaves, or 3 tablespoons shredded green cabbage, or 2 pieces vegetable marrow, or 3 tablespoons fresh peas.

BEEF HOT POT
For babies of 10 months onwards.
D E G W Serves I

25–40 g (I–I½ oz) lean braising steak
I small potato
I small carrot
7.5 cm (3 in) piece celery
¼ small onion
I tablespoon chopped parsley
225 ml (8 fl oz) stock (page 19), or water

Dice the beef. Peel and dice the potato. Dice the carrot and celery. Finely chop the onion. Put all the ingredients, including the parsley, into a saucepan, bring to the boil, cover and simmer gently for 1¼ hours or until the meat is very tender. Put all the ingredients through a baby food mill, moistening with stock from the pan to the required consistency.

To make Lamb Hot Pot, use lean, boneless shoulder or leg of lamb instead of beef and 25 g (1 oz) pot barley instead of the potato.

GRILLED CHICKEN LIVER
For babies of seven months onwards.
D E G W Serves I

I chicken liver,
or I tablespoon lamb's liver
2 teaspoons oil
¼ teaspoon chopped thyme

Lay a small square of foil on the grill rack. Heat the grill to the highest temperature, getting the foil hot. Cut away any green patches from the chicken liver as these will make it taste bitter; if you are using lamb's liver, cut out any tubes or stringy pieces. Lightly brush the liver with oil and lay it on the hot foil, sprinkled with the thyme. Grill for about 1½ minutes, turning once, until it is cooked through but still very soft. Put through a baby food mill.

GREEN LENTILS WITH RICE AND TOMATOES
D E G W Serves I

2 tomatoes
25 g (I oz) green lentils
25 g (I oz) brown rice
I tablespoon chopped parsley
150 ml (5 fl oz) mineral or tap water

Halve the tomatoes. Put all the ingredients into a saucepan, bring to the boil, cover and simmer for 45 minutes or until both lentils and rice are tender, and most of the water has been absorbed. Drain off any excess water. Sieve the ingredients or put them through a baby food mill. For older babies, skin the tomatoes and mash all the ingredients together.

LENTILS WITH RICE
D E G W Serves I

I small carrot
¼ small onion
I tomato
25 g (I oz) split red lentils
25 g (I oz) brown rice, or millet
½ tablespoon chopped parsley
225 ml (8 fl oz) mineral or tap water

Slice the carrot and onion thinly, and halve the tomato. Put all the ingredients into a saucepan, bring to the boil and simmer, covered, for 45 minutes or until both lentils and rice (or millet) are soft. Drain off any excess water. Sieve all the ingredients or put them through a baby food mill. For older babies, skin the tomatoes and mash all the ingredients together.

LENTIL AND OATMEAL SOUP
D E W Serves I

I small carrot
½ small celery stick
¼ small onion
I tablespoon split red lentils
I tablespoon porridge oats
225 ml (8 fl oz) stock (page 19), or water
I teaspoon chopped parsley

Finely chop the carrot, celery and onion. Put all the ingredients into a saucepan, bring to the boil and simmer, covered, for 40 minutes or until the lentils are very soft. Put the soup through a baby food mill.

HARICOT BEANS WITH WATERCRESS AND TOMATOES
D E Serves I

25 g (I oz) cooked haricot beans (page 12)
I small potato
4 sprigs watercress
2 tomatoes
I teaspoon wheatgerm

Scrub the potato and cut it in half. Remove the tougher stems from the watercress. Halve the tomatoes. Put the potato, watercress and tomatoes into a vegetable steamer, lower over lightly simmering water and steam for 20 minutes, covered, until the potato is tender. Skin the potato and tomatoes.

Put the beans, potato, watercress and tomatoes through a sieve or baby food mill. Mix in the wheatgerm. For older babies, mash the beans with the watercress, tomatoes and wheatgerm, and mash the potato separately.

BUTTERBEANS WITH VEGETABLES AND CHEESE
E G W Serves I

25 g (I oz) cooked butterbeans (page 12)
I small potato
I small carrot, or 2 cauliflower florettes, or
4 spinach leaves, or 4 broccoli spears
¼ small onion
2 teaspoons curd cheese,
or low fat soft cheese,
or 15 g (½ oz) Edam cheese, grated

Scrub the potato and cut it in half. Thinly slice the carrot. Keep the cauliflower florettes whole. Roughly chop the spinach. Remove the tougher parts of the broccoli stems. Thinly slice the onion. Put the potato, chosen vegetable and onion into a vegetable steamer, lower over lightly simmering water and steam, covered, for 20 minutes or until the vegetables are tender.

Put the beans and vegetables through a sieve or baby food mill and mix in the cheese. For older babies, mash the beans with the cheese, and serve with all the vegetables in a separate mash; or mash the onion with the potato and leave the other vegetable mashed on its own.

BUTTERBEANS WITH TOMATO AND RICE
D E G W Serves I

50 g (2 oz) cooked butterbeans (page 12)
2 tomatoes
¼ small onion (optional)
pinch dried mixed herbs
4 tablespoons cooked brown rice

Cut the skin from the tomatoes and finely chop the flesh. Thinly slice the onion, if using. Put both into a saucepan with the herbs and simmer for 10 minutes so that they make a thick sauce. Mix in the butterbeans and rice and heat them through. Mash everything together.

PASTA WITH MUSHROOMS AND CHEESE
E Serves I

2 button mushrooms
25 g (I oz) wholewheat pasta
2 teaspoons curd cheese,
or other low fat soft cheese
½ teaspoon lemon juice

Wash the mushrooms and boil them with the pasta in unsalted water for 15 minutes or until tender. Drain, and put them through a baby food mill. Mix in the cheese and the lemon juice.

PASTA WITH TOMATOES AND CHEESE
E Serves I

25 g (I oz) wholewheat pasta
2 tomatoes
25 g (I oz) curd cheese,
or other low fat soft cheese,
or 15 g (½ oz) Edam cheese, grated

Boil the pasta in unsalted water for 15 minutes or until tender. Drain. Grill the tomatoes and skin them. Put the pasta and tomatoes through a baby food mill, and mix in the cheese.

PASTA WITH TOMATOES AND WALNUTS
D E Serves I

25 g (I oz) wholewheat pasta
2 tomatoes
15 g (½ oz) walnuts

Boil the pasta in unsalted water for 15 minutes or until tender. Drain. Grill the tomatoes and skin them. Put the pasta and tomatoes through a baby food mill. Finely grind the walnuts and mix with the pasta and tomatoes.

VEGETABLE DISHES · SALADS

POTATO AND CELERY MASH
Ⓓ Ⓔ Ⓖ Ⓦ Serves I

I very small potato
I celery stick
½ small onion
I tablespoon chopped parsley

Peel and chop the potato. Chop the celery. Thinly slice the onion. Steam them together for 20 minutes or until all are tender. Mash them together and mix in the parsley: the celery keeps the potatoes moist so there is no need for milk or butter.

POTATO AND PARSNIP MASH
Ⓓ Ⓔ Ⓖ Ⓦ Serves I

I small potato
I small parsnip
½ small onion

Peel and finely chop the potato and parsnip. Thinly slice the onion. Steam for 15 minutes, then mash them together.

TOMATO RICE
Ⓓ Ⓔ Ⓖ Ⓦ Serves I

25 g (I oz) long grain brown rice
150 ml (5 fl oz) stock (page 19), or water
½ teaspoon tomato purée
I tablespoon chopped parsley

Put the rice into a saucepan with the stock, tomato purée and parsley. Bring it to a gentle boil, cover and simmer for 45 minutes or until the rice is tender and all the stock absorbed.

MUSHROOM RICE
Ⓓ Ⓔ Ⓖ Ⓦ Serves I

25 g (I oz) brown rice
150 ml (5 fl oz) stock (page 19), or water
3 button mushrooms
I tablespoon chopped parsley

Put the rice, stock and mushrooms into a saucepan. Bring to a gentle boil and simmer for 45 minutes. Drain if necessary and stir in the parsley.

CARROT, BANANA AND NUT SALAD
Ⓔ Ⓖ Ⓦ Serves I

I small carrot
½ banana
15 g (½ oz) unsalted peanuts, or walnuts
2 teaspoons natural yoghurt
small sliver of garlic (optional)

Finely grate the carrot and mash the banana. Mix them together. Finely grind the nuts and mix them into the carrot and banana. Mix in the yoghurt and crushed garlic, if using.

TOMATO AND WATERCRESS SALAD
Ⓔ Ⓖ Ⓦ Serves I

2 tomatoes
I tablespoon very finely chopped watercress leaves
2 teaspoons curd cheese
2 teaspoons natural yoghurt

Scald, skin, seed and mash the tomatoes. Mix with the watercress and add the cheese and yoghurt.

Instead of the watercress you could grate in the flesh of a quarter of a small red pepper.

CARROT, BANANA AND TAHINI SALAD
E G M Serves I

1 small carrot
½ banana
1 teaspoon tahini
2 teaspoons natural yoghurt
small sliver of garlic

Finely grate the carrot and mash the banana. Mix them together and mix in the tahini, yoghurt and garlic.

CARROT AND APPLE SALAD
E G M Serves I

1 small carrot
¼ sweet dessert apple
2 teaspoons curd cheese
2 teaspoons natural yoghurt

Peel and finely grate the carrot and apple. Mix them together and mix in the curd cheese and yoghurt.

AVOCADO AND TOMATO SALAD
E G M Serves I

½ ripe avocado
1 large tomato
2 teaspoons curd cheese,
or 1 tablespoon ground almonds
small sliver of garlic (optional)

Peel and mash the avocado. Scald, skin, seed and mash the tomato, and mix it with the avocado. Mix in the cheese and crushed garlic, if using.

SEMOLINA AND ALMONDS
E Serves I

2 tablespoons wholewheat semolina
110 ml (4 fl oz) milk
1 teaspoon apple and pear spread
15 g (½ oz) ground almonds
juice ½ small orange

Put the semolina into a saucepan and stir in the milk. Bring to a gentle boil, stirring, and continue to stir for 2 minutes or until the semolina becomes thick. Take the pan from the heat and blend in the apple and pear spread, almonds and orange juice.

You can substitute cashew nuts for the almonds – there is no need to blanch them before grinding.

SEMOLINA WITH RAISINS
E Serves I

2 tablespoons wholewheat semolina
110 ml (4 fl oz) milk
10 raisins

Put the semolina into a saucepan and stir in the milk. Add the raisins and bring to the boil, stirring. Stir for 2 minutes or until the semolina is thick. Put the mixture through a baby food mill to break up the raisins.

SEMOLINA AND APPLE DELIGHT
E Serves I

1 small dessert apple
2 tablespoons wholewheat semolina
110 ml (4 fl oz) milk
2 teaspoons sugar-free jam

Heat the oven to 200°C/400°F/Gas Mark 6. Core the apple and score it round with a sharp knife. Put it into an ovenproof dish and add water to come halfway up the side. Put it into the oven for 20 minutes or until the apple is soft. Skin it and mash the flesh.

Put the semolina into a saucepan and stir in the milk. Bring to the boil, stirring, and stir for 2 minutes or until it becomes thick. Take the pan from the heat and mix in the apple pulp together with the jam.

BABY CEREAL WITH STRAWBERRIES
E Serves 1

3 strawberries
3 tablespoons baby cereal
6 tablespoons boiling water
2 teaspoons natural yoghurt

Sieve the strawberries for young babies; for older babies they can be mashed. Put the cereal into a bowl and mix it to the required consistency with the water. Mix in the strawberries and the yoghurt.

BABY CEREAL WITH BANANA
E Serves 1

3 tablespoons baby cereal
6 tablespoons boiling water
$\frac{1}{2}$ banana
juice $\frac{1}{2}$ small orange
2 teaspoons natural yoghurt

Put the cereal into a bowl and mix it to the required consistency with the water. Sieve the banana, or mash it for older babies. Mix it into the cereal with the orange juice and yoghurt.

BABY CEREAL WITH AVOCADO
D E Serves 1

3 tablespoons baby cereal
6 tablespoons boiling water
$\frac{1}{4}$ ripe avocado
juice $\frac{1}{2}$ small orange

Put the cereal into a bowl and mix it to the required consistency with the water. Sieve or mash the avocado. Mix it into the cereal together with the orange juice.

PORRIDGE AND STRAWBERRIES
E W Serves 1

2 tablespoons rolled oats
150 ml (5 fl oz) mineral or tap water
3 strawberries
2 teaspoons natural yoghurt

Put the oats into a saucepan with the water and bring to the boil, stirring. Stir for 5 minutes or until the porridge is thick, then put it through a baby food mill. Put the strawberries through the mill. Mix them into the porridge and add the yoghurt.

For older babies the strawberries may be mashed and mixed into the unsieved porridge before adding the yoghurt.

PORRIDGE AND APRICOTS
E W Serves 1

4 dried whole apricots
150 ml (5 fl oz) mineral or tap water
2 tablespoons rolled oats
juice $\frac{1}{2}$ small orange
2 teaspoons natural yoghurt

Soak the apricots in the water overnight. The next day, put them into a saucepan with the water and oats, and bring to the boil, stirring. Stir for 5 minutes or until the porridge is thick. Put the apricots and porridge through a baby food mill and mix in the orange juice and yoghurt.

You can substitute 2 large prunes for the apricots in this recipe.

FRUITY COCONUT DESSERT
D E G W Serves 1

2 large plums, or 1 small cooking apple
25 g (1 oz) stoned dates
4 tablespoons unsweetened fruit juice
15 g ($\frac{1}{2}$ oz) desiccated coconut

Stone and chop the plums, or peel, core and chop the apple. Chop the dates. Put both ingredients into a saucepan with the juice, cover and set on a low heat for 10 minutes or until the fruit is soft and juicy. Stir in the coconut and put through the blender or food processor to make a purée.

FRUIT DESSERTS

APRICOT AND CHEESE CREAM
E G W Serves I

125 g (4 oz) dried whole apricots
150 ml (5 fl oz) unsweetened orange
or apple juice
50 g (2 oz) quark,
or other low fat soft cheese
2 tablespoons natural yoghurt

Soak the apricots in the fruit juice for 6–8 hours. Drain them, reserving the juice to drink, and purée the apricots in a blender or food processor. Add the cheese and yoghurt and blend again. Put the purée into a dish and chill for 1 hour.

RHUBARB AND DATE CREAM
D E Serves I

50 g (2 oz) rhubarb
25 g (1 oz) stoned dates
110 ml (4 fl oz) prune juice,
or unsweetened orange juice
2 teaspoons wholewheat semolina,
or baby cereal

Finely chop the rhubarb and the dates. Put them into a saucepan with the juice, cover, and set over a low heat for 10 minutes or until the rhubarb is soft. Sprinkle in the semolina and stir until the mixture is thick. Serve hot or cold.

DATE AND ALMOND CREAM
E G W Serves I

40 g (1½ oz) stoned dates
3 tablespoons prune juice,
or any other unsweetened fruit juice
1 tablespoon ground almonds
4 tablespoons natural yoghurt

Chop the dates and simmer in the juice for 3 minutes. Cool, and mash them with the juice. Mix with the almonds and yoghurt.

MASHED BANANAS

Mashed banana is always a favourite with toddlers. It is naturally sweet and has a deliciously soft texture. Vary the ways in which you serve it: mash it with honey; mix in a little yoghurt; or mix in a little curd cheese. A spoonful of sugar-free jam can be added to any of these.

Try to make the mashed banana look attractive instead of just a splodge. For example, put it round the edges of a plate with yoghurt or soft cheese in the centre and a big blob of sugar-free jam in the centre of that.

BANANA WITH NUTS
E G W Serves I

1 ripe banana
25 g (1 oz) almonds, hazelnuts, unsalted
peanuts or cashew nuts
1 tablespoon natural yoghurt
juice ½ small orange

Sieve or mash the banana. Blanch and grind the almonds, hazelnuts or peanuts, or simply grind the cashew nuts. Mix them into the banana together with the yoghurt and orange.

BANANA AND CHEESE
E Serves I

1 ripe banana
25 g (1 oz) curd cheese,
or other low fat soft cheese
juice ½ small orange
1 teaspoon wheatgerm

Sieve or mash the banana. Mix it with the cheese, orange juice and wheatgerm.

CHAPTER FIVE

COOKING FOR TODDLERS

Individual and Family Meals for Pre-School Children

You no longer have a baby; you now have a small person who is rapidly establishing her independence and her preferences. She is growing fast and using up vast amounts of energy at play and at nursery school. She will be able to eat what everybody else in the family eats – provided it is made from fresh, natural ingredients and is not salted, rich or fatty. The family mealtime will also be a time to learn about good table manners and sociability.

Daily needs

It is a great temptation to satisfy your child's growing appetite with convenience foods such as biscuits and crisps. However, by supplying calories from these sources you are robbing your child of essential vitamins. All the foods that you give her should be as nutritious as possible and contribute to health as well as satisfying hunger. In between meals your child will almost certainly want snacks, but even these can be high in vitamins, minerals and fibre. Have the following on hand: wholegrain biscuits, oatcakes, sesame seed crackers, rice puffs, cheese, fresh fruit, crisp vegetables and flavoured natural yoghurt.

Refusing food

A baby up to eighteen months old will normally only refuse food if she doesn't like it or she isn't feeling hungry. After this time she will let you know about definite and genuine preferences for foods. Often the first sign is that she now wants to *see* what she is eating. She would much rather have her food in separate heaps upon the plate than in an indiscriminate mush. This is a reasonable demand that can easily be accommodated,

especially now your child has teeth. Genuine dislikes are formed too. If she always spits out or leaves a certain food on her plate, this could be a genuinely disliked food. It may be the flavour or the texture.

If she pushes the entire plate of food away saying she doesn't want it, ask her, without losing your temper, to try again. You will know if she means it. She has now realized that she can influence the world around her. By refusing food she can gain your attention or change your mood. Swallow hard and offer something else that you know she likes. If she refuses three times in a row, take the food away and offer nothing else. By the next mealtime, hunger will most likely have produced a willing eater.

If your child just sits and plays with her food, she may not be hungry. Give her about twenty minutes and then simply take the plate away; provided her average daily nutrition has been sound, one missed meal won't matter.

The atmosphere at mealtimes should be as relaxed and happy as possible. Praise, encouragement and fun will reward your child if she eats her food. If there is trouble, a non-reaction is far better than any reaction. 'You don't want it? Right, let's take it away then.' That's all you have to do. There might be tears but at least she knows that she is not going to be punished for it.

There are all kinds of cups, plates and napkins available to make mealtimes fun. Try bendy straws, cups with feet and hats and brightly coloured plates with favourite cartoon characters on them. Most are made from cheap, safe and durable plastic. It helps to make food look attractive on the plate. You could arrange it in shapes or faces: even the youngest children will appreciate the fact that you have taken a little care.

Food fads
Some children develop such a preference for one particular type of food that they demand it at every meal. If it is a nutritious food, you can offer it once a day and simply offer whatever the rest of the family is going to have at other meals. If your child complains, just explain that she has had that food once today, now she must have what everyone else wants.

Teaching your child to feed herself
By the age of eighteen months your child will be able to use a small spoon to feed herself. This is another means by which she establishes her independence. If you are concerned about the mess, get the largest bib possible, with sleeves if necessary. If the food on her plate is difficult to pick up, she may use her fingers until she is able to master a spoon.

Coping with outside influences
When your child is old enough to play with other children, you will need to establish your policy on sweet eating (pages 82–3). She will be invited to parties, perhaps eat at playgroup or with a friend. Don't send her off with a diet sheet. Just let her eat what she is given. She may find it strange, she may not like it, or she may find it a tremendous novelty if it is not food she is accustomed to eating at home. If you know she has been given white bread with chocolate spread and she asks for it again, say something like 'our food is different'. From the age of about three you can start explaining to your child why you eat certain foods and why other foods are not very good for you. If she still asks for chocolate spread, you must have the courage of your convictions to refuse.

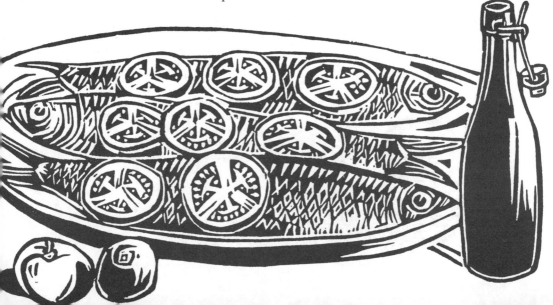

COCK-A-LEEKIE
D E G W Serves 1

50 g (2 oz) chicken breast
1 leek
1 small parsnip
1 small carrot
1 tablespoon chopped parsley
275 ml (10 fl oz) stock (page 19), or water

Cut the chicken into small, thin slivers. Wash the leek well, cut it in half lengthways and thinly slice it. Finely chop the parsnip and the carrot. Put all the ingredients into a saucepan, bring to the boil and simmer for 40 minutes. It may be necessary to cut the chicken up further before serving.

COD BAKED WITH TOMATOES
E G W Serves 1

50–75 g (2–3 oz) cod fillet, or other white
fish, skinned
1 tablespoon lemon juice
1 tablespoon chopped parsley
1 tablespoon Cheddar cheese, grated
2 tomatoes
3 tablespoons milk

Heat the oven to 180°C/350°F/Gas Mark 4. Put the cod into an ovenproof dish and sprinkle it with lemon juice, parsley and grated cheese. Skin and finely chop the tomatoes, and put them on top of the fish. Pour over the milk. Cover the dish with foil and put it into the oven for 20 minutes or until the fish is cooked through. Alternatively, microwave for 3 minutes covered with plastic wrap.

PORK WITH ONIONS
D E G W Serves 1

1 very small pork chop, or 50 g (2 oz) lean
boneless pork
1 small onion
150 ml (5 fl oz) stock (page 19), or water
pinch dried sage, or 1 fresh sage leaf,
finely chopped

Trim any fat or bone from the pork and cut it into small, thin slivers. Thinly slice the onion. Bring the stock to the boil in a small saucepan and add the pork, onion and sage. Cover and simmer for 15 minutes or until the pork is very tender. Lift out the pork and onion with a perforated spoon. Finely chop the pork if necessary.

Use the stock as gravy to pour over steamed potatoes and a green vegetable such as cabbage, kale or broccoli.

LAMB AND OATMEAL
D E W Serves 1

1 small lamb chop, or 50 g (2 oz) lean meat
from shoulder or leg of lamb
½ small onion
150 ml (5 fl oz) stock (page 19), or water
1 tablespoon chopped green part of leek
1 tablespoon porridge oats
1 teaspoon chopped fresh thyme,
or pinch dried

Cut all the lean meat from the chop and cut it into very small, thin pieces. Finely chop the onion. Put the stock into a small saucepan and bring it to the boil. Put in the lamb, onion, leek, oats and thyme, cover, and simmer gently for 20 minutes or until the lamb is very tender. Lift it out with a perforated spoon.

The oatmeal thickens the gravy, which is very good poured over accompanying vegetables.

STEAK AND MUSHROOMS
D E G W Serves 1

25–40 g (1–1½ oz) lean rump steak
4 button mushrooms
150 ml (5 fl oz) stock (page 19), or water
4 drops Worcestershire sauce
2 tablespoons chopped parsley

Cut the steak into small, thin slivers. Thinly slice the mushrooms. Bring the stock to the boil in a small saucepan and add the Worcestershire sauce. Put in the steak, mushrooms and parsley and simmer, uncovered, for 10 minutes or until the steak is really tender. Lift the meat and vegetables out with a perforated spoon and finely chop the steak.

Use the stock as a gravy for steamed vegetables.

RABBIT WITH BACON
D E G W Serves 1

50 g (2 oz) rabbit meat (back is best)
2.5 cm (1 in) square piece lean bacon
½ small onion
½ sage leaf
150 ml (5 fl oz) stock (page 19), or water

Cut the meat into small, thin slivers. Very finely chop the bacon. Thinly slice the onion. Very finely chop the sage. Put all the ingredients into a saucepan, bring to the boil, cover, and simmer for 20 minutes or until the rabbit is completely tender. Lift out the meat with a perforated spoon.

Use the stock as gravy to pour over vegetables.

LAMB WITH LEEKS AND MUSHROOMS
D E G W Serves 1

1 small lamb chop, or 50 g (2 oz) lean meat
from shoulder or leg of lamb
1 medium leek
4 button mushrooms
150 ml (5 fl oz) stock (page 19), or water
1 teaspoon chopped fresh thyme,
or pinch dried

Cut all the lean meat from the chop and cut it into small thin slivers. Cut the leek in half lengthways, wash it well and thinly slice it. Thinly slice the mushrooms. Bring the stock to the boil in a small saucepan. Put in the lamb, leek, mushrooms and thyme, cover and simmer for 15 minutes or until the lamb is completely tender. Lift the lamb and vegetables out with a perforated spoon. Finely chop the lamb.

Use the stock as gravy to pour over steamed carrots and potatoes.

CHICKEN LIVERS WITH TOMATO GRAVY
D E G W Serves 1

1–2 chicken livers
½ small onion
150 ml (5 fl oz) stock (page 19), or water
¼ teaspoon tomato purée
1 teaspoon chopped fresh thyme,
or pinch dried

Cut the livers into very small, thin slices. Thinly slice the onion. Put the stock into a small saucepan and bring to the boil. Stir in the tomato purée and thyme and add the onion. Cover and simmer for 10 minutes. Put in the liver, cover and simmer for a further 5 minutes or until it is very tender and just cooked through. Lift it out with a perforated spoon.

Use the stock as gravy for the liver and for steamed vegetables.

HOT DISHES · SALADS FOR ONE

PIGEON BREAST WITH MUSHROOMS
D E Serves 1

½ pigeon breast
1 teaspoon wholewheat flour
50 g (2 oz) open mushrooms
½ small onion
275 ml (10 fl oz) stock (page 19), or water
1 tablespoon chopped parsley

Cut the pigeon breast into small, thin slivers and toss them in the flour. Thinly slice the mushrooms and onion. Put them into a saucepan with the stock and parsley, bring to the boil and simmer for 30 minutes or until the meat is very tender. Lift the meat and vegetables out with a perforated spoon and serve the stock as a gravy.

GREEN LENTILS WITH TOMATOES
D E G W Serves 1

25 g (1 oz) green lentils
½ small onion
1 celery stick
1 tiny piece garlic
pinch dried mixed herbs
150 ml (5 fl oz) stock (page 19), or water
½ teaspoon tomato purée
2 tomatoes

Chop the onion, celery and garlic. Put all the ingredients except the tomatoes into a saucepan. Bring to the boil, cover and simmer for 50 minutes or until the lentils are soft and most of the stock absorbed. Skin and finely chop the tomatoes. Mix them into the lentils and heat them through just before serving.

Serve with brown rice, millet, hot burghul wheat or kasha.

MUNG BEANS WITH VEGETABLE JUICE
D E G W Serves 1

50 g (2 oz) cooked mung beans (page 12)
½ small onion
½ small carrot
2 button mushrooms
150 ml (5 fl oz) tomato and vegetable juice

Finely chop the onion, carrot and mushrooms. Bring the vegetable juice to the boil in a small saucepan and put in the vegetables and beans. Cover and simmer for 15 minutes or until the carrots are soft.

Serve with savoury rice or with pasta.

CORN AND WHITE BEAN SALAD
E G W Serves 1

2 tablespoons sweetcorn
1 tablespoon natural yoghurt
2 tablespoons cooked flageolets or haricot beans (page 12)
2 teaspoons chopped parsley
1 small beetroot, cooked
small handful mustard and cress

Dressing
2 teaspoons salad oil
1 teaspoon wine vinegar

Mix the sweetcorn into the yoghurt, and in a separate bowl mix the beans, parsley and dressing together. Dice the beetroot and chop the mustard and cress. Arrange piles of the mixtures, the beetroot and the mustard and cress around the plate. Have wholewheat bread or biscuits to go with it.

SALADS FOR ONE

BROWN BEAN AND CORN SALAD
D E G W Serves 1

2 tablespoons cooked pinto beans (page 12)
2 tablespoons sweetcorn
1 tablespoon chopped parsley
1 tomato

Dressing
1½ teaspoons salad oil
1 teaspoon wine vinegar

Beat together the oil and vinegar. Mix it with all the other ingredients except the tomato and pile in the centre of a plate. Arrange tomato slices round the edge.

SALMON SALAD
D G W Serves 1

1–2 tablespoons tinned salmon
1–2 small tomatoes
small piece cucumber
2–3 sprigs watercress
1 tablespoon mild mayonnaise

Scald, skin and finely chop the tomatoes. Peel and finely chop the cucumber. Chop the watercress. Arrange the salmon, tomatoes, cucumber and watercress round the edge of a plate and put the mayonnaise in the centre.
  You can substitute drained flaked tuna fish for the salmon.

HAM, APPLE AND CELERY SALAD
D E G W Serves 1

50 g (2 oz) cooked lean ham
1 small dessert apple
1 celery stick

Finely dice the ham, apple and celery. Put the ham in the centre of a small plate and arrange 2 piles of celery and 2 of apple on opposite sides around it.
  A little dressing made with oil and cider vinegar or lemon juice can be sprinkled over the celery and apple.

EGG, BEETROOT AND POTATO SALAD
D G W Serves 1

1 egg, hard-boiled
1 tablespoon mayonnaise (optional)
1 small cooked beetroot
2 small cooked new potatoes

Mash the egg, with the mayonnaise if using, and put it in the centre of a small plate. Finely dice the beetroot and potatoes and put them in rings round the egg.
  You could add a tiny parsley sprig to the egg or scatter chopped parsley over the potatoes.

AVOCADO AND CHEESE SALAD
E G W Serves 1

½ small ripe avocado
½ small red pepper
2 tablespoons sweetcorn
1 tablespoon curd cheese,
or other low fat soft cheese

Finely chop the avocado and red pepper. Arrange portions of the vegetables round the edge of a plate and put the cheese in the centre.

EGG, TOMATO AND CUCUMBER SALAD
D G W Serves 1

1 egg, hard-boiled
1 tablespoon mayonnaise (optional)
1 medium tomato
4–6 cucumber slices

Mash the egg, with the mayonnaise if using, and put it in the centre of a small plate. Cut the tomato into 8 small wedges and arrange them with the cucumber slices round the egg.

MR CHEESY SALAD
E G W Serves 1

2 tablespoons cottage cheese
1–2 teaspoons chopped chives (optional)
small amounts of mustard and cress, red
pepper and celery

Mix together the cheese and chives. Put
the cheese to one side of a small plate and
make it into a flat circle. Finely chop
about 1 tablespoon mustard and cress and
use it for the hair. Make eyes and nose
from small cubes of red pepper and a
mouth from a curved strip. Make 4
matchstick pieces of celery and use them
for legs and arms.

Serve extra pieces of celery separately
and accompany the salad with Sesame
Oatcakes (page 113).

MR SUNSHINE SALAD
E G W Serves 1

4–5 sprigs watercress
2 tomatoes
1 medium carrot
25 g (1 oz) Cheddar cheese, grated
raisins for face

Chop the watercress and use it to cover
the base of a medium-sized plate. Thinly
slice the tomatoes and arrange them in a
circle in the centre of the watercress. Cut
the carrot into matchstick pieces and
arrange them round the tomatoes to make
the sun's rays. Put the cheese on top of the
tomatoes. Make eyes, a nose and a mouth
with the raisins.

Serve with wholewheat bread.

COD BAKED IN A PARCEL
E G W Serves 2 adults and 2 children

450 g (1 lb) cod fillet
juice 1 lemon
freshly ground black pepper
75 g (3 oz) Cheddar cheese, grated
225 g (8 oz) tomatoes
2 green peppers

Heat the oven to 180°C/350°F/Gas Mark 4.
Skin the cod and cut it into 1.5 cm ($\frac{1}{2}$ in)
cubes. Grease a large sheet of foil and put
the cod on top, sprinkled with lemon juice
and pepper. Scatter the cheese over the
top. Scald, skin and finely chop the tomatoes. Core, seed and finely chop the peppers. Put them on top of the cheese. Bring
the sides of the foil together and seal them;
seal the ends by rolling them upwards. Lay
the parcel on a baking sheet and put it into
the oven for 20 minutes.

Serve straight from the foil.

HERRINGS WITH TOMATOES
D E G W Serves 2 adults and 2 children

3 herrings
3 tablespoons water
3 tablespoons dry cider
(or use 6 tablespoons water)
6 small tomatoes

Heat the oven to 180°C/350°F/Gas Mark 4.
Fillet the herrings or ask the fishmonger
to do it for you. Lay them in a large, flat,
ovenproof dish, and pour in the water and
cider. Cut each tomato into four slices and
lay them on the herring fillets. Cover the
dish with foil and bake the herrings for 20
minutes or until cooked through.

FAMILY FISH DISHES

MILDLY MUSTARD PLAICE
D E G W Serves 2 adults and 2 children

3 large or 6 small plaice fillets
½ teaspoon Dijon mustard
juice 1 large lemon
4 tablespoons chopped parsley

Heat the oven to 180°C/350°F/Gas Mark 4. Lay the plaice fillets in a large, flat, ovenproof dish, overlapping as little as possible: if the fillets overlap more than about 2.5 cm (1 in) use two dishes. Put the mustard into a small bowl and gradually beat in the lemon juice. Pour the mixture over the fish and scatter the parsley over the top. Cover the dish with foil and put it into the oven for 20 minutes or until the fish is cooked through.

LEMON OATY HERRINGS
D E W Serves 2 adults and 2 children

3 herrings
juice 1 lemon
1 teaspoon mustard powder
40 g (1½ oz) rolled oats

Fillet the herrings, or ask the fishmonger to do it for you. Lay the fillets on a large plate, overlapping as little as possible, and pour over the lemon juice. Sprinkle the mustard powder over the fillets for the adults. Leave the herrings for 30 minutes at room temperature.

Heat the grill to high and if you have an open wire rack cover it with foil. Coat the herring fillets in the oats. Lay them on the hot rack, skin side down. Grill them for 4 minutes or until the top has browned.

COD STEAKS WITH CORN
D E G W Serves 2 adults and 2 children

6 frozen cod steaks
1 × 350 g (12 oz) tin sweetcorn
1 teaspoon arrowroot or cornflour
150 ml (5 fl oz) vegetable or tomato juice
3 tablespoons oil
2 tablespoons chopped parsley (optional)

Thaw the cod steaks. Put the sweetcorn through a blender or food processor with the arrowroot and vegetable juice.

Heat the grill to high. Put the oil into a flat heatproof dish and heat it under the grill. Turn the cod steaks in the oil and put them under the grill for 2 minutes. Turn them over and return them to the grill for 1 minute. Pour over the blended corn. Return the dish to the grill for 10 minutes, or until the cod steaks cook through and the corn mixture thickens slightly and browns on top.

Serve scattered with parsley.

WHITE FISH WITH ORANGE AND TOMATO YOGHURT
E G W Serves 2 adults and 2 children

575 g (1¼ lb) cod or haddock fillet
150 ml (5 fl oz) natural yoghurt
juice 1 medium orange
2 tablespoons tomato purée
4 tablespoons chopped parsley

Heat the oven to 180°C/350°F/Gas Mark 4. Skin the fillets, cut them into small serving pieces and put them into a flat, ovenproof dish. Beat together the remaining ingredients and spoon them over the fish. Cover the dish with foil and put it into the oven for 25 minutes or until the fish is cooked through.

FAMILY MEALS WITH CHICKEN

NUTTY STUFFED CHICKEN

E Serves 2 adults and 2 children

1 × 1.35 kg (3 lb) roasting chicken
50 g (2 oz) walnuts
125 g (4 oz) fresh wholewheat breadcrumbs
4 tablespoons chopped parsley
2 tablespoons chopped chives
4 tablespoons natural yoghurt

Heat the oven to 200°C/400°F/Gas Mark 6. Grind or finely chop the walnuts and mix them with the breadcrumbs and herbs. Add the yoghurt and mix well. Put the mixture into the chicken and tie its legs together. Set it on a rack in a roasting tin, cover it completely with foil and put it into the oven for 1 hour. Remove the foil, and continue cooking for a further 20 minutes or until the skin is golden brown.

CHICKEN WITH PARSLEY AND LEMON

D E G W Serves 2 adults and 2 children

1 × 1.35 kg (3 lb) roasting chicken
4 tablespoons oil
2 medium onions
1 clove garlic
6 tablespoons chopped parsley
grated rind and juice ½ lemon

Heat the oven to 200°C/400°F/Gas Mark 6. Cut the chicken into 8 serving pieces. Brush them with half the oil. Heat the grill to high and grill the chicken until it is just brown on both sides – about 5 minutes altogether.

Slice the onions and finely chop the garlic. Soften both in the remaining oil over a low heat. Pack the chicken, onions and parsley into a small casserole and add the lemon rind and juice. Cover the casserole and put into the oven for 45 minutes.

CHICKEN WITH MIXED VEGETABLES

E G W Serves 2 adults and 2 children

1 × 1.35 kg (3 lb) roasting chicken
350 g (12 oz) leeks
6 celery sticks
3 medium carrots
15 g (½ oz) butter
275 ml (10 fl oz) stock (page 19)
150 ml (5 fl oz) dry cider
(or use 425 ml (15 fl oz) stock)
2 tablespoons chopped parsley

Heat the oven to 180°C/350°F/Gas Mark 4. Cut the chicken into 8 serving pieces and the leeks and celery into 2.5 cm (1 in) pieces. Slice the carrots. Melt the butter in a flameproof casserole on a moderate heat. Put in the chicken joints, skin side down first. Brown them on both sides and remove them. Mix the vegetables into the butter, cover and cook over a low heat for 5 minutes. Pour in the stock and cider and bring to the boil. Replace the chicken, cover the casserole and put it into the oven for 1 hour.

Remove the chicken and vegetables and keep them warm. Skim any fat from the juices in the casserole. Bring the juices to the boil, add the parsley and simmer for 2 minutes. Pour them over the chicken for serving.

Jacket potatoes are the best accompaniment.

FAMILY MEALS WITH BEEF

BEEFBURGERS
E G W Serves 2 adults and 2 children

575 g (1¼ lb) good quality minced beef
½ small onion
½ teaspoon dried mixed herbs
4 tablespoons natural yoghurt

Put the beef into a bowl. Grate in the onion. Add the herbs and yoghurt and mix well. Form the mixture into six burger shapes, using a burger press if you have one. Put them on a plate and refrigerate for 30 minutes so that they set into shape.

Heat the grill to high and if you have an open wire rack, cover it with foil pierced here and there with a fork or skewer. Lay the burgers on the hot foil and grill them for 4 minutes on each side or until they are cooked through.

BEEF AND CELERY CASSEROLE
D E Serves 2 adults and 2 children

575 g (1¼ lb) stewing beef
1 head celery
1 large onion
1 clove garlic
575 ml (1 pint) stock (page 19)
1 tablespoon wholewheat flour
juice 1 small orange
1 tablespoon chopped thyme
2 tablespoons chopped parsley

Heat the oven to 180°C/350°F/Gas Mark 4. Cut the beef into 2.5 cm (1 in) cubes. Chop the celery. Finely chop the onion and garlic. Put 150 ml (5 fl oz) of the stock into a flameproof casserole. Put in the onion and garlic and cook them on a medium heat until all the stock has evaporated and they are beginning to brown. Raise the heat and add the beef, stirring it around until it browns. Sprinkle in the flour. Pour in the remaining stock and bring to the boil. Add the orange juice and herbs. Cover, and put the casserole into the oven for 1 hour 30 minutes or until the meat is tender.

Serve with jacket or mashed potatoes, and green vegetables and carrots.

BRAISED BEEF WITH MUSHROOMS
D E G W Serves 2 adults and 2 children

575 g (1¼ lb) braising steak
125 g (4 oz) mushrooms
2 medium onions
575 ml (1 pint) stock (page 19)
4 tablespoons chopped parsley

Heat the oven to 180°C/350°F/Gas Mark 4. Cut the meat into pieces about 2.5 × 5 cm (1 × 2 in). Thinly slice the mushrooms and onions. Put 150 ml (5 fl oz) stock into a flameproof casserole and bring it to the boil over a high heat. Put in the onions and cook until they are soft and all but about 2 tablespoons of the stock has evaporated. Add the meat and stir it around until it browns. Pour in the remaining stock and bring it to the boil. Add the mushrooms and parsley, cover the casserole and put it into the oven for 1 hour 30 minutes.

Serve with jacket potatoes, carrots and a green vegetable.

BEEF WITH SWEDE AND CARROTS
D E G W Serves 2 adults and 2 children

450 g (1 lb) lean minced beef
350 g (12 oz) carrots
350 g (12 oz) swede
1 large onion
1 tablespoon chopped thyme
1 tablespoon chopped marjoram
4 tablespoons chopped parsley
275 ml (10 fl oz) stock (page 19)
2 tablespoons tomato purée

Coarsely grate the carrots and swede. Finely chop the onion. Oil a heavy saucepan and put it over a high heat. Put in the beef, break it up well and stir until it browns. Mix in the vegetables and herbs, pour in the stock and bring to the boil. Stir in the tomato purée. Cover and simmer for 45 minutes or until the beef and vegetables are completely tender.

FAMILY MEALS WITH LAMB

LAMB AND AUBERGINE CASSEROLE

D E G W Serves 2 adults and 2 children

575 g (1¼ lb) lean boneless lamb
(either buy a small half shoulder and
bone it yourself, or use boneless chops,
or the lean meat cut from the neck)
225 g (8 oz) aubergine
(about one medium-sized)
1 tablespoon fine sea salt
1 large onion
1 clove garlic
1 × 400 g (14 oz) tin tomatoes in juice
up to 575 ml (1 pint) stock (page 19)
2 tablespoons oil
½ teaspoon paprika
1 bayleaf

Heat the oven to 180°C/350°F/Gas Mark 4.
Dice the aubergine. Put the dice into a
colander, sprinkle them with the salt and
press them down gently with a weight,
such as a saucer or shallow bowl. Leave to
drain for 20 minutes, then rinse with cold
water and pat dry with kitchen paper.
Finely chop the onion and garlic. Drain
the tomatoes and make the juice up to
575 ml (1 pint) with the stock. Cut the lamb
into 2 cm (¾ in) dice.

Heat the oil in a flameproof casserole
over a high heat, put in the lamb and stir it
about to brown it. Lower the heat, add the
aubergine, onion, tomatoes and garlic and
scatter in the paprika. Stir for 2 minutes,
then pour in the stock and bring to the
boil. Add the bayleaf, cover the casserole
and put it in the oven for 1 hour 20
minutes.

Serve with jacket potatoes or wholewheat pasta, and a green vegetable.

LAMB WITH HARICOT BEANS

D E G W Serves 2 adults and 2 children

900 g (2 lb) neck of lamb
1 medium onion
1 carrot
1 celery stick
bouquet garni
1 teaspoon black peppercorns
1.725 litres (3 pints) water
175 g (6 oz) haricot beans
2 tablespoons tomato purée
1 tablespoon chopped thyme
1 tablespoon chopped marjoram
2 tablespoons chopped parsley

Soak the haricot beans overnight and boil
for 10 minutes. Drain. Cut the onion in
half, split the carrot lengthways and
break up the celery. Put all three into a
large saucepan with the lamb, bouquet
garni, peppercorns and water. Bring to
the boil and skim off any scum that rises to
the surface. Cover and simmer for 2 hours
or until the lamb is very tender. Lift out
the lamb, cut all the meat from the bones
and dice it. Strain and reserve the stock.

Put 575 ml (1 pint) of the reserved stock
into a saucepan. Bring to the boil and add
the beans, tomato purée and herbs. Cover
and simmer until the beans are soft.

Reserve some of the meat for the baby.
Put the rest into the pan with the beans
and cook for a further 5 minutes to reheat.

Finely chop the meat for the baby. Put
some beans separately on her plate and
spoon some of the hot liquid over the meat:
this should be enough to reheat it.

Serve with a green vegetable.

LAMB IN YOGHURT
Ⓔ Ⓖ Ⓦ

lamb chops – two small each per adult, one
small each per young child or baby

Marinade
1 clove garlic
150 ml (5 fl oz) natural yoghurt
juice ½ lemon
1 tablespoon tomato purée
2 tablespoons chopped parsley
1 tablespoon chopped thyme
1 tablespoon chopped marjoram
(or 1 teaspoon dried mixed herbs if no fresh
herbs are available)
freshly ground black pepper

For the baby
150 ml (5 fl oz) stock (page 19)

Crush the garlic in a large, flat dish, and
mix in all the ingredients for the
marinade. Turn the chops in it and leave
them for at least 4 hours at room
temperature.

Chops for adults can be grilled, or laid
on a rack in a roasting tin and cooked in
the oven at 200°C/400°F/Gas Mark 6 for 25
minutes. For the baby, cut away all the fat
and remove the bones. Cut the meat into
small, thin slivers. Bring the stock to the
boil in a small saucepan, put in the lamb,
cover, and simmer for 20 minutes or until
the meat is very tender. Lift out the lamb
with a perforated spoon. Use the stock as
gravy for steamed vegetables.

HERBY GRILLED LIVER
Ⓓ Ⓔ Ⓖ Ⓦ Serves 2 adults and 2 children

450–575 g (1–1¼ lb) lamb's liver
6 tablespoons olive or sunflower oil
2 tablespoons chopped parsley
½ tablespoon chopped thyme
¼ tablespoon chopped marjoram
1 teaspoon chopped rosemary

Cut the liver into small, thin pieces. Mix
the oil and herbs together, fold in the liver
and let it stand for 30 minutes at room
temperature.

Heat the grill to high, and if you have an
open wire rack, cover it with foil. Grill the
pieces of liver for about 2 minutes each
side, so they are cooked through but still
soft.

LAMB'S LIVER IN VEGETABLE JUICE
Ⓓ Ⓔ Ⓖ Ⓦ Serves 2 adults and 2 children

450–575 g (1–1¼ lb) lamb's liver
1 large carrot
1 celery stick
1 medium onion
150 ml (5 fl oz) stock (page 19)
1 × 330 ml (11½ fl oz) tin tomato and
vegetable juice
1 tablespoon chopped thyme

Cut the liver into small, thin slices. Chop
the carrot and celery into matchstick
pieces and finely chop the onion. Put the
stock into a frying pan, skillet or large
shallow saucepan and bring to the boil.
Put in the vegetables and cook them until
all the stock has evaporated. Pour in the
vegetable juice and bring it to the boil.
Add the thyme, cover, and simmer for 5
minutes. Put in the liver, cover again and
cook for a further 5 minutes or until the
liver is tender and cooked through.

SPICED ROAST PORK

The spice and garlic flavours produced by roasting pork in this way stay only on the outside of the meat, so if the children would rather have a plain flavour make sure that they get the inside pieces.

D E G W Serves 6

1 × 1.35–1.575 kg (3–3½ lb)
knuckle end leg of pork
1 teaspoon black peppercorns
½ teaspoon allspice berries (optional)
pinch fine sea salt
1 clove garlic
4 rosemary sprigs

Heat the oven to 180°C/350°F/Gas Mark 4. Crush together the peppercorns, allspice berries, salt and garlic. Score the skin of the pork and rub it thoroughly with the crushed mixture. Make small slits in the skin and poke in the rosemary sprigs. Put the pork on a rack in a roasting tin and put it into the oven for 2 hours 30 minutes.

Serve with jacket potatoes and a selection of green vegetables.

PORK CHOPS AND APPLES

E G W Serves 2 adults and 2 children

3 pork chops
2 dessert apples
1 medium onion
oil, butter or margarine for frying
275 ml (10 fl oz) stock (page 19)
½ teaspoon chopped rosemary

Trim any excess fat from the chops. Peel, core and chop the apples. Thinly slice the onion. Oil a heavy frying pan and place it over a moderate heat. Put in the chops, brown them on both sides and remove them. Lower the heat, put in the onion and apples and stir them for 2 minutes. Pour in the stock and bring to the boil. Replace the chops and scatter in the rosemary. Cover and cook on a low heat for 25 minutes or until the chops are very tender.

Serve with jacket or boiled potatoes, carrots and cauliflower or cabbage.

CRUSTY TOPPED HARICOT BEANS

Serves 2 adults and 2 children

225 g (8 oz) haricot beans
125 g (4 oz) button mushrooms
4 celery sticks
1 medium onion
2 tablespoons oil
2 tablespoons wholewheat flour
275 ml (10 fl oz) stock (page 19)
4 tablespoons chopped parsley
1 egg
150 ml (5 fl oz) natural yoghurt
50 g (2 oz) mature Cheddar cheese, finely grated
2 tablespoons wheatgerm

Soak the haricot beans overnight and boil for 10 minutes. Drain. Heat the oven to 200°C/400°F/Gas Mark 6. Thinly slice the mushrooms. Finely chop the celery and onion. Heat the oil in a flameproof casserole over a low heat. Stir in the celery and onion, cover and cook gently for 10 minutes. Stir in the flour and then the stock. Mix in the mushrooms, beans and parsley. Cover the casserole and put into the oven for 40 minutes.

Beat the egg. Mix in the yoghurt and cheese and spoon the mixture evenly over the beans. Scatter the wheatgerm over the top, and return the casserole to the oven, uncovered, for 20 minutes or until the top is golden brown.

Serve the beans straight from the casserole. Accompany them with jacket potatoes or wholewheat pasta, and carrots and a green vegetable or a salad.

COLD DESSERTS

RHUBARB AND CUSTARD
Serves 2 adults and 2 children

350 g (12 oz) rhubarb, weighed before
trimming
75 g (3 oz) sultanas
4 tablespoons water
6 tablespoons concentrated apple juice
1 teaspoon cornflour
2 eggs
275 ml (10 fl oz) milk
few drops vanilla essence

Chop the rhubarb into lengths of about 2.5 cm (1 in). Put it into a saucepan with the sultanas and water. Cover and set over a low heat for 15 minutes or until the fruit is soft and can be broken up with a fork. Mix in 3 tablespoons of the concentrated apple juice, then put the rhubarb into a serving dish and leave it to get quite cold.

Put the cornflour into a bowl. Beat the eggs together well and gradually mix them into the cornflour, making a smooth paste. Mix in the remaining concentrated apple juice. Put the milk into a saucepan, add the vanilla essence and bring to just below boiling point. Take it from the heat and gradually mix it into the eggs. Rinse out the saucepan, leaving a thin film of water in the bottom. Pour in the custard mixture and stir over a low heat, without letting it boil, until it becomes thick and coats the back of a wooden spoon. (Use a double boiler if you have one, with hot but not boiling water in the base.) Take the pan from the heat and cool the custard completely.

Pour the custard over the rhubarb and chill in the refrigerator for one hour before serving.

For family meals, serve just as it is. For more special occasions the top could be decorated with chopped nuts, angelica or glacé cherries.

APPLE AND STRAWBERRY LAYER
D E Serves 2 adults and 2 children

675 g (1½ lb) cooking apples
7.5 cm (3 in) piece cinnamon stick
6 tablespoons water
125 g (4 oz) sugar-free strawberry jam
50 g (2 oz) vegetable margarine
125 g (4 oz) fresh wholewheat breadcrumbs

Peel, core and chop the apples. Put them into a saucepan with the cinnamon stick and water. Cover and set over a low heat for 15 minutes or until the apples are soft and can be beaten to a thick purée. Take the pan from the heat, remove the cinnamon stick and beat in the strawberry jam. Cool completely.

Melt the margarine in a large frying pan on a high heat. Put in the breadcrumbs and stir them around until they brown. Take them from the heat and cool.

Put one-third of the apples into a serving dish, then half the crumbs, and another third of the apples, the remaining crumbs and then the remaining apples. Chill for 1 hour or until firm.

Serve plain or with natural yoghurt.

APPLES AND CUSTARD
G W Serves 2 adults and 2 children

450 g (1 lb) cooking apples
50 g (2 oz) pressed dates
3 tablespoons concentrated apple juice
4 tablespoons water
½ teaspoon ground cinnamon
custard as for Rhubarb and Custard (left)

Peel, core and chop the apples. Finely chop the dates. Put them both into a saucepan with the concentrated apple juice and water. Sprinkle in the cinnamon, cover, and set over a low heat for 15 minutes or until the apples can be beaten to a thick purée. Pour into a dish and cool completely.

Make the custard, cool it and pour over the apples. Chill for 1 hour before serving.

COLD DESSERTS

FLAVOURED YOGHURTS
E G W

Flavoured yoghurts make a quick and healthy end to a meal. Since the bought kinds very often contain sugar, preservative or artificial colouring, it is best to make your own, either from home-made yoghurt or using bought natural yoghurts. For a rich creamy flavour, look out for the Greek yoghurts which are becoming available in supermarkets.

Into every 275 ml (10 fl oz) natural yoghurt, mix one of the following:
- 3–4 tablespoons any sugar-free jam;
- 2 tablespoons honey;
- 2 tablespoons honey plus 2–3 tablespoons ground nuts;
- 1 small or ½ large banana, mashed;
- 50–75 g (2–3 oz) chopped dates: if you have a blender or food processor, work them with the yoghurt to make a rough but sweet purée;
- 1 small dessert apple, baked and puréed or mashed;
- apple as above plus chopped raisins or sultanas;
- 1 small ripe peach, skinned and mashed, plus 2 teaspoons tahini, if liked;
- 75 g (3 oz) strawberries or raspberries, sieved or mashed, plus 2 tablespoons honey or sugar-free jam;
- 1 small very ripe pear, peeled and mashed;
- 1 small dessert apple, grated;
- 1 small dessert apple, grated, plus 50 g (2 oz) chopped raisins, sultanas or dates;
- 2 tablespoons crunchy peanut butter (page 120) plus 50 g (2 oz) chopped dates or 2 tablespoons honey;
- 50 g (2 oz) fruits tinned in natural juice plus 2 tablespoons of their juice. For tart fruits such as blackcurrants, add a little honey or sugar-free jam to sweeten;
- whole dried apricots or prunes, soaked overnight in unsweetened fruit juice, drained and finely chopped, plus 2–3 tablespoons of the juice.

FROZEN YOGHURT
G W Serves 2 adults and 2 children

2 egg yolks
50 g (2 oz) any sugar-free jam, or honey
575 ml (1 pint) natural yoghurt
½ teaspoon vanilla essence

Beat the egg yolks well. Bring the jam or honey to just below boiling point and beat it into the egg yolks until the mixture is light and fluffy. Beat in the yoghurt and vanilla essence. Cool, chill and freeze as for ice-cream.

Fruit Flavourings
Add one of the following before freezing:
- 225 g (8 oz) ripe strawberries, mashed or sieved;
- 225 g (8 oz) ripe raspberries, mashed or sieved;
- 225 g (8 oz) black cherries, stoned and chopped;
- 2 ripe peaches, puréed or chopped;
- 2 bananas, mashed;
- 125 g (4 oz) whole dried apricots, soaked and roughly chopped or puréed.

JUNKET
E G W Serves 2 adults and 2 children

575 ml (1 pint) full cream milk
5 ml (1 teaspoon) junket rennet
(available from most grocers,
supermarkets and chemists)
1 tablespoon clear honey
freshly grated nutmeg (optional)

Warm the milk to blood heat. Stir in the rennet and honey until just dissolved, without heating any further. Pour into a flat dish. Put the junket in a warm place to set, grating some nutmeg over the top after the first 30 minutes. It should be ready to eat in two hours.

COLD DESSERTS

MILK SHAKES

Treat these as desserts or as meals in a hurry rather than drinks. Start by using only 150 ml (5 fl oz) milk per child, as milk shakes can be quite filling. Whip the mixture for about 20 seconds in a blender or food processor to make it frothy. For a really special shake, top with a small scoop of home-made ice-cream.

Put 275 ml (10 fl oz) milk into the machine with one of the following:

- 1 small ripe banana, sliced;
- 1 small very ripe peach, chopped, or equivalent tinned in natural juice;
- 50 g (2 oz) strawberries, mashed or sieved: use fresh, frozen or tinned in natural juice;
- 1 dessert apple, baked until very soft, plus 1 tablespoon concentrated apple juice;
- blackcurrants tinned in natural juice, sieved with their juice: use 2 tablespoons resulting purée;
- 3 tablespoons concentrated apple juice;
- 2 tablespoons apple and pear spread;
- 1 tablespoon honey;
- 2 teaspoons honey plus 2 teaspoons sieved carob powder.

DRIED FRUIT WHIZ

E G W Serves 2 adults and 2 children

125 g (4 oz) dried whole apricots
125 g (4 oz) prunes
275 ml (10 fl oz) unsweetened fruit juice
150 ml (5 fl oz) natural yoghurt

Soak the apricots and prunes in the juice overnight; or put them into a saucepan with the juice, bring them to the boil and leave for 4 hours. Drain the fruits, reserving the juice. Halve and stone the prunes. Put all the fruits through a blender or food processor with the juice. Add the yoghurt and blend again.

The whiz can be served just as it is or scattered with chopped mixed nuts, flaked almonds, a grated sugar-free carob bar or some Oat Crunch (page 31).

BLACKCURRANT JELLY

E G W Serves 2 adults and 2 children

1 × 220 g (7½ oz) tin blackcurrants in apple juice
2 tablespoons honey (optional)
15 g (½ oz) gelatine
4 tablespoons water
275 ml (10 fl oz) natural yoghurt

Put the blackcurrants and honey into a saucepan and warm them over a low heat until the honey dissolves. In a small pan, soak the gelatine in the water for 5 minutes. Melt it over a low heat and stir it into the blackcurrants. Cool slightly and then stir in the yoghurt. Pour the jelly either into a dish or into a lightly oiled 575 ml (1 pint) mould. Leave in a cool place for 2 hours to set.

STRAWBERRY WHIP

E W Serves 2 adults and 2 children

225 g (8 oz) ripe strawberries, or frozen strawberries, thawed
225 g (8 oz) curd cheese
125 g (4 oz) cream cheese
(or 350 g (12 oz) curd cheese)
2 tablespoons sugar-free strawberry jam, or honey
4 tablespoons Oat Crunch (page 31)

Rub the strawberries through a sieve. Cream the cheeses together in a bowl. Beat in the jam or honey and gradually beat in the strawberry purée. Pile the whip into one large bowl or into individual bowls. Scatter the oat crunch over the top.

ICE-CREAM

Home-made ice-cream, even if you use single cream, will be cheaper and certainly more nutritious than most bought varieties. To give a lighter texture and flavour, and in the interests of economy and a healthy diet, most of the ice-creams here are made with a mixture of cream and yoghurt. You can also make ice-creams using milk or soya milk, or use all yoghurt.

When the ice-cream has been mixed, cool it first, then chill it in the refrigerator for 30 minutes. Pour the mixture into a shallow freezing tray: this enables the mixture to freeze quickly. Leave it in the freezing compartment of the refrigerator, turned to its lowest setting, or in the coldest part of the freezer for 3 hours or until it has frozen to a slush. Take it out, turn the mixture into a large bowl and whisk it well to break up the ice particles. Put it into a covered plastic container and freeze for a further 4 hours or until quite firm.

The ice-cream can be eaten immediately or stored in the freezer for up to 3 months, or in the freezing compartment of the refrigerator for up to 2 weeks, according to the star rating.

Before serving, put the ice-cream into the refrigerator for 1 hour so that it softens gradually. Serve it with an ice-cream scoop or a tablespoon dipped in hot water: dip it again between each scoop.

STRAWBERRY ICE-CREAM
E G W Serves 4

350 g (12 oz) ripe strawberries, or frozen strawberries, thawed
225 ml (8 fl oz) double cream
125 g (4 oz) sugar-free strawberry jam, or soft honey
225 ml (8 fl oz) natural yoghurt

Rub the strawberries through a sieve. Whip the cream until it stands in peaks. Whip in the jam or honey and then the yoghurt. Thoroughly mix in the strawberries. Freeze as above.

APRICOT JAM ICE-CREAM
G W Serves 4

1 vanilla pod, or 1 teaspoon vanilla essence
275 ml (10 fl oz) single cream
125 g (4 oz) sugar-free apricot jam, or honey
3 egg yolks
275 ml (10 fl oz) natural yoghurt

Split the vanilla pod and put it into a saucepan with the cream. Bring them to just below boiling point and leave to cool. Remove the vanilla pod. If you are using vanilla essence, add it after heating the cream.

Melt the jam on a low heat and bring it to just below boiling point. Beat it into the egg yolks until the mixture is light and fluffy. Whip in the cream and then the yoghurt. Cool, chill and freeze (see left).

VANILLA AND HONEY ICE-CREAM
E G W Serves 4

275 ml (10 fl oz) double cream
75 g (3 oz) soft honey
¼ teaspoon vanilla essence
275 ml (10 fl oz) natural yoghurt

Whip the cream until it stands in peaks. Whip in the honey, vanilla essence and finally the yoghurt. Freeze (see left).

HOT CAROB SAUCE FOR ICE-CREAM
E G W

1 × 40 g (1½ oz) sugar-free carob bar
15 g (½ oz) arrowroot
275 ml (10 fl oz) milk

Finely grate the carob bar. Put the arrowroot into a bowl and mix in 6 tablespoons of the milk. Put the remaining milk into a saucepan and warm it. Stir it into the arrowroot. Pour the mixture back into the pan and bring to the boil, stirring. Simmer for 2 minutes, stirring all the time. Take the pan from the heat and let the mixture come off the boil. Quickly beat in the carob to make a smooth sauce.

BANANA MILK ICE
E G W Serves 6

4 ripe bananas
50 g (2 oz) apple and pear spread
25 g (1 oz) arrowroot
850 ml (1½ pints) milk, or soya milk

Mash the bananas with the apple and pear spread. Put the arrowroot into a bowl and gradually mix in 150 ml (5 fl oz) milk so you have a thin, smooth paste. Put the remaining milk into a saucepan and bring to just below boiling point. Stir the boiled milk into the arrowroot. Return the mixture to the saucepan and bring it to the boil, stirring. Boil for 2 minutes to thicken, stirring all the time. Stir in the banana mixture thoroughly. Cool, chill and freeze as for ice-cream.

CAROB MILK ICE
E G W Serves 6

2 × 40 g (1½ oz) sugar-free carob bars
25 g (1 oz) arrowroot
850 ml (1½ pints) milk, or soya milk

Finely grate the carob bars. Put the arrowroot into a bowl and gradually mix in 150 ml (5 fl oz) of the milk to make a smooth paste. Put the remaining milk into a saucepan and bring it to just below boiling point. Stir it into the arrowroot. Return the mixture to the saucepan and bring it to the boil, stirring. Boil for 2 minutes to thicken, stirring all the time, then take the pan from the heat and cool the mixture for 2 minutes. Add the grated carob and beat well to melt it and mix it in. Cool, chill and freeze as for ice-cream.

BAKED SPONGE PUDDING
Serves 6

50 g (2 oz) margarine
50 g (2 oz) apple and pear spread
125 g (4 oz) wholewheat flour
1 teaspoon bicarbonate of soda
flavouring (optional, see below)
1 egg
4 tablespoons milk
topping (see below)

Heat the oven to 180°C/350°F/Gas Mark 4. Cream the margarine with the apple and pear spread. Mix the flour with the bicarbonate of soda and one of the flavourings below, if using. Beat the egg. Gradually beat the flour into the margarine, alternating with the egg and the milk. Put one of the toppings below into an 850 ml (1½ pint) shallow, ovenproof dish. Spread the sponge mixture over the top and bake for 40 minutes or until golden.

When cooked, let the pudding cool in its dish for about 5 minutes, then turn it out carefully on to a flat serving plate.

Flavourings
Add with the bicarbonate of soda one of the following:
- ½ teaspoon ground mixed spice
- ¼ teaspoon ground cloves
- ½ teaspoon ground cinnamon
- ⅛ nutmeg, finely grated, or ¼ teaspoon ground nutmeg.

Toppings
Apple and Raisin 450 g (1 lb) cooking apples, peeled, cored and chopped, plus 75 g (3 oz) raisins and 2 tablespoons apple and pear spread.

Plum and Date 350 g (12 oz) plums, halved and stoned, plus 75 g (3 oz) stoned dates, chopped, and 3 tablespoons concentrated apple juice.

Dried Fruit 125 g (4 oz) prunes or whole apricots or a mixture, soaked in 275 ml (10 fl oz) unsweetened fruit juice overnight. Stone the prunes before using. Add both fruit and juice to the dish.

Tinned Fruit 1 × 225 g (8 oz) tin fruit in natural juice: use the juice as well as the fruit.

HOT PUDDINGS

BAKED BANANA SLICES
D E G W Serves 4

Use four medium-sized, firm bananas with no brown patches. Cut them into slices 6 mm ($\frac{1}{4}$ in) thick and put them into an ovenproof dish. Add one of the flavourings below, then cover with foil and put into a preheated 200°C/400°F/Gas Mark 6 oven for 10 minutes to heat through.

Flavourings
- grated rind and juice 1 orange plus 50 g (2 oz) raisins or sultanas;
- grated rind and juice 1 orange plus 2 tablespoons honey;
- 4 tablespoons sugar-free apricot jam;
- 3 tablespoons sugar-free marmalade;
- jam or marmalade as above plus 2 tablespoons ground almonds;
- 75 g (3 oz) chopped dates plus 6 tablespoons unsweetened pineapple or apple juice;
- 4 tablespoons concentrated apple juice.

BREAD AND BUTTER PUDDING
Serves 4

225 g (8 oz) wholewheat bread
butter, or margarine
225 g (8 oz) stoned dates
3 eggs
275 ml (10 fl oz) milk

Heat the oven to 200°C/400°F/Gas Mark 6. Thinly slice the bread and cut off any tough crusts. Lightly butter the slices and cut them into quarters. Finely chop the dates. Put one-third of the bread in the bottom of a greased, ovenproof dish. Scatter over half the dates. Put in another third of the bread, the remaining dates and the remaining bread.

Beat the eggs into the milk. Pour the mixture over the bread and dates and bake the pudding for 25 minutes or until the custard is set and the top browned.

BAKED APPLES
D E G W

These are easy to prepare and make an economical dessert, especially if the oven is already on to cook the main dish. Use either small to medium-sized cooking apples or crisp eating apples. Cooking apples have a better flavour, although they will probably need extra sweetening after they are cooked. Dessert apples have a mild, sweet flavour of their own.

To cook baked apples, heat the oven to 200°C/400°F/Gas Mark 6. Allow one apple per person. Core each one and score it with a sharp knife round the centre – this will prevent it from bursting. Place the apples upright in a flat, ovenproof dish. Fill them with one of the fillings and pour in about 1.5 cm ($\frac{1}{2}$ in) water or fruit juice. Bake for 20 minutes so that the middles soften but the apples stay whole.

For very young children, remove the soft apple and the filling from the skin and mash them together.

Fillings
Quantities for 4 apples:
- 125 g (4 oz) dates or figs, finely chopped and mixed with 2 tablespoons sugar-free jam or honey;
- 125 g (4 oz) sultanas or raisins mixed with 2 tablespoons sugar-free jam or honey;
- 75 g (3 oz) ground almonds mixed with grated rind and juice 1 medium orange plus 50 g (2 oz) raisins;
- 75 g (3 oz) ground almonds or other nuts mixed with 3 tablespoons sugar-free jam or marmalade;
- 50 g (2 oz) each shelled walnuts and dried whole apricots minced together or finely chopped in a blender or food processor, plus 2 tablespoons concentrated apple juice;
- 50 g (2 oz) each shelled walnuts and dates, raisins or sultanas minced together or finely chopped in a food processor or blender, plus 2 tablespoons concentrated apple juice;
- 50 g (2 oz) each almonds or hazelnuts and dried whole apricots minced together or finely chopped in a food processor or blender, plus 2 tablespoons concentrated apple juice.

HOT PUDDINGS

STEAMED CAROB PUDDING
D Serves 4

75 g (3 oz) stoned dates
6 tablespoons unsweetened orange juice
50 g (2 oz) carob powder
125 g (4 oz) wholewheat flour
1 teaspoon bicarbonate of soda
2 eggs
125 g (4 oz) vegetable margarine

Sauce
275 ml (10 fl oz) unsweetened orange
or pineapple juice
1 tablespoon arrowroot

Finely chop the dates. Put them into a saucepan with the orange juice, bring to the boil and simmer for 5 minutes. Put them through a blender or food processor. Sieve the carob powder and mix it with the flour and bicarbonate of soda. Beat the eggs. Cream the margarine and gradually beat in the blended dates. Beat in the flour mixture, alternating with the eggs. Put the mixture into a greased 850 ml (1½ pint) pudding basin. Cover it with buttered greaseproof paper and then aluminium foil. Tie the cover down securely and lower the pudding into a saucepan of boiling water. Cover and steam for 1 hour 30 minutes, topping up the water when necessary.

Turn the pudding out of the basin and serve it hot with the sauce: put the arrowroot into a bowl and mix in 6 tablespoons of the fruit juice. Put the remaining juice into a saucepan and bring to the boil. Stir in the arrowroot mixture and continue stirring until the sauce is thick. Take the pan from the heat.

GRILLED APPLE SLICES
E G W Serves 4

4 cooking apples
25 g (1 oz) butter
3 tablespoons honey
2 teaspoons ground cinnamon
natural yoghurt

Peel and core the apples, and cut them into rings 6 mm (¼ in) thick. Arrange them in a shallow heatproof dish, overlapping as little as possible. Melt the butter in a saucepan over a low heat, and brush it over the apples. Put the honey into the saucepan with the cinnamon, melt over a low heat and spoon over the apples.

Heat the grill to high. Put the dish under the grill so that the rings are about 5 cm (2 in) from the heat. Cook for about 3 minutes or until brown and bubbling. Turn them over and brown the other side. Serve the rings immediately, topped with yoghurt.

OATY TOPPED APRICOTS
D E Serves 4

175 g (6 oz) dried whole apricots
225 ml (8 fl oz) unsweetened orange juice
75 g (3 oz) jumbo oats
15 g ($\frac{1}{2}$ oz) wheatgerm
25 g (1 oz) desiccated coconut
15 g ($\frac{1}{2}$ oz) sunflower seeds,
or chopped toasted hazelnuts,
or chopped mixed nuts
3 tablespoons sunflower oil

Soak the apricots overnight in the orange juice. Alternatively, put them into a saucepan with the juice and bring to the boil. Take the pan from the heat and leave the apricots to soak for 4 hours.

Heat the oven to 200°C/400°F/Gas Mark 6. Drain and quarter the apricots, and put them with their juice into a pie dish. In a bowl, mix together the oats, wheatgerm, coconut and seeds or nuts. Add the oil and mix well, making sure that all the dry ingredients are well coated. Cover the apricots with the mixture. Put the dish into the oven for 30 minutes or until the oats are golden brown on top.

Serve hot or cold accompanied, if wished, with natural yoghurt. This topping can be used instead of the usual crumble mixture on top of any fresh fruits such as apples, rhubarb or plums.

BROWN RICE PUDDING
E G W Serves 4

50 g (2 oz) short grain brown rice
50 g (2 oz) honey, or maple syrup, or sugar-free jam, or apple and pear spread
575 ml (1 pint) milk
$\frac{1}{8}$ nutmeg, freshly grated,
or $\frac{1}{4}$ teaspoon ground nutmeg

Heat the oven to 140°C/275°F/Gas Mark 1. Put the rice into a bowl. Put the sweetener into a saucepan and melt it over a low heat; leave to cool. Mix it into the rice and add the milk and nutmeg to taste. Pour the mixture into a pie dish and bake for 3 hours, stirring well after the first hour.

APPLE OR RAISIN RICE PUDDING
E G W

Make the pudding mixture in the same way as Brown Rice Pudding, but flavour it with a pinch of ground cloves instead of nutmeg. Chop 2 dessert apples or 75 g (3 oz) raisins and put them into the bottom of the pie dish before adding the pudding mixture. Bake as for Brown Rice Pudding but do not stir.

APRICOT RICE PUDDING
E G W Serves 4

125 g (4 oz) dried whole apricots
275 ml (10 fl oz) water,
or unsweetened orange juice
50 g (2 oz) sugar-free apricot jam
50 g (2 oz) short grain brown rice
575 ml (1 pint) milk
freshly grated nutmeg

Put the apricots into a saucepan with the water or orange juice, and bring them to the boil. Remove from the heat and leave to soak for 4 hours. Put the apricots through a blender or food processor with 6 tablespoons of the juice, and spread the purée in the bottom of a pie dish. Make a rice pudding mixture in the same way as for Brown Rice Pudding and pour it over the apricots. Bake as for Brown Rice Pudding, but do not stir.

PASTRY · TARTS · PIES

EASY SHORTCRUST PASTRY
E

225 g (8 oz) wholewheat flour
pinch fine sea salt
125 g (4 oz) margarine, or butter
4 tablespoons water

Put the flour and salt into a bowl. Make a well in the centre, add the margarine and water, and using a fork or pastry blender gradually mix them into the flour. Press the mixture together with your fingers so that you have a smooth dough. Leave it in a cool place for 15 minutes before using.

OIL PASTRY
D E

225 g (8 oz) wholewheat flour
pinch fine sea salt
6 tablespoons corn oil
4 tablespoons water

Rub the oil into the flour and salt and mix to a dough with the water. Gather it all together into a ball. This is very crumbly pastry to handle, but it has a deliciously crisp texture when cooked. You may find it easier to roll it out between 2 sheets of greaseproof paper, or you can press it into the flan or pie dish with your knuckles, and avoid rolling it out altogether. Use and bake it like ordinary pastry.

TAHINI TART
E Serves 6

shortcrust pastry made with 125 g (4 oz)
wholewheat flour
150 ml (5 fl oz) tahini
150 ml (5 fl oz) natural yoghurt
2 tablespoons dried skimmed milk powder
50 g (2 oz) honey

Heat the oven to 200°C/400°F/Gas Mark 6. Roll out the pastry and line an 18 cm (7 in) tart tin. Thoroughly mix together all the ingredients for the filling – this is easiest in a blender or food processor. Put the mixture into the pastry base and bake for 20 minutes or until the top is golden and risen. Cool completely before serving.

APPLE AND BLACKBERRY PIE
D Serves 4

shortcrust pastry made with 225 g (8 oz)
wholewheat flour, with ½ teaspoon
bicarbonate of soda added before the fat
450 g (1 lb) cooking apples
1 × 225 g (8 oz) tin blackberries in
apple juice
1 tablespoon arrowroot, or cornflour
2 tablespoons cold water
beaten egg for glaze

Heat the oven to 200°C/400°F/Gas Mark 6. Peel, core and chop the apples. Put them into a saucepan with the blackberries and their juice. Bring to the boil, cover and simmer for 15 minutes or until the apples are soft and can be beaten to a rough purée. Put the arrowroot into a bowl. Mix in the water, then add to the apples. Stir with a wooden spoon until the mixture boils and thickens – about 1½ minutes. Take the pan from the heat and let the mixture cool to room temperature.

Using about two-thirds of the pastry, line a 20 cm (8 in) diameter, 4–5 cm (1½–2 in) deep, sloping-sided pie dish. Put in the filling, cover it with the remaining pastry and trim and seal the edges. Brush the top of the pie with the beaten egg. Bake for 30 minutes or until the pastry is golden.

Serve warm.

APPLE BATTER
Serves 6

shortcrust pastry made with 225 g (8 oz)
wholewheat flour
675 g (1½ lb) cooking apples
75 g (3 oz) honey, or apple and pear spread
1 teaspoon ground mixed spice
75 g (3 oz) wholewheat flour
2 eggs
100 ml (3½ fl oz) milk
100 ml (3½ fl oz) water

Heat the oven to 200°C/400°F/Gas Mark 6.
Roll out the pastry and line a Swiss roll
tin. Peel, core and thinly slice the apples.
Put them into a bowl and mix in the honey
or apple and pear spread and spice. Spread
the mixture evenly over the pastry base.

Put the flour and salt into a bowl and
make a well in the centre. Beat the eggs
together and pour into the well. Gradually
begin to mix in flour from the sides, then
beat in the milk and water. Pour the batter
over the apples and bake for 30 minutes or
until set and golden. Cool in the tin.

Serve warm or cold, cut in slices.

FRUITY PLUM PIE
D Serves 4

shortcrust pastry made with 125 g (4 oz)
wholewheat flour
675 g (1½ lb) dessert plums
50 g (2 oz) raisins
50 g (2 oz) apple and pear spread
beaten egg for glaze

Heat the oven to 200°C/400°F/Gas Mark 6.
Stone and slice the plums and put them
into a bowl with the raisins. Mix in the
apple and pear spread. Put the mixture
into a small pie dish and put a pie funnel in
the centre. Cover with the pastry and
brush the top with beaten egg. Bake for 25
minutes or until the top is golden.

Serve warm.

QUICK BOILED SEMOLINA PUDDING
E Serves 4

575 ml (1 pint) milk
(or ¾ milk and ¼ unsweetened fruit juice)
40 g (1½ oz) wholewheat semolina

Warm the milk in a saucepan. Sprinkle in
the semolina and the chosen sweetener
(see below). Bring the mixture to the boil,
stirring. Stir over the heat for 2 minutes or
until thick. Pour into bowls.

Sweeteners for Boiled Semolina Pudding

● up to 75 g (3 oz) sultanas or raisins, or
a mixture
● 4–6 tablespoons concentrated apple
juice
● 3 tablespoons honey
● 3 tablespoons apple and pear spread.

Add after cooking:
● 3–4 tablespoons sugar-free jam.

MOULDED SEMOLINA PUDDINGS

These puddings are made thicker for setting in a mould, and are eaten cold. Make
them in the same way as the boiled pudding, using 50 g (2 oz) semolina instead of
40 g (1½ oz). Flavour and sweeten in the
same way. Pour the mixture into a lightly
wetted mould and leave it in a cool place
for 2 hours to set. Turn out on a plate to
serve. Fresh fruit makes a good
accompaniment.

Or try one of the following recipes.

LEMON MOULDED PUDDING
E Serves 4

Thinly pare the rind from one lemon. Put
it into the milk and leave for 10 minutes on
a very low heat without boiling. Strain,
then use the milk to make the pudding.
Use 3 tablespoons honey as the sweetener.

SEMOLINA PUDDINGS

VANILLA MOULDED PUDDING
E Serves 4

Flavour the milk as for Lemon Moulded Pudding, using a vanilla pod, or add ½ teaspoon of vanilla essence to the milk – in this case there is no need to infuse the milk over heat for 10 minutes. Make the pudding and add 3–4 tablespoons sugar-free strawberry jam before pouring into the mould.

ALMOND MOULDED PUDDING
E Serves 4

Flavour the milk with ¼ teaspoon almond essence. Make the pudding and sweeten it by adding 3–4 tablespoons sugar-free apricot or raspberry jam before pouring into the mould.

SEMOLINA AND CAROB MOULD
E Serves 4

1 × 40 g (1½ oz) sugar-free carob bar
575 ml (1 pint) milk
50 g (2 oz) wholewheat semolina
2 tablespoons concentrated apple juice

Finely grate the carob bar. Warm the milk in a saucepan, sprinkle in the semolina and add the concentrated apple juice. Stir over the heat for 2 minutes or until thick. Take the pan from the heat and quickly beat in the carob. Pour the mixture into a lightly wetted mould and leave in a cool place for 2 hours to set.
Serve with natural yoghurt.

BASIC BAKED SEMOLINA PUDDING
E Serves 4

40 g (1½ oz) wholewheat semolina
575 ml (1 pint) milk, flavoured as for moulded puddings if wished
sweetener as for boiled puddings (opposite)

If using raisins or sultanas as the sweetener, bring them to the boil in a little water and leave to stand for 1 hour.
Heat the oven to 150°C/300°F/Gas Mark 2. Butter an ovenproof dish about 5 cm (2 in) deep, and put in the semolina. Warm the milk and stir in the sweetener, if using. Pour over the semolina. Bake the pudding for 3 hours.
Alternatively, put either a thick layer of sugar-free jam, or cooked and chopped or puréed fruits, or soaked dried fruits in the bottom of the dish. Soak the semolina in the milk in a separate bowl for 3 hours and pour into the dish just before cooking. Bake as above.
Baked Semolina Pudding will develop a brown skin, which some children love but others hate. To prevent it from developing, cover the dish with oiled foil before putting it into the oven.

PEACHY SEMOLINA
E Serves 4

1 × 300 g (14 oz) tin peaches in natural juice
up to 575 ml (1 pint) milk
40 g (1½ oz) wholewheat semolina
¼ teaspoon almond essence (optional)

Heat the oven to 150°C/300°F/Gas Mark 2. Drain the peaches. Measure the juice, and make it up to 575 ml (1 pint) with the milk. Put the semolina into a bowl and pour in the milk mixture. Add the almond essence if using. Leave for 3 hours.
Put the peaches into the bottom of a greased ovenproof dish. Pour the semolina and milk over the top and cover with oiled foil if you want to prevent a brown skin forming. Bake for 3 hours.

CHAPTER SIX

SCHOOLDAYS

Breakfasts, High Teas, Sweets and Treats for Hungry Scholars

Now that your child is at school, his
nutritional demands are as great or even greater than they
were when he was a toddler. He is coping with new environments,
his brain is working harder than ever and he is burning up energy
in the playground with his friends. His stomach, however, is still
not as large as an adult's, and if it is filled with fizzy drinks and
sugary sweets there will not be enough room for the
nutritious foods that he needs.

Daily needs
Make sure that twice a day your child
eats protein foods. These can be meat,
fish, eggs, cheese, pulses or other
types of vegetarian protein foods
(pages 20–1). All the carbohydrates
that he eats should be unrefined –
wholewheat breads and biscuits,
brown rice, wholewheat pasta and
oatmeal. Fresh fruits and vegetables
should also be eaten twice a day if
possible. Fruits will provide the sweet
element in the diet. Very fatty foods
are not good for children or adults,
but do not cut fats out of his diet
altogether. Use good-quality vegetable
oils in cooking and a little margarine
or butter for spreading on bread. If
possible give yoghurt every day. This
will provide calcium. Milk is also a
good source of calcium and can be an
excellent snack when children come
home tired from school.

Breakfast
It is important for a school child to
start the day right. If he has no
breakfast, he will tire quickly and by
mid-morning his concentration will
begin to flag. Begin with freshly
squeezed orange juice or fresh fruit,
and then a choice of a whole grain
cereal, poached, boiled or scrambled
eggs, cheese on toast, beans on toast,

drop scones or sardine patties (page
85). If your child is not a hungry
person in the morning, try giving him
a supercharged milk drink (page 35).
Although recommended for pregnant
women, this contains a wide range of
nutrients that will also suit an active
child.

Sweets
There is bound to come a time when
your child wants to be like all his
schoolfriends and buy sweets and
crisps from the local shop. It is
unrealistic of you to expect fresh fruit
to fill the gap every time. What are
you going to do at Easter, for
example, when the ubiquitous
commercial product is a chocolate egg
with a gooey sugar centre? Will there
be boxes of chocolates at Christmas?
    The accepted argument against
proprietary brands of sweets is that
they consist mainly of sugar and food
colouring. They provide no
nourishment or fibre, they dull a
child's appetite for other nutrient-rich
foods, and they are a significant
contributor to tooth decay. Even the
doting relative who provides your
child with sweets as treats would
accept these arguments, but the idea
of giving children sweets is still all
too popular.

If your child's friends take sweets to school and he does not want to be left out, look around the healthfood shop: there are all kinds of fruit and nut bars, yoghurt or carob-coated peanuts and bags of banana chips. Alternatively, let your child take some home-made sweets (pages 91–5) to school. Although all sweets cause tooth decay, these will at least allow you to provide some nutrients in the treats that you give your child, and you can be sure that you are keeping the sugar in his diet to a minimum.

Problems will arise if the other children are given money to spend in the sweet shop on the way home. Try explaining to your child just why your home-made sweets are better. If necessary, give him plenty so that he can share them with the other children. If he really is miserable and worried about the situation, then let him be like the others once or even twice a week. If you weigh up the amount of sweets that he eats against the amount of nutritious foods you are giving him at home, you will see that there is nothing to worry about.

Home-made sweets
Provided you have a cupboard well stocked with nuts and dried fruits, semolina, carob powder and carob bars you should be able to make a variety of sweets quickly and easily. With dried fruit sweets, for example, there is no need for sugar thermometers and pans of boiling water, and no risk of scalding your eager helpers in the process. Other useful ingredients are desiccated coconut, tahini and the fruit juice in which the dried fruits were soaked.

It is not more expensive to make your own sweets. Commercial brands are no longer cheap and a few dried fruits will go a long way and will be more filling. It is obviously quicker to go to a shop and buy sweets, but instead you could turn sweetmaking into a weekly fun occasion. Let your children, within reason, choose the ingredients and help with shaping the mixture into balls or animal shapes or anything else that takes their fancy. This way, your sweets and treats will be far more appreciated than those bought from shops.

MUESLI

Use jumbo oats rather than the porridge oats. They can be used alone or mixed with rolled barley, wheat and rye: use half oats and make up the remaining weight with a mixture of the rest. (All these can normally be bought from healthfood shops.) Additions to muesli could be:

- chopped or ground nuts
- sesame seeds
- sunflower seeds
- raisins and sultanas
- chopped dates, figs and dried apricots
- banana chips
- toasted coconut flakes.

For young children use 2 tablespoons dry mixture and make it more palatable by soaking it overnight in a little natural yoghurt, milk or, provided it contains plenty of dried fruits, cooled boiled water or still mineral water. You will be surprised at how much it swells.

SUPER MUESLI
Ⓓ Ⓔ

225 g (8 oz) jumbo oats
65 g (2½ oz) rolled wheat
65 g (2½ oz) rolled barley
65 g (2½ oz) rolled rye
(or 125 g (4 oz) each rolled wheat and barley, omitting rye; or 450 g (1 lb) jumbo oats only)
175 g (6 oz) raisins
75 g (3 oz) stoned dates
50 g (2 oz) dried apricots
40 g (1½ oz) toasted coconut flakes
40 g (1½ oz) dried banana chips
125 g (4 oz) chopped nuts (can be all one type or a mixture)
50 g (2 oz) sunflower seeds

Chop the dates and apricots. Mix all the ingredients together and store in an airtight container. For young children 2 tablespoons of the dry mixture soaked overnight in milk, natural yoghurt or cooled boiled water makes one serving.

PORRIDGE
Ⓔ Ⓦ Serves 4

700 ml (1¼ pints) water
125 g (4 oz) porridge oats

Put the water into a saucepan and bring it to the boil. Scatter in the oats. Boil for 3 minutes, stirring. Remove from the heat and leave to stand for 5 minutes before serving, during which time the porridge should become thick. You can make porridge replacing half the water with milk, or make it entirely with milk.

Serve the porridge with sweet or savoury ingredients. For sweet toppings, choose from honey, molasses, sugar-free jam, chopped dried fruits and nuts, soaked dried fruits, cooked fresh fruits, fruits tinned in their own juice, or yoghurt. For a savoury topping, try chopped grilled bacon, chopped grilled mushrooms, grilled tomato slices, grilled smoked mackerel or herrings.

Fruity porridge is another variation: add 50–75 g (2–3 oz) dried fruits to the water or milk when you add the porridge. Choose between raisins, sultanas, chopped dried apricots, or chopped figs; or use a mixture.

BREAKFAST DISHES

CHEESY DROP SCONES

The batter improves if allowed to stand for a while, so make it the night before and cook the scones in the morning.

Makes 12

50 g (2 oz) wholewheat flour
$\frac{1}{4}$ teaspoon bicarbonate of soda
25 g (1 oz) butter
125 g (4 oz) cottage cheese
2 eggs
1 tablespoon milk
$\frac{1}{2}$ teaspoon yeast extract
oil for cooking

Mix the flour with the bicarbonate of soda. Melt the butter and beat it into the cottage cheese. Beat the eggs, then beat them into the mixture, followed by the flour and milk. Add the yeast extract and beat well to make sure that it becomes evenly mixed.

Lightly oil a heavy frying pan and set it on a high heat. When it is very hot, pour 1 tablespoon of the mixture into the pan and cook it until the top is just beginning to set and the underside is browned. Turn it over and brown the other side. If the pan is big enough, cook several together. When done, lift the scones on to a clean tea cloth and wrap them up to keep them soft and warm. Cook the remaining batter in the same way, re-oiling the pan if necessary.

Serve spread with curd cheese, low fat soft cheese, or with butter or margarine.

SARDINE PATTIES

These are for the family that likes a hearty savoury breakfast. Make them the night before and simply grill them in the morning.

E G Serves 4

1 × 125 g (4 oz) tin sardines in oil
450 g (1 lb) potatoes
4 tablespoons milk
1 tablespoon tomato purée (optional)
25 g (1 oz) bran
4 tablespoons oil

Scrub the potatoes. Cut them into chunks and steam them until tender. Skin them and mash with the milk. Drain the sardines and mash them. Mix them into the potatoes, with the tomato purée if using. Form the mixture into eight round, flat cakes and coat them in the bran.

Just before cooking, heat the grill to high. Brush the patties with the oil and grill them for 3 minutes on each side or until browned and heated through.

EGG CUSTARDS

G W Serves 2 adults and 2 children

4 eggs
150 ml (5 fl oz) milk
butter

Heat the oven to 190°C/375°F/Gas Mark 5. Beat the eggs with the milk and divide the mixture between four lightly buttered ramekin dishes or individual soufflé dishes (or other small, ovenproof dishes). Stand them on a baking sheet for ease of handling and to prevent them tipping up in the oven. Bake the custards for 20 minutes.

Serve hot, with wholewheat toast and freshly ground black pepper.

HIGH TEAS

BAKED BEANS

Instead of haricot beans, you can successfully use pinto or cannellini beans in this recipe, or brown or red kidney beans.
Ⓓ Ⓔ Ⓖ Ⓦ Serves 4

225 g (8 oz) haricot beans
1 large onion
4 tablespoons oil
575 ml (1 pint) vegetable
or meat stock (page 19)
2 teaspoons honey
2 teaspoons molasses
2 tablespoons tomato purée
2 tablespoons white wine vinegar

Put the beans into a saucepan and cover them with water. Bring to the boil, boil for 10 minutes and then soak them in the same water for 2 hours. Drain.

Heat the oven to 180°C/350°F/Gas Mark 4. Thinly slice the onion and soften it in the oil in a large, flameproof casserole over a low heat. Pour in the stock and bring it to the boil. Stir in the honey, molasses, tomato purée and wine vinegar. Put in the beans, cover the casserole and put it in the oven for 1 hour 30 minutes.

These are ideal for serving on wholewheat toast. Serve them as they are or topped with grated cheese and a sprinkling of wheatgerm.

TUNA QUICHE
Serves 4

shortcrust pastry made with 175 g (6 oz)
wholewheat flour (page 79)
175 g (6 oz) tomatoes
1 × 100 g (3½ oz) tin tuna
2 eggs
200 ml (7 fl oz) milk

Heat the oven to 200°C/400°F/Gas Mark 6. Line a 20 cm (8 in) tart tin with the pastry. Thinly slice the tomatoes and lay them in the base. Drain and flake the tuna and put it evenly on top of the tomatoes. Beat the eggs with the milk and pour them over the top. Bake the quiche for 30 minutes or until the filling is set and beginning to brown on top.

Serve hot or cold; to reheat, put into a hot oven for 10 minutes.

NUTTY PIE
Serves 4

shortcrust pastry made with 125 g (4 oz)
wholewheat flour (page 79)
50 g (2 oz) walnuts
50 g (2 oz) hazelnuts
50 g (2 oz) fresh wholewheat breadcrumbs
1 teaspoon dried mixed herbs
2 eggs
150 ml (5 fl oz) milk

Heat the oven to 200°C/400°F/Gas Mark 6. Use the pastry to line an 18 cm (7 in) tart tin. Very finely chop or grind the nuts and mix them with the breadcrumbs and herbs. Beat the eggs together and gradually incorporate them in the mixture. Finally add the milk. Pour the mixture into the pastry shell and bake for 30 minutes or until the filling is set and golden.

Serve hot or cold; to reheat, put into a hot oven for 10 minutes.

RED LEICESTER QUICHE
Serves 4

shortcrust pastry made with 125 g (4 oz)
wholewheat flour (page 79)
1 medium onion
15 g (½ oz) butter
75 g (3 oz) Red Leicester cheese, grated
2 eggs
2 tablespoons tomato purée
150 ml (5 fl oz) milk

Heat the oven to 200°C/400°F/Gas Mark 6. Use the pastry to line a 20 cm (8 in) tart tin. Thinly slice the onion and cook it in the butter until it is soft and beginning to turn golden. Spread the onion in the pastry base and scatter the cheese over the top. Beat the eggs with the tomato purée and beat in the milk. Pour the mixture over the cheese. Bake the quiche for 30 minutes or until the filling is set and beginning to brown.

Serve hot or cold; to reheat, put into a hot oven for 10 minutes.

HIGH TEAS

RED BEAN BAPS
E

4 wholewheat baps
225 g (8 oz) cooked red
kidney beans (page 12)
1 small red pepper
125 g (4 oz) Cheddar cheese, grated
1 tablespoon tomato purée
¼ teaspoon Tabasco sauce

Heat the oven to 200°C/400°F/Gas Mark 6. Split the baps in half. Divide the beans between the bottom portions of the baps. Core and seed the pepper and cut it into strips. Put them on top of the beans. Mix the cheese with the tomato purée and Tabasco sauce. Divide the mixture between the baps and sandwich them back together again. Put the baps, two at a time, into roasting bags, lay them on a baking sheet and put them into the oven for 10 minutes.

CHEESE AND TOMATO TOASTS
Serves 4

8 large slices wholewheat bread
175 g (6 oz) Red Leicester or Cheddar
cheese, grated
1 tablespoon tomato purée
4 tablespoons milk
butter or margarine for toast (optional)
3–4 tomatoes (optional)

Cream the cheese with the tomato purée and milk. Toast the bread on one side only, turn it over and butter the other side if wished. Spread the cheese mixture over the toast and return the slices to the grill until the cheese melts and bubbles. You will get an attractive marbling effect with the orange cheese and red purée. You can lay sliced tomatoes on top just as the cheese begins to melt, which will heat through as the toasts finish cooking.

SWEETCORN BAPS
E

4 wholewheat baps
4 small tomatoes
6 tablespoons tinned sweetcorn
4 teaspoons peach chutney
175 g (6 oz) Edam cheese, grated

Heat the oven to 200°C/400°F/Gas Mark 6. Split the baps in half. Cut each tomato into four slices and lay them on the bottom portions of the baps. Mix together the corn, chutney and cheese. Divide the mixture between the baps and sandwich them back together again. Put the baps, two at a time, into roasting bags, lay them on a baking sheet and put them into the oven for 10 minutes.

CHEESE AND TOMATO PASTA
Serves 4

225 g (8 oz) wholewheat macaroni,
or other pasta shapes
350 g (12 oz) tomatoes
25 g (1 oz) butter, or margarine
2 tablespoons wholewheat flour
275 ml (10 fl oz) milk
2 tablespoons tomato purée
125 g (4 oz) Cheddar cheese, finely grated

Heat the oven to 200°C/400°F/Gas Mark 6. Boil the pasta in lightly salted water for 12–15 minutes, or until tender. Drain. Chop the tomatoes. (If you have time and don't mind doing it, scald and skin them first.) Mix them into the macaroni, and pour all into an ovenproof dish.

Melt the butter in a saucepan on a moderate heat. Stir in the flour, cook it gently for 2–3 minutes, then gradually add the milk. Bring to the boil, stirring. Simmer for 2 minutes. Take the pan from the heat and beat in the tomato purée and two-thirds of the cheese. Pour the sauce over the macaroni. Scatter the remaining cheese over the top and put the dish into the oven for 20 minutes or until the cheese has melted and is just beginning to brown round the edges.

HIGH TEAS

PASTA AND CAULIFLOWER CHEESE

Pasta spirals work very well in this dish.
Serves 4

225 g (8 oz) wholewheat pasta shapes
1 medium cauliflower
25 g (1 oz) butter, or margarine
2 tablespoons wholewheat flour
275 ml (10 fl oz) milk
125 g (4 oz) Cheddar cheese, finely grated
1 tablespoon wheatgerm

Heat the oven to 200°C/400°F/Gas Mark 6. Boil the pasta shapes in lightly salted water for 12–15 minutes or until tender. Drain. Break the cauliflower into small florettes and steam them for 10 minutes or until just tender. Mix the pasta and cauliflower in a flat, ovenproof dish.

Melt the butter or margarine in a saucepan on a medium heat. Stir in the flour, cook it gently for 2–3 minutes, then gradually add the milk. Bring to the boil, stirring. Simmer for 1 minute or until you have a thick sauce. Take the pan from the heat and beat in two-thirds of the cheese. Pour the sauce over the cauliflower and pasta. Scatter the remaining cheese and then the wheatgerm over the top, and put the dish into the oven for 15 minutes or until the cheese has melted and the top is beginning to brown.

SAVOURY RICE
D E G W Serves 4

225 g (8 oz) long grain brown rice
2 tablespoons oil
1 small onion (optional)
575 ml (1 pint) stock (page 19)

Heat the oil in a saucepan on a low heat. Thinly slice the onion, if using, and soften it. Put in the rice and stir for $\frac{1}{2}$ minute. Pour in the stock and bring to the boil. Cover and simmer gently for 45 minutes, or until the rice is soft and all the water has been absorbed.

Vary the rice as suggested below.

Flavourings
Add one of the following during cooking:
● 4 chopped celery sticks softened with the onion;
● 125 g (4 oz) mushrooms, sliced and cooked with the onion;
● 175 g (6 oz) carrots, added after the stock has boiled;
● 1 tablespoon tomato purée, added with the stock.

Variations
Fork these in after the rice has cooked:
● 125 g (4 oz) grated Cheddar or Edam cheese plus 4 chopped tomatoes;
● 1 × 125 g (4 oz) tin sardines plus 4 chopped tomatoes;
● 1 × 100 g (3$\frac{1}{2}$ oz) tin tuna plus 4 tablespoons chopped parsley;
● 125 g (4 oz) peanuts (very good if celery or carrots are used);
● 125 g (4 oz) diced ham or corned beef;
● 125 g (4 oz) cooked red kidney beans (page 12) plus 50 g (2 oz) grated cheese and 4 chopped tomatoes.

Right: Pancakes with Scrambled Egg Filling, top (p. 89); Cheese and Tomato Toasts, bottom (p. 87).

Overleaf from left to right: Banana Cake (p. 133), Sesame-Coated Drumsticks (p. 128), Lentil Minestrone (p. 118), All-in-One Burghul Salad (p. 124).

PANCAKES

PANCAKES
Basic mixture makes 8 pancakes

125 g (4 oz) wholewheat flour
pinch fine sea salt
1 egg
1 egg yolk
150 ml (5 fl oz) milk
150 ml (5 fl oz) water
1 tablespoon oil
oil for frying

Put the flour and salt into a mixing bowl and make a well in the centre. Beat together the egg and egg yolk and put them in the well. Gradually begin to beat in the flour from the sides. Mix together the milk and water and beat them into the flour a little at a time, until you have used half. Beat well, making sure the batter is smooth. Beat in the oil and then the remaining milk and water. Leave the batter to stand for 30 minutes.

Heat 1 tablespoon oil in an 18 cm (7 in) omelette pan on a medium heat. Put in 3 tablespoons of the batter and tip the pan to spread it out quickly. Cook until the underside is speckled brown, the top is set and the edges are beginning to look lacy. Turn it over and cook until the underside has browned. Lift the pancake on to a plate. Cook the others in the same way and leave to cool.

To fill the pancakes, put a portion of one of the fillings that follow on one end in a long shape, and roll up from that end. Lay the pancakes in a flat, ovenproof dish and cover them with foil. Reheat if necessary in a preheated 200°C/400°F/Gas Mark 6 oven for 10 minutes.

The pancakes will be soft and moist so there is no need to make a sauce for them, but they can be scattered with grated Cheddar cheese.

SCRAMBLED EGG PANCAKE FILLING
Fills 8 pancakes

4 eggs
50 g (2 oz) mature Cheddar cheese, finely grated
50 g (2 oz) mushrooms
225 g (8 oz) tomatoes
25 g (1 oz) butter

Beat the eggs with the cheese. Finely chop the mushrooms. Scald, skin and chop the tomatoes. Melt the butter in a saucepan on a low heat. Put in the mushrooms and cook them for 2 minutes. Pour in the egg and cheese mixture and cook it, stirring, until it sets into a scramble. Stir in the tomatoes. Cool the mixture before filling the pancakes.

TUNA AND TOMATO PANCAKE FILLING
Fills 8 pancakes

1 × 200 g (7 oz) tin tuna
225 g (8 oz) tomatoes
1 small onion
2 tablespoons oil
2 tablespoons tinned sweetcorn
2 tablespoons chopped parsley (optional)

Scald, skin and chop the tomatoes. Finely chop the onion. Drain and flake the tuna. Heat the oil in a frying pan on a low heat. Soften the onion, take the pan from the heat and mix in the tomatoes, tuna, sweetcorn and parsley. Cool the mixture before filling the pancakes.

Left: Mr Sunshine Salad (p. 64).

BAKED POTATOES

Scrub medium to large, even-sized potatoes. Prick them twice on both sides with a fork. Lay the potatoes on the oven rack, turn the oven to 200°C/400°F/Gas Mark 6 and leave the potatoes for 1 hour 30 minutes. (If you are putting the potatoes into a preheated oven, cook them for 1 hour 15 minutes.) When done, they should have soft, fluffy middles and delicious crispy skins. Split the potatoes in half and serve with a nut of butter or margarine, or with one of the toppings that follow.

LENTIL BAKED POTATO TOPPING
D E G W For 4 potatoes

75 g (3 oz) split red lentils
2 medium carrots
1 small onion
1 large celery stick
2 tablespoons oil
½ clove garlic (optional)
275 ml (10 fl oz) stock (page 12)
½ teaspoon yeast extract

Finely grate the carrots. Finely chop the onion and celery. Heat the oil in a saucepan over a low heat and stir in the carrots, onion, celery and crushed garlic. Cover and cook them gently for 5 minutes. Stir in the lentils and cook, stirring, for 1 minute. Pour in the stock and yeast extract and bring to the boil. Cover and simmer gently for 30 minutes or until the lentils are soft.
  Split the potatoes in half and pile on the topping.

SARDINE BAKED POTATO TOPPING
D E G W For 4 potatoes

2 × 125 g (4 oz) tins sardines in tomato sauce
150 ml (5 fl oz) tomato and vegetable juice

Mash the sardines with their sauce. Put them into a saucepan and stir in the juice. Bring to a gentle boil, stirring, then pour over the baked potatoes. Chopped parsley may be added to the mixture if wished, or sprinkled over the top before serving.

CORN AND EGG BAKED POTATO TOPPING
D For 4 potatoes

1 × 350 g (12 oz) tin sweetcorn, drained
2 eggs, hard-boiled
15 g (½ oz) vegetable margarine
1 tablespoon wholewheat flour
150 ml (5 fl oz) stock (page 19)

Melt the margarine in a saucepan over a low heat. Stir in the flour and then the stock. Bring to the boil, stirring. Put in the sweetcorn and chopped egg and heat them through. Split the baked potatoes in half and pile the mixture on top.

HAM AND TOMATO BAKED POTATO TOPPING
D E G W For 4 potatoes

225 g (8 oz) cooked lean ham (page 119)
1 × 200 g (7 oz) tin tomatoes in juice
pinch dried mixed herbs (optional)

Finely dice the ham. Mash the tomatoes with their juice or put both through a blender or food processor. Put them into a saucepan and bring to the boil. Add the ham and herbs and simmer for 2 minutes. Split the potatoes in half and pour the mixture over.
  A small chopped onion can be softened in 2 tablespoons oil in the saucepan before adding the tomatoes.

ICED LOLLIES

ICED LOLLIES
The Basic Principles

Iced lollies are summer favourites with children of all ages. Making them yourself has two advantages: you can keep a ready supply in the freezer, and you can be confident that they contain healthy ingredients only.

You can buy lolly moulds from most cookware shops. The best are those that make use of disposable rolled paper sticks: if you use those with reusable plastic sticks you will have to wait until one batch of lollies is eaten before you can make another. Each mould holds about 5 tablespoons of liquid so you will need 275 ml (10 fl oz) of liquid for 4 lollies – but measure your moulds to make sure before you start. Push the sticks into the moulds, fill with liquid and freeze the lollies on a flat tray until solid – about 3 hours. Push them out of the moulds and store in pairs with greaseproof paper in between in polythene bags. They will keep in the freezer for up to 2 months. If you have upright moulds, you can half-fill them with fruit juice and freeze; then top with another coloured mixture to make two-colour lollies.

LEMON BARLEY
ICED LOLLIES
D E

50 g (2 oz) pot barley
575 ml (1 pint) water
juice 1 lemon
1 tablespoon honey

Put the barley and water into a saucepan. Bring to the boil, cover and simmer for 30 minutes. Strain and measure the liquid: there should be just under 275 ml (10 fl oz). Top up, if necessary, with hot water. Add the liquid to the lemon juice and stir in the honey. Leave the mixture until it is quite cold before pouring it into the moulds and freezing.

PEACH AND YOGHURT
ICED LOLLIES
E G W

150 ml (5 fl oz) natural yoghurt
juice from 1 × 225 g (8 oz) tin
peaches in apple juice
4 peach slices

Put all the ingredients through a blender or food processor. Pour into moulds and freeze.

BLACKCURRANT ICED LOLLIES
D E G W

1 × 225 g (8 oz) tin blackcurrants in
apple juice
unsweetened pineapple juice, if necessary

Put the blackcurrants and their juice through a sieve, rubbing the blackcurrants well to make a thick liquid. Top up to the required amount with pineapple juice, pour into moulds and freeze.

PINEAPPLE ICED LOLLIES
D E G W

1 × 225 g (8 oz) tin pineapple in natural juice
unsweetened pineapple juice, if necessary

Put the pineapple plus its juice into a blender or food processor and work it to a thick liquid. Measure, and add pineapple juice if necessary to make it up to 275 ml (10 fl oz). Pour into moulds and freeze.

PRUNE AND APPLE
ICED LOLLIES
D E G W

225 ml (8 fl oz) prune juice
2 tablespoons concentrated apple juice

Mix the juices together, stirring well to prevent the apple juice from sinking to the bottom of the jug. Pour into lolly moulds and freeze.

HOME-MADE SWEETS

DRIED FRUIT AND NUT SWEETS

Delicious sweets can be made from soft pastes of ground nuts or dried fruits. For nuts, follow the recipe for Almond Paste (right). The ground mixed nuts obtainable from health food shops are ideal, although they may be on the dry side, in which case increase the amount of concentrated apple juice. If you grind your own nuts, use equal quantities of each type. Brazil nuts, walnuts or unsalted peanuts all have a strong flavour and are much better mixed, but hazelnuts can be used on their own.

Dried fruits also make an excellent basis for sweets. Choose from raisins, sultanas, dates, figs, apricots and prunes. Soak two or more types in fruit juice to make them easy to chop or purée, then mix them with finely ground sunflower seeds, which give a mild creamy flavour, or with ground peanuts, brazil nuts, hazelnuts or almonds; use walnuts sparingly as they have quite a strong flavour.

A paste of dried fruit and nuts, or just nuts, can be rolled out between sheets of rice paper, left to become firm and cut into squares or bars (see the recipes that follow for detailed instructions); or roll the paste into small balls with dampened hands; or flatten it out to a thickness of about 1 cm ($\frac{3}{8}$ in) and cut it into squares. If you decide to roll it into balls, or if you are not using rice paper, you will find a coating of some sort will make the sweets keep better and reduce stickiness. The most effective is skimmed milk powder, but you can also use desiccated coconut, ground or chopped nuts, wheatgerm, finely crushed Shredded Wheat or a crunchy oat cereal which you have ground or crushed. Dried fruit or nut sweets will keep well in airtight containers.

ALMOND PASTE

Almond paste can be used to make cake decorations or sweets of many colours and shapes.

D E G W

125 g (4 oz) ground almonds
4 tablespoons concentrated apple juice
(if using bought ground almonds you may
need 1 tablespoon extra)

Put the almonds in a bowl. Mix in the concentrated apple juice to make a sticky but workable paste. Add food colourings of your choice: deep colours like blues and purples must be quite strong since the paste is a pale browny colour when uncoloured.

When handling almond paste dampen your hands, your work surface and your rolling pin with cold water. Stamp out shapes with small biscuit cutters for sticking directly on to fruit cakes; or mould the paste like Plasticine to make small flowers, animals, birds or whatever you wish. Balls of paste can be coated like dried fruit sweets, to vary the taste and texture; or try removing the stones from semi-dried dates and stuffing them with small 'sausages' of paste in different colours.

FIG, DATE AND BRAZIL NUT SWEETS

D E G W

125 g (4 oz) dried figs
125 g (4 oz) stoned dates
125 g (4 oz) brazil nuts, ground
rice paper (optional)

Finely mince together all the ingredients. Knead with your fingers to make sure that the fruits and nuts are evenly mixed. With dampened hands, either form the mixture into small balls and coat them in skimmed milk powder; or spread it out on a sheet of rice paper to a thickness of about 6 mm ($\frac{1}{4}$ in). Lay another sheet on top and go over it with a rolling pin to flatten it evenly. Leave for 2 hours to become firm and then cut into squares.

HOME-MADE SWEETS

RAISIN, DATE AND PEANUT SWEETS

E

50 g (2 oz) pressed dates
75 g (3 oz) raisins
4 tablespoons apple or unsweetened orange juice
50 g (2 oz) unroasted peanuts
2 tablespoons bran
3 tablespoons skimmed milk powder

Chop the dates and put them in a saucepan with the raisins and fruit juice. Bring to the boil on a gentle heat and simmer for 2 minutes, stirring occasionally. Take the pan from the heat. Finely grind the peanuts. Put the dates, raisins, ground peanuts and bran into a blender or food processor and work to a rough purée.

Form the mixture into small balls about 1.5 cm ($\frac{1}{2}$ in) in diameter and roll them in skimmed milk powder.

APRICOT, APPLE AND SUNFLOWER SEED BARS

D E G W

50 g (2 oz) dried whole apricots
50 g (2 oz) dried apple rings
1 tablespoon soya flour
1 tablespoon concentrated apple juice
150 ml (5 fl oz) water
50 g (2 oz) sunflower seeds
rice paper

Put the apricots and apple rings into a saucepan and sprinkle in the soya flour. Mix the concentrated apple juice with the water and stir them into the pan. Set over a very low heat, stirring frequently, for 10 minutes, so the liquid thickens and the fruits begin to soften. Take it from the heat. Finely grind the sunflower seeds. Put them into a blender or food processor with the fruit mixture and work to a rough purée. Cool it completely.

Spread the mixture out to a thickness of about 6 mm ($\frac{1}{4}$ in) on a sheet of rice paper. Lay another sheet on top and go over it with a rolling pin to flatten it evenly. Leave the mixture for 2 hours to firm and then cut it into bars or small squares.

BANANA SQUARES

D E G W

125 g (4 oz) dried bananas
25 g (1 oz) dried apple rings
6 tablespoons apple juice
25 g (1 oz) sunflower seeds
rice paper

Chop the bananas and apple rings. Put them into a saucepan with the apple juice, bring to the boil and simmer, uncovered, for 5 minutes, or until the bananas and apples have begun to soften and the juice has been reduced to about 2 tablespoons. Finely grind the sunflower seeds. Work the bananas, apples and remaining juice to a rough purée in a blender or food processor. Add the ground sunflower seeds and blend again. Leave until cool.

Spread the mixture out to a thickness of about 6 mm ($\frac{1}{4}$ in) on a sheet of rice paper. Cover with another sheet and go over it with a rolling pin to flatten it evenly. Leave uncovered for 2 hours to become firm, then cut the 'sandwich' into small squares or bars.

Store in an airtight container.

CHEWY DATE SQUARES

D E W

225 g (8 oz) stoned or pressed dates
225 g (8 oz) apple and pear spread
110 ml (4 fl oz) sunflower oil
225 g (8 oz) porridge oats

Heat the oven to 190°C/375°F/Gas Mark 5. Finely chop the dates. Melt the apple and pear spread in the sunflower oil over a low heat, stirring continuously. Mix in the dates and porridge oats and take the pan from the heat. Press the mixture into a shallow, oiled 18 cm (7 in) square tin. Bake it for 15 minutes. Cut it into small squares while it is hot and leave them in the tin to cool completely before lifting them out.

These keep exceptionally well in an airtight container.

HOME-MADE SWEETS

NO-COOK CAROB FUDGE
D E G W

2 × 40 g (1½ oz) carob bars
125 g (4 oz) tahini
50 g (2 oz) desiccated coconut

Break up the carob bars. Put them into a bowl in a saucepan of cold water and set over a low heat for the carob to melt. Do not let the water boil or splash into the carob, as this will make it grainy. Take the bowl from the water and immediately stir in the tahini and coconut. Spread the carob mixture on a sheet of oiled greaseproof paper on a baking tray to a thickness of about 6 mm (¼ in). Leave in a cool place until the fudge has set. Cut it into 2.5 cm (1 in) squares.

LITTLE EGGS
D E G W

2 × 40 g (1½ oz) carob bars
125 g (4 oz) ground almonds
4 tablespoons concentrated apple juice
few drops yellow food colouring

Put the almonds into a bowl and mix them to a stiff paste with the concentrated apple juice. Take away one-quarter of the paste, colour it yellow, and with damp hands roll it into 6 small balls. Divide the rest of the paste into 6, and cover the yellow balls with uncoloured paste, making egg shapes.

Break up the carob bars and put them into a small basin in a saucepan of water. Set over a low heat for the carob to melt. Do not let the water boil or splash into the carob. Dip one side of each egg into the melted carob. Lay the eggs on a sheet of greaseproof paper, carob side up. Leave until the carob has set. Dip the eggs again and put them on the paper dry side down. Leave them for at least 2 hours to set completely.

HOLLOW EASTER EGGS
D E G W

You will need an Easter egg mould, preferably a fairly small one. Make sure that the mould is clean and dry and grease it lightly by rubbing it with oiled kitchen paper. Stand it rounded side down and support it with screws of cooking foil. You will need 4 × 40 g (1½ oz) carob bars to make an egg 7.5–10 cm (3–4 in) high.

Break up the carob bars (if you only have one half of a mould, melt the carob in 2 batches). Put the carob into a basin in a saucepan of cold water and set it over a low heat until the carob has melted. Do not let the water boil and do not let any of the water splash into the carob, as this will make it grainy.

Once the carob has melted, take the pan from the heat. Using a pastry brush, coat the inside of the mould with half the melted carob. Leave until the carob has hardened, keeping the remaining carob melted and warm. Brush the mould again, making the layer as thick as possible. Leave to cool and harden completely at room temperature.

When it is quite hard, insert the point of a sharp knife between the carob and the mould. Gently twist it and the carob shell should come out.

When you have made two half shells, hold them carefully together. Brush more melted carob over the join and hold the halves together until it begins to set. Gently lay the egg down and leave it until the join has set completely.

Wrap the eggs in aluminium foil.

CAROB COATED NUTS
D E G W

Break up sugar-free carob bars and put them into a basin in a saucepan of cold water. Set over a low heat until the carob has melted: do not let the water boil or splash into the carob, as this will make it grainy. Take the pan from the heat. Dip whole almonds, hazelnuts, brazil nuts and walnut halves into the carob. Lift them out with a teaspoon and leave on oiled greaseproof paper until completely set.

HOME-MADE SWEETS · POPCORN

SEMOLINA-BASED SWEETS

If semolina is made thick enough it will set to a soft, jelly-like consistency which can be quite delicious if flavoured with dried fruits and fruit juice. The sweets are rich in fibre and very economical, as a little will go a very long way. You can also eat them as a pudding, topped with natural yoghurt and a sprinkling of Oat Crunch (page 31) or a spoonful of sugar-free jam.

APRICOT AND RAISIN SQUARES
E

125 g (4 oz) dried whole apricots
425 ml (15 fl oz) unsweetened orange juice
75 g (3 oz) wholewheat semolina
75 g (3 oz) raisins
3 tablespoons skimmed milk powder
(optional)

Put the apricots into a saucepan with the orange juice and bring them to the boil. Take the pan from the heat and leave the apricots to soak for 4 hours. Drain, then put them through a blender or food processor with 4 tablespoons of the juice. Put the remaining juice into a saucepan and bring it to the boil. Stirring briskly, sprinkle in the semolina and add the apricot purée and raisins. Stir until the mixture is very thick. Lay a sheet of oiled greaseproof paper on a baking tray. Spread the mixture on the paper to a thickness of about 1 cm ($\frac{3}{8}$ in). Leave it for about 2 hours in a cool place to set to a jelly-like consistency. Cut it into small squares and coat them in skimmed milk powder, if using.

DATE AND ORANGE SQUARES
E

175 g (6 oz) stoned dates
275 ml (10 fl oz) unsweetened orange juice
65 g (2$\frac{1}{2}$ oz) wholewheat semolina
3 tablespoons skimmed milk powder
(optional)

Finely chop the dates. Put them into a saucepan with the orange juice, bring to the boil and simmer for 2 minutes. Stirring briskly, scatter in the semolina. Keep stirring until the mixture is very thick. Take the pan from the heat. Lay a sheet of oiled greaseproof paper on a baking tray. Spread the mixture on the paper to a thickness of about 1 cm ($\frac{3}{8}$ in) and leave for about 2 hours in a cool place to set to a jelly-like consistency. Cut it into small squares and coat in milk powder.

POPCORN
D E G W

50 g (2 oz) popping corn
1 tablespoon oil

Use a saucepan with a tightly fitting lid. Heat the oil over a medium heat. Put in the corn and cover the pan tightly. Shake the pan on the heat until the corn stops popping. Remove the lid and sprinkle with a flavouring while still hot.

If children are helping you, you can let them put the seeds into the cold pan, cover and then set it on the heat. It seems to work just as well and certainly gives more pleasure since the children have then done everything for themselves.

Flavourings
- 2 tablespoons melted honey
- 2 tablespoons maple syrup
- 2 tablespoons melted apple and pear spread
- stir in 3 tablespoons desiccated coconut or 2 tablespoons sesame seeds with any of the above
- 2 tablespoons melted malt extract
- $\frac{1}{4}$ teaspoon fine salt
- $\frac{1}{4}$ teaspoon paprika
- $\frac{1}{4}$ teaspoon turmeric plus $\frac{1}{4}$ teaspoon curry powder.

CHAPTER SEVEN

HEALTHY BAKING

Scones, Breads, Cakes, Biscuits and Buns

There is something homely about a
kitchen filled with the warmth and smell of freshly
baked cakes and biscuits, bread and scones. It provides a
real welcome for children home from school, as well as snacks and
light meals that are nutritious and good to eat. Apart from the
satisfying aspect of producing your own foods, you can also be
confident that your family are eating high-fibre, low-sugar
goodies that are free from artificial additives, for even
bought bread made from stoneground wholewheat
flour can contain preservatives.

Wholewheat flour
There is no real difficulty in using
wholewheat flour for baking but you
should not expect exactly the same
results as you would get from white
flour. Wholewheat flour contains all
the bran and germ of the wheat,
which means that you will not be able
to achieve a light-as-air texture.
However, wholewheat products can be
light and they do have a real flavour.
They are also more satisfying and so,
although the initial ingredients may
be slightly more expensive than white
flour and sugar, your money will go
as far in the long run.

Wholewheat bread
To ensure that the family always has
a supply of good wholewheat bread,
there is nothing better than making
your own. Once you have tried, you
will find that the time you spend
making it is quite small. While the
dough is rising you are free to get on
with other jobs. You can even leave it
to rise in a cool place overnight or
while you're out at work. Follow the
basic instructions and you will see
how easy breadmaking is. If you have
a freezer, it is a good idea to make up

1.35 kg (3 lb) flour at a time (simply
treble the ingredients) and put two
loaves into the freezer after they have
cooled. Thaw them at room
temperature for a couple of hours or
in a hot oven for 15 minutes.

One hundred per cent wholewheat
or wholemeal flour (page 13) makes
the best everyday loaf. For a change
use half wholemeal and half granary
bread meal; or half wholemeal and
half whole rye flour (this makes a
nutty-tasting, heavier loaf); or three-
quarters wholemeal and one-quarter
fine or medium oatmeal (this makes a
crumbly loaf that does not rise quite
so well). Two tablespoons of bran or
wheatgerm can also be added to every
450 g (1 lb) of flour. Non-wheat flours
need to be used with a wheat flour so
that the mixture contains enough
gluten (the starch that reacts with the
yeast to make the bread rise).

Bread without added salt will have a slightly sweet, bland flavour. If you do add salt, use fine sea salt or pure rock salt – 2 teaspoonfuls per 450 g (1 lb) flour. Even if the salt is fine, it is best to dissolve it in water before adding it to the flour so that it mixes in evenly. In recipes where the salt is added dry to the flour, use fine salt.

You can use dried or fresh yeast, but you will probably find that you have the best results with fresh. It will keep stored in a covered polythene container (not metal) in the refrigerator for up to two weeks or for several months in the freezer. Dried yeast is available in ready-to-use form; you just mix it into the dry ingredients or allow it to froth up in warm water. Use 25 g (1 oz) fresh yeast or 15 g ($\frac{1}{2}$ oz) dried per 450 g (1 lb) flour.

You will need 275 ml (10 fl oz) liquid to every 450 g (1 lb) flour. For an ordinary loaf, water is all that is needed. Use it at around blood heat (37°C/98.5°F): it should feel just lukewarm when you dip your fingers in it. Half milk and half water makes a softer loaf. You can also use beaten eggs to make up some of the liquid, but although this makes a light loaf it will not keep as well as one made with water alone.

Cakes

In any cake recipe, you can replace the given amount of refined sugar with apple and pear spread. However, most of the time I use dried fruits as sweeteners. Admittedly they cost more than sugar, and cakes made with them take slightly longer to prepare, but you will soon get into the routine and find that all your efforts are worthwhile – and nutritious.

In some of the recipes, you will see that I have reduced the amount of fat by using a mixture of corn oil and fruit juice or water. This produces a rather batter-like consistency and a beautifully light cake.

SCONES
The Basic Principles

Of all baked goodies, scones are the easiest to make, they always taste good and as they contain only a small amount of fat and little or no sweetener they make a healthy snack. Using the same basic mixture you can make them plain, sweet or savoury. Here are some basic tips to help you make up your own versions.

Flour 100% wholewheat or wholemeal flour is the best type to use most of the time. For a change you can replace 25 g (1 oz) of the flour with the same weight of bran: this makes nutty-flavoured, high-fibre scones which are soft in the middle and slightly crisp on the outside.

For soft-textured, crumbly scones, replace up to half the flour with medium oatmeal. Granary bread meal can also be used. As it is lower in fibre than wholewheat flour, replace 25 g (1 oz) of the flour with the same weight of bran.

Raising Agent Use $\frac{1}{2}$ teaspoon bicarbonate of soda to every 225 g (8 oz) flour or flour mixture.

Salt Use $\frac{1}{2}$ teaspoon fine sea salt to every 225 g (8 oz) flour or flour mixture.

Fat For every 225 g (8 oz) flour or flour mixture you will need 40 g (1$\frac{1}{2}$ oz) butter or soft vegetable margarine. Rub it into the flour with your fingertips as though you were making pastry.

Liquid A fermented or soured milk product helps make the scones rise and gives them a soft, light texture. Use natural yoghurt, buttermilk or ordinary milk which you have allowed to go sour. If you haven't any of these use fresh milk mixed with $\frac{1}{2}$ teaspoon cream of tartar per 150 ml (5 fl oz).

PLAIN SCONES
E Makes about 12

225 g (8 oz) wholewheat flour
$\frac{1}{2}$ teaspoon fine sea salt
$\frac{1}{2}$ teaspoon bicarbonate of soda
40 g (1$\frac{1}{2}$ oz) butter or margarine
150 ml (5 fl oz) natural yoghurt,
or buttermilk, or sour milk,
or fresh milk with $\frac{1}{2}$ teaspoon cream of
tartar dissolved in it

Heat the oven to 200°C/400°F/Gas Mark 6. Put the flour into a bowl. Put in the salt and bicarbonate of soda and toss with your fingers to distribute them evenly. Rub in the butter or margarine. (Add any flavourings at this point – see below.) Make a well in the centre, put in the liquid and, using a fork or a round-bladed knife, gradually mix in flour from the edges of the well until you can draw it all into a dough with your fingers: it will be slightly sticky and uneven. Put it on to a floured work surface. Flour your hands and gently squeeze the dough together until it becomes smooth. This should only take about a minute. Coat the kneaded dough in a light dusting of flour and roll it out to a thickness of 2 cm ($\frac{3}{4}$ in). Cut it into squares or triangles, or stamp it into 4–5 cm (1$\frac{1}{2}$–2 in) rounds with a pastry cutter. Lay them on a floured baking sheet. Alternatively, the dough can be rolled into an 18 cm (7 in) round and put into a floured tin. Score the top into sections. Bake the scones or scone round for 15 minutes or until just beginning to colour. Lift on to a wire rack to cool.

Flavourings and Additions to Savoury Scones

- 2–3 tablespoons chopped parsley
- 2 tablespoons chopped chives
- 2 tablespoons chopped thyme
- 1 teaspoon dried mixed herbs
- 1 teaspoon paprika
- 50 g (2 oz) chopped walnuts
- 75 g (3 oz) Cheddar or Cheshire cheese, finely grated.

SWEET SCONES

Scones made with wholewheat flour have such a good flavour that if dried fruit and a little spice are added you may well find that no extra sweetening is necessary. For every 225 g (8 oz) flour or flour mixture add 75–125 g (3–4 oz) dried fruits such as raisins, sultanas, currants, chopped pressed dates or a mixture. Toss them into the flour after you have rubbed in the fat.

Spiced Fruit Scones

Add one of the following to the flour:
- $\frac{1}{8}$ nutmeg, freshly grated, or $\frac{1}{4}$ teaspoon ground nutmeg
- $\frac{1}{2}$ teaspoon ground mixed spices
- $\frac{1}{2}$ teaspoon ground cinnamon
- 1 teaspoon caraway seeds.

These spices can also be added if you use one of the sweeteners below instead of dried fruits.

Additional Flavourings for Sweet Scones

For every 225 g (8 oz) flour or flour mixture add one of the following, at the same time as adding the liquid:
- 50 g (2 oz) stoned dates, simmered for 2 minutes in 4 tablespoons fruit juice and put through a blender or food processor;
- 50 g (2 oz) dried apple rings soaked in a mixture of 150 ml (5 fl oz) each apple juice and water for 4 hours, drained and put through a blender or food processor;
- 50 g (2 oz) honey;
- 50 g (2 oz) molasses (this will darken the colour).

Add the following before rubbing in the fat:
- 50 g (2 oz) dark Barbados sugar.

DATE SCONES ·
E Makes about 12

225 g (8 oz) wholewheat flour
50 g (2 oz) stoned dried dates
4 tablespoons prune or unsweetened orange juice
$\frac{1}{2}$ teaspoon bicarbonate of soda
pinch fine sea salt
50 g (2 oz) raisins
50 g (2 oz) sultanas
3 tablespoons corn oil
150 ml (5 fl oz) natural yoghurt

Heat the oven to 200°C/400°F/Gas Mark 6. Finely chop the dates and put them into a saucepan with the juice. Set over a moderate heat and bring to the boil. Simmer gently for 2 minutes, then mash them or put through a blender or food processor.

Put the flour, soda and salt into a mixing bowl. Toss in the raisins and sultanas. Make a well in the centre and put in the oil and yoghurt and mix well. Turn the dough on to a floured work surface and knead it lightly so it becomes smooth. Roll out the dough to a thickness of 2 cm ($\frac{3}{4}$ in). Stamp it into 4 cm ($1\frac{1}{2}$ in) rounds and put them on a floured baking sheet. Bake the scones for 15 minutes or until they are just beginning to colour. Lift them on to wire racks to cool.

The scones can be flavoured with $\frac{1}{2}$ teaspoon ground mixed spice added to the flour.

OATMEAL AND MOLASSES SCONE ROUND
E

175 g (6 oz) wholewheat flour
50 g (2 oz) medium oatmeal
½ teaspoon ground ginger
½ teaspoon fine sea salt
½ teaspoon bicarbonate of soda
40 g (1½ oz) butter, or margarine
50 g (2 oz) molasses
150 ml (5 fl oz) sour milk, or natural yoghurt, or buttermilk

Heat the oven to 200°C/400°F/Gas Mark 6. Put the flour and oatmeal into a bowl. Add the ginger, salt and bicarbonate of soda and mix well. Rub in the butter or margarine and make a well in the centre. Gently melt the molasses in a saucepan and pour it into the flour and oatmeal. Pour in the milk, yoghurt or buttermilk and mix everything to a dough – it will be quite moist. Put the dough into a greased 18 cm (7 in) diameter sponge tin or skillet and score it into twelve sections. Bake for 20 minutes or until firm. Turn it on to a wire rack to cool.

Serve the scone plain or buttered. It is deliciously crumbly and semi-sweet.

CHEESE TOPPED SCONES
E Makes about 12

225 g (8 oz) wholewheat flour
½ teaspoon fine sea salt
½ teaspoon bicarbonate of soda
2 tablespoons chopped parsley (optional)
40 g (1½ oz) butter, or margarine
100 g (3½ oz) mature Cheddar cheese, finely grated
150 ml (5 fl oz) natural yoghurt, or buttermilk, or sour milk

Heat the oven to 200°C/400°F/Gas Mark 6. Put the flour into a bowl with the salt, bicarbonate of soda and parsley. Rub in the butter or margarine. Toss in two-thirds of the cheese. Make a well in the centre and pour in the yoghurt, buttermilk or sour milk. Mix everything to a dough and turn it on to a floured work surface. Knead it lightly until it becomes smooth. Divide the dough into 8 pieces. Make each one into a flat round about 2 cm (¾ in) thick, and lay them on a floured baking sheet. Bake for 15 minutes. Put the remaining cheese on top and return the scones to the oven for a further 5 minutes.

Serve warm, or cool the scones completely on a wire rack. They can be eaten just as they are, or split, buttered and filled with mustard and cress and a slice of tomato.

BRAN AND MARMITE SCONES

E Makes about 12

200 g (7 oz) wholewheat flour
25 g (1 oz) bran
½ teaspoon fine sea salt
½ teaspoon bicarbonate of soda
40 g (1½ oz) butter, or margarine
1 teaspoon Marmite,
or yeast extract
2 tablespoons boiling water
150 ml (5 fl oz) natural yoghurt, or
buttermilk, or sour milk

Heat the oven to 200°C/400°F/Gas Mark 6.
Put the flour into a bowl and toss in the
bran, salt and bicarbonate of soda. Rub in
the butter or margarine. Make a well in
the centre. Dissolve the yeast extract in
the boiling water and pour it into the well.
Add the yoghurt and mix everything to a
dough. Turn it out on to a floured surface
and knead it lightly. Roll out to a thickness of 2 cm (¾ in) and stamp it into 4 cm
(1½ in) rounds. Lay them on a floured
baking sheet and bake for 15 minutes or
until they are just beginning to colour.
Lift them on to a wire rack to cool.

These can be served plain but are best
split, spread with butter or margarine and
sandwiched back together again with
watercress sprigs or a slice of cheese in
the middle.

For a change, add 50 g (2 oz) chopped
walnuts with the bran and 2 tablespoons
chopped chives.

DATE AND RAISIN MUFFINS

Makes 18

125 g (4 oz) stoned dates
150 ml (5 fl oz) hot black tea
225 g (8 oz) wholewheat flour
2 tablespoons bran
2 tablespoons wheatgerm
1 teaspoon bicarbonate of soda
125 g (4 oz) raisins
3 tablespoons oil
1 egg
225 ml (8 fl oz) milk

Heat the oven to 190°C/375°F/Gas Mark 5.
Finely chop the dates and put them into a
saucepan with the tea. Bring to the boil
and simmer for 2 minutes. Put them
through a blender or food processor with
the tea.

Mix together the flour, bran,
wheatgerm, bicarbonate of soda and raisins. Make a well in the centre and put in
the oil and beaten egg. Beat in some of the
flour mixture from the sides of the well
and then gradually beat in the milk. Beat
all together well. Divide the mixture between 18 oiled bun tins. Bake the muffins
for 20 minutes or until they are risen and
firm. Lift them on to wire racks to cool.

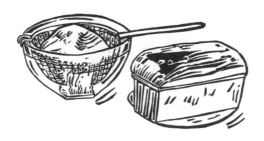

TEA BREADS

DATE AND RAISIN TEA BREAD

Tea bread is a cross between a bread and a cake. This one is dark brown, rich and light. It is delicious served plain, spread with curd cheese and sugar-free jam or eaten with cheese and apples.

225 g (8 oz) wholewheat flour
125 g (4 oz) stoned dates
150 ml (5 fl oz) hot black tea
I teaspoon bicarbonate of soda
25 g (I oz) margarine
I egg
110 ml (4 fl oz) milk
125 g (4 oz) raisins

Heat the oven to 180°C/350°F/Gas Mark 4. Finely chop the dates and put them into a saucepan with the tea. Set them on a low heat and simmer for 5 minutes. Put the dates through a blender or food processor with the tea.

Put the flour and bicarbonate of soda into a bowl. Make a well in the centre and put in the margarine, beaten egg, milk and date purée. Beat everything to a smooth, thick batter. Mix in the raisins. Put the mixture into a greased 450 g (1 lb) loaf tin and bake for 1 hour or until firm and risen, and a skewer stuck in the centre comes out clean.

Turn the bread on to a wire rack to cool.

MALTED TEA BREAD

225 g (8 oz) wholewheat flour
I teaspoon bicarbonate of soda
¼ nutmeg, freshly grated, or ½ teaspoon ground nutmeg
50 g (2 oz) butter, or margarine
25 g (I oz) malt extract
150 ml (5 fl oz) milk
I egg
50 g (2 oz) raisins
50 g (2 oz) sultanas

Heat the oven to 180°C/350°F/Gas Mark 4. In a large bowl, mix together the flour, bicarbonate of soda and nutmeg. Rub in the butter or margarine. Make a well in the centre.

Put the malt extract and milk into a saucepan and stir over a low heat until the malt extract has melted. Cool them a little and pour into the flour. Beat the egg, add it to the flour and mix thoroughly with a wooden spoon to make a smooth, dropping consistency. Fold in the raisins and sultanas. Put the mixture into a greased 450 g (1 lb) loaf tin and bake for 1 hour or until the bread is golden brown and risen, and a skewer inserted in the centre comes out clean.

TEA BREADS

MILK AND HONEY TEA BREAD

E

150 g (5 oz) honey
275 ml (10 fl oz) milk
50 g (2 oz) butter
50 g (2 oz) stoned dates
350 g (12 oz) wholewheat flour
1 tablespoon baking powder
½ teaspoon bicarbonate of soda
50 g (2 oz) raisins

Heat the oven to 180°C/350°F/Gas Mark 4. Put the honey, milk and butter into a saucepan and set them on a low heat, stirring occasionally. When the honey and butter are melted, take the pan from the heat and let the mixture cool. Finely chop the dates.

Put the flour into a mixing bowl and toss in the baking powder, bicarbonate of soda, dates and raisins. Make a well in the centre and pour in the milk and honey mixture. Using a wooden spoon, beat everything to a thick batter. Pour into a buttered 900 g (2 lb) loaf tin and bake for 1 hour, or until a skewer inserted in the centre comes out clean.

HONEY BUN

E

225 g (8 oz) wholewheat flour
½ teaspoon fine sea salt
½ teaspoon bicarbonate of soda
50 g (2 oz) raisins
50 g (2 oz) sultanas
50 g (2 oz) margarine
75 g (3 oz) honey
150 ml (5 fl oz) natural yoghurt

Heat the oven to 200°C/400°F/Gas Mark 6. Put the flour into a bowl and toss in the salt, bicarbonate of soda and dried fruits with your fingertips. Make a well in the centre. Put the margarine and honey into a saucepan and melt them over a low heat. Pour them into the well and gradually beat in flour from the sides. Add the yoghurt and beat until it is like a thick cake mixture. Pour it into a greased 18 cm (7 in) diameter cake tin and bake for 25 minutes or until a skewer inserted in the centre comes out clean. Turn it on to a wire rack to cool.

In texture this falls somewhere between a scone and a cake, and it can be served either plain or buttered: slice it horizontally in two, spread with butter and sandwich it back together again.

BASIC WHOLEWHEAT LOAF

For notes on breadmaking, see pages 96–7.

D E

450 g (I lb) wholewheat flour
275 ml (10 fl oz) warm water
25 g (I oz) fresh yeast, or 15 g (½ oz) dried
I teaspoon honey, if using dried yeast
2 teaspoons fine sea salt

Put half the water into a bowl and crumble in the fresh yeast. If you are using dried yeast, stir in the honey until it dissolves then sprinkle the yeast on top. Leave the mixture in a warm place to become frothy – about 15 minutes. Dissolve the salt in the remaining water.

Put the flour into a bowl and make a well in the centre. Pour in the frothy yeast and gradually mix in some of the flour from the sides of the well. Add the salt water and mix everything to a dough. Turn it on to a floured board and knead until it is quite smooth and no longer feels sticky. To knead, push the bread away from you with the palms of your hands and bring it back with your fingertips. Do this several times. This makes a fat sausage shape. Take the ends and bring them to the middle, turn the dough round and continue kneading. The process usually takes about three minutes, and you may well need to flour your hands several times.

When the dough is ready, put it back into the bowl and cut a cross in the top: this will help it to rise evenly. Cover the bowl with a clean, dry tea cloth and put it into a warm place for about 1–2 hours for the dough to double in size.

Heat the oven to 200°C/400°F/Gas Mark 6. Oil a 450 g (1 lb) loaf tin. Knead the dough very lightly again, for about 1 minute only. Form it into a long shape and put it into the prepared tin. Knock it down very lightly with the back of your hand. Cover with the cloth again and leave until the dough has risen above the top of the tin. This is called proving and will take about 20 minutes.

Bake the loaf for 40–50 minutes or until it has a golden crust and sounds hollow when tapped. Turn it out on to a wire rack and let it cool completely before slicing.

Variations

The top of the loaf can be slashed with a sharp knife before proving, either straight down the middle or several times diagonally. For a shiny, glazed effect, brush the top with beaten egg before proving. Cracked wheat, sesame seeds or poppy seeds can be scattered over the egg.

WHOLEMEAL BARM BRACK

E

bread dough made with 450 g (I lb)
wholewheat flour
175 g (6 oz) currants
175 g (6 oz) raisins or sultanas
beaten egg for glaze

Make up the bread dough according to the basic recipe. Knead, and when it is smooth gradually knead in the fruits. Leave to rise like ordinary bread.

Heat the oven to 200°C/400°F/Gas Mark 6. Oil two 225 g (8 oz) bread tins. Knead the dough again. Divide it in two, shape each piece and put them into the tins. Brush the tops with beaten egg, then cover with a tea cloth and leave in a warm place for 15 minutes to prove.

Bake the loaves for 40 minutes or until they sound hollow when tapped. Turn them on to a wire rack to cool completely.

Serve plain or buttered. One loaf could be frozen if wished and thawed when needed at room temperature.

WHEAT, OATMEAL AND BRAN BREAD

400 g (14 oz) wholewheat flour
350 ml (12 fl oz) warm water
2 teaspoons molasses
40 g (1½ oz) fresh yeast, or 20 g (¾ oz) dried
2 teaspoons fine sea salt
125 g (4 oz) medium oatmeal
25 g (1 oz) bran
25 g (1 oz) butter, or margarine
beaten egg for glaze
4 tablespoons rolled oats

Put half the water into a bowl. Add the molasses and stir until it dissolves. Crumble in the fresh yeast or sprinkle in the dried. Leave the mixture in a warm place until frothy – about 15 minutes. Dissolve the salt in the remaining water.

Put the flour, oatmeal and bran into a mixing bowl. Rub in the butter or margarine. Make a well in the centre. Pour in the yeast mixture and stir in a little flour from the sides of the well. Add the salt water and mix everything to a dough. Turn it out on a floured work surface and knead until it is smooth. Return the dough to the bowl, cover with a clean tea cloth and leave in a warm place for 1 hour or until doubled in size.

Heat the oven to 200°C/400°F/Gas Mark 6. Knead the dough again and divide it into two. Form each piece into a high round shape and lay them on floured baking sheets. Brush the loaves with the beaten egg and scatter the rolled oats over the top. Cover with a tea cloth and leave in a warm place for 15 minutes to prove.

Bake the loaves for 40 minutes or until they sound hollow when tapped. Lift them on to a wire rack and cool completely before slicing.

SOFT MILK ROLLS
E Makes 16

450 g (1 lb) wholewheat flour
150 ml (5 fl oz) warm water
25 g (1 oz) fresh yeast, or 15 g (½ oz) dried
1 teaspoon honey, if using dried yeast
1 teaspoon fine sea salt
40 g (1½ oz) butter, or margarine
150 ml (5 fl oz) warm milk

Put the water into a bowl and crumble in the fresh yeast. If you are using dried yeast, stir in the honey until it dissolves, then sprinkle the yeast on top. Leave the mixture in a warm place to become frothy – about 15 minutes.

Put the flour and salt into a bowl. Rub in the butter or margarine. Make a well in the centre. Pour in the yeast mixture, the milk and any flavouring (see below). Mix everything to a dough. Turn on to a floured board and knead until smooth. Return the dough to the bowl. Cover with a clean tea cloth and leave in a warm place for 1 hour or until it has doubled in size.

Heat the oven to 200°C/400°F/Gas Mark 6. Knead the dough again and divide it into 16 pieces. Form each one into a round and place them on a large floured baking sheet. Cover the rolls with the tea cloth and leave them in a warm place for about 20 minutes so they almost double in size.

Bake the rolls for 20 minutes. To keep them soft, wrap them in two clean tea cloths as soon as they come out of the oven and leave them until they are quite cold. They can also be cooled on a wire rack, which gives them a thin, crisp crust.

Flavourings
● 1 teaspoon dried mixed herbs;
● 2 tablespoons chopped fresh chives plus 2 tablespoons chopped fresh parsley;
● 75 g (3 oz) finely grated Cheddar cheese, used on its own or with herbs;
● 1 tablespoon tomato purée stirred into the milk, plus herbs if wished.

HOT CROSS BUNS
Makes 12

450 g (1 lb) wholewheat flour
200 ml (7 fl oz) milk
75 g (3 oz) butter
50 g (2 oz) honey
25 g (1 oz) fresh yeast, or 15 g ($\frac{1}{2}$ oz) dried
$\frac{1}{2}$ teaspoon fine sea salt
$\frac{1}{2}$ teaspoon ground cinnamon
$\frac{1}{2}$ teaspoon ground mixed spice
$\frac{1}{4}$ nutmeg, freshly grated, or $\frac{1}{2}$ teaspoon
ground nutmeg
175 g (6 oz) currants
50 g (2 oz) candied peel, finely chopped
2 eggs

Crosses and Glaze
shortcrust pastry made with
125 g (4 oz) '85%' flour
1 egg
3 tablespoons milk

Put the milk, butter and honey into a saucepan and set over a low heat for the butter and honey to melt. Remove them and cool the mixture to lukewarm. Sprinkle in the yeast and leave it for about 5 minutes to froth.

Put the flour into a bowl with the salt, spices and fruits. Toss with your fingers to mix. Beat the eggs together. Make a well in the centre and pour in the yeast mixture and the eggs. Mix well to make a moist dough. Turn it on to a floured board and knead well, taking the sides into the centre, until it feels elastic. Return it to the bowl and cut a cross in the top. Cover the bowl with a clean, dry tea cloth and leave it in a warm place for 1 hour 30 minutes or until the dough has doubled in size.

Heat the oven to 200°C/400°F/Gas Mark 6. Knead the dough again and divide it into 12 pieces. Form each into a round bun and place on floured baking sheets. Roll out the pastry and cut it into thin strips; use it to make the crosses on the buns. Beat the milk into the egg to make the glaze and brush the buns with it. Leave them in a warm place for 10 minutes to prove.

Put a tray of hot water in the bottom of the oven: this will keep the buns soft. Bake them for 20 minutes or until browned and lift them on to wire racks to cool.

CAKES
The Basic Method

In all the recipes that follow the instructions are for hand mixing. If you want to use a large blender or food processor, blend the fruits and juice first and then simply add all the remaining ingredients and whiz. If the cake is to contain whole fruits, such as the sultanas and raisins in the simnel and Christmas cakes (page 110), turn the basic mixture into a bowl before folding them in: otherwise you might find that you have blended the dried fruit as well!

RAISIN CAKE
D

225 g (8 oz) wholewheat flour
1 teaspoon bicarbonate of soda
50 g (2 oz) molasses
125 g (4 oz) apple and pear spread
4 eggs
125 ml (4 fl oz) corn oil
125 ml (4 fl oz) unsweetened orange juice
125 g (4 oz) raisins

Heat the oven to 180°C/350°F/Gas Mark 4. Mix the flour and bicarbonate of soda in a bowl and make a well in the centre. Put the molasses and apple and pear spread into a saucepan and melt them over a low heat. Pour them into the well in the flour. Beat together the eggs and add them to the well. Gradually begin to beat in flour from the sides. Beat in the oil and the orange juice a little at a time. Fold in the raisins. Put the mixture into an oiled 18 × 25 cm (7 × 10 in) cake tin. Bake for 25 minutes or until firm and golden. Turn the cake on to a wire rack to cool completely.

Serve cut into squares.

FRUITY APPLE CAKE
D

125 g (4 oz) dried apple rings
50 g (2 oz) stoned dates
575 ml (1 pint) apple juice
225 g (8 oz) wholewheat flour
1 teaspoon bicarbonate of soda
½ teaspoon ground mixed spice
½ teaspoon ground cinnamon
110 ml (4 fl oz) corn oil
4 eggs
125 g (4 oz) raisins
125 g (4 oz) sultanas

Put the apple rings and dates into a saucepan with the apple juice. Bring them to the boil, take them from the heat and leave them to soak for at least 2 hours. Drain the fruits, reserving the juice. Put them through a blender or food processor with 110 ml (4 fl oz) of the juice.

Heat the oven to 170°C/325°F/Gas Mark 3. In a bowl, mix together the flour, bicarbonate of soda and spices. Make a well in the centre. Put in the blended fruits and oil and gradually beat in flour from the sides of the well. Beat the eggs together, then beat them into the flour, a little at a time, to make a smooth thick batter. Fold in the raisins and sultanas. Put the mixture into an oiled 20 cm (8 in) diameter cake tin and bake for 1 hour or until a skewer inserted in the centre comes out clean. Turn the cake on to a wire rack to cool.

APPLE AND RAISIN CAKE
D

75 g (3 oz) dried apple rings
175 g (6 oz) raisins
275 ml (10 fl oz) unsweetened apple juice
175 g (6 oz) wholewheat flour
1 teaspoon bicarbonate of soda
1 teaspoon ground mixed spice
6 tablespoons corn oil
3 eggs

Put the apple rings and one-third of the raisins into a saucepan with the apple juice. Bring to the boil, remove from the heat and leave to soak for 4 hours. Drain the fruits, reserving the juice. Put them through a blender or food processor with 6 tablespoons of the juice.

Heat the oven to 180°C/350°F/Gas Mark 4. Put the flour into a bowl and toss in the bicarbonate of soda and the spice. Make a well in the centre and put in the blended fruits, oil and beaten eggs. Beat everything to make a thick batter. Put the mixture into an oiled 20 cm (8 in) diameter cake tin. Bake for 50 minutes or until a skewer stuck in the centre comes out clean. Turn on to a wire rack to cool.

For a fruitier cake add up to 125 g (4 oz) extra raisins or sultanas.

HONEY CAKE
D

125 g (4 oz) honey
175 g (6 oz) wholewheat flour
1 teaspoon bicarbonate of soda
6 tablespoons corn oil
6 tablespoons unsweetened pineapple
or orange juice
3 eggs

Put the honey into a small saucepan and allow it to melt over a low heat. Cool.

Heat the oven to 180°C/350°F/Gas Mark 4. Put the flour into a bowl and mix in the bicarbonate of soda. Make a well in the centre. Put in the honey, oil, fruit juice and beaten eggs and beat everything to a thick batter. Put the mixture into an oiled 20 cm (8 in) cake tin and bake for 40 minutes or until firm and springy. Turn on to a wire rack to cool.

BASIC APRICOT CAKE
Ⓓ

175 g (6 oz) dried whole apricots
275 ml (10 fl oz) unsweetened orange juice
175 g (6 oz) wholewheat flour
I teaspoon bicarbonate of soda
6 tablespoons corn oil
3 eggs

Heat the oven to 180°C/350°F/Gas Mark 4. Put the apricots into a saucepan with the orange juice and bring to the boil. Take them from the heat and leave to soak for 4 hours. Drain, then put them through a blender or food processor with 6 tablespoons of the juice.

Put the flour into a bowl with the bicarbonate of soda. Make a well in the centre and put in the oil, beaten eggs and apricots. Gradually beat in flour from the edges of the well until you have a thick batter. Put the mixture into an oiled 20 cm (8 in) diameter cake tin. Bake for 40 minutes or until firm and golden and a skewer stuck into the centre comes out clean. Turn the cake on to a wire rack to cool.

For a Cherry Cake, add 1 teaspoon almond essence with the oil, eggs and apricots. When everything is well mixed, fold in 125 g (4 oz) halved glacé cherries.

For an Apricot and Date Cake, replace half the apricots with stoned, chopped dates and soak with the apricots as above.

APRICOT AND SUNFLOWER CAKE

125 g (4 oz) dried whole apricots
275 ml (10 fl oz) unsweetened orange juice
125 g (4 oz) butter, softened, or margarine
2 eggs
125 g (4 oz) wholewheat flour
I teaspoon bicarbonate of soda
50 g (2 oz) sunflower seeds

Soak the apricots in the orange juice for 8 hours. Drain, and put them through a blender or food processor with 6 tablespoons of the juice.

Heat the oven to 180°C/350°F/Gas Mark 4. Cream the butter or margarine and beat in the puréed apricots. Beat the eggs together. Mix the flour with the bicarbonate of soda. Beat it into the butter and apricots, alternately with the eggs. Mix in the sunflower seeds and put the mixture into a greased 20 cm (8 in) diameter cake tin. Bake for 20 minutes or until the cake feels firm and springy. Cool in the tin for 5 minutes, then turn it on to a wire rack to cool completely.

CAKES

DATE, WALNUT AND BANANA CAKE
E

225 g (8 oz) stoned dates
150 ml (5 fl oz) prune juice
125 g (4 oz) walnuts
1 banana
450 g (1 lb) wholewheat flour
1 teaspoon bicarbonate of soda
50 g (2 oz) margarine
225 ml (8 fl oz) milk

Heat the oven to 180°C/350°F/Gas Mark 4. Finely chop the dates and put them into a saucepan with the prune juice. Bring to the boil, simmer for 5 minutes and then put them through a blender or food processor. Finely chop the walnuts. Mash the banana.

Put the flour into a large mixing bowl with the bicarbonate of soda. Rub in the margarine and gradually mix in the walnuts. Make a well in the centre and put in the blended dates and the banana. Gradually beat in flour from the sides of the well. Beat in the milk a little at a time. Put the mixture into a greased 20 × 26 cm (8 × 11 in) cake tin. Bake for 30 minutes or until firm. Turn on to a wire rack to cool.

This is good cut into slices and buttered. It freezes well, and as it is rather large it is a good idea to freeze half.

BREAD PUDDING
Although called a pudding, this is cut in slices and eaten like a cake.

225 g (8 oz) wholewheat bread, one day old or more, without tough crusts
275 ml (10 fl oz) milk
1 teaspoon ground cinnamon
1 medium carrot
1 medium cooking apple
175 g (6 oz) raisins
175 g (6 oz) sultanas
75 g (3 oz) sugar-free marmalade
2 eggs
125 g (4 oz) margarine, or butter

Roughly crumble the bread. Put it into a bowl, pour in the milk and stir in the cinnamon. Leave for 45 minutes.

Heat the oven to 170°C/325°F/Gas Mark 3. Finely grate the carrot. Peel, core and grate the apple. Mix these into the bread together with the raisins, sultanas and marmalade. Beat the eggs and mix them in. Melt the margarine or butter and beat half into the mixture. Use some of the remainder to grease an 18 × 25 cm (7 × 10 in) cake tin. Fill it with the mixture in an even layer and pour the remaining margarine or butter over the top. Leave for 5 minutes.

Bake the pudding for 1 hour or until it is firm and the top browned. Cool it in the tin. Turn it out and store in plastic wrap.

SIMNEL CAKE

A delicious cake, traditionally made by servant girls for Mothering Sunday. It is now often baked for Easter, and the 11 almond paste balls are said to represent the apostles; if you prefer you could form them into egg shapes.

D

125 g (4 oz) prunes
275 ml (10 fl oz) apple juice
125 g (4 oz) stoned dates
225 g (8 oz) wholewheat flour
1 teaspoon ground mixed spice
4 eggs
175 g (6 oz) vegetable margarine
175 g (6 oz) sultanas
175 g (6 oz) raisins
175 g (6 oz) ground almonds
6 tablespoons concentrated apple juice

Put the prunes into a saucepan with the apple juice. Bring to the boil, remove from the heat and let them soak for 4 hours. Drain, reserving the juice. Stone and finely chop them. Finely chop the dates. Put both dates and prunes into a saucepan with 150 ml (5 fl oz) of the juice. Bring to the boil and simmer for 5 minutes. Put them through a blender or food processor.

Heat the oven to 150°C/300°F/Gas Mark 2. Mix the flour with the spice. Beat the eggs together. In a large mixing bowl, cream the margarine then beat in the eggs, alternating with the flour. Beat in the blended fruits and the sultanas and raisins. Put half the mixture in a greased 20 cm (8 in) diameter cake tin.

Mix the ground almonds with the concentrated apple juice until you have a stiff, marzipan-like paste. Divide it in half. Dampen a work board and a rolling pin and roll out one portion of the almond paste to a diameter of about 17.5 cm (7 in), i.e. slightly smaller than your cake tin. Using a palette knife or fish slice, lift it on to the cake mixture in the tin. Cover it completely with the remaining cake mixture and put it into the oven for 50 minutes.

Meanwhile, divide the remaining paste into 11 small pieces. Roll them into balls or egg shapes and flatten them slightly. Remove the cake from the oven and arrange the almond paste balls around the edge of the cake. Return the cake to the oven for 10 minutes or until the almond paste is firm and beginning to brown. Turn the cake on to a wire rack to cool – the balls will now be quite hard and will not be badly damaged by turning out.

CHRISTMAS CAKE

D

225 g (8 oz) stoned dates
275 ml (10 fl oz) unsweetened orange juice
(or use half juice and half rum)
225 g (8 oz) wholewheat flour
1 teaspoon ground mixed spice
1 medium carrot
175 g (6 oz) vegetable margarine
4 eggs
175 g (6 oz) sultanas
175 g (6 oz) raisins
125 g (4 oz) glacé cherries, halved

Finely chop the dates. Soak them in the orange juice for 12 hours. Put them through a blender or food processor.

Heat the oven to 160°C/300°F/Gas Mark 2. Line a 20 cm (8 in) diameter cake tin with oiled greaseproof paper. Mix the flour with the spice. Grate the carrot. In a large mixing bowl, cream the margarine and beat in the carrot. Beat the eggs together and mix them in gradually, alternating with the flour. Beat in the blended dates and fold in the sultanas, raisins and cherries. Put the mixture into the prepared tin and bake for 1 hour or until a skewer inserted in the centre comes out clean. Cool the cake in the tin for 5 minutes, then turn it on to a wire rack to cool.

This cake should be stored in plastic wrap in the refrigerator, and will keep for up to 2 weeks. Decorate it with coloured almond paste (page 92) rolled out to a thickness of about 1 cm ($\frac{3}{8}$ in) and cut into star, bell and tree shapes with small cutters. The paste is very sticky so you will not need jam to make the shapes stay in position.

DATE AND PEANUT ROCK CAKES

These are best made in a mixer or food processor.

D E Makes 16

125 g (4 oz) stoned dates
110 ml (4 fl oz) prune juice
125 g (4 oz) wholewheat flour
½ teaspoon bicarbonate of soda
75 g (3 oz) Peanut Butter (page 120)
1 tablespoon corn oil

Heat the oven to 180°C/350°F/Gas Mark 4. Finely chop the dates. Put them into a saucepan with the prune juice, bring to the boil and simmer for 3 minutes. Put them through a blender or food processor with the juice.

Put all the ingredients into a blender or food processor and work them to a stiff cake mixture. Three-quarters fill 16 small, oiled bun tins. Bake the cakes for 12 minutes or until firm but not coloured. Lift them on to a wire rack to cool.

COCONUT AND PINEAPPLE CAKES

D Makes 12

125 g (4 oz) dried pineapple snacks
6 tablespoons unsweetened pineapple or orange juice
125 g (4 oz) wholewheat flour
50 g (2 oz) desiccated coconut
1 teaspoon bicarbonate of soda
4 tablespoons corn oil
2 eggs

Heat the oven to 180°C/350°F/Gas Mark 4. Put the pineapple snacks into a saucepan with the fruit juice, bring to the boil and simmer for 5 minutes. Put them through a blender or food processor.

In a large mixing bowl, mix together the flour, coconut and bicarbonate of soda. Make a well in the centre. Put in the oil, beaten eggs and pineapple purée and beat until you have a smooth batter. Divide the mixture between 12 small, oiled bun tins. Bake the cakes for 15 minutes or until firm and just beginning to turn golden. Lift them on to a wire rack to cool.

HONEY CAKES

D Makes 15

125 g (4 oz) honey
125 g (4 oz) wholewheat flour
½ teaspoon bicarbonate of soda
5 tablespoons corn oil
4 tablespoons water
2 eggs

Put the honey into a small saucepan, melt it over a low heat then leave to cool.

Heat the oven to 180°C/350°F/Gas Mark 4. Put the flour and bicarbonate of soda into a mixing bowl. Make a well in the centre and put in the oil, water and honey. Gradually mix in flour from the sides of the well. Beat the eggs together and beat them into the mixture until you have a smooth, thick batter. Half-fill 15 small, greased bun tins. Bake the cakes for 15 minutes or until they are golden brown and risen.

BAKEWELL TARTS

D E Makes 12

shortcrust pastry made with 125 g (4 oz) wholewheat flour (page 79)
50 g (2 oz) dried whole apricots
150 ml (5 fl oz) unsweetened orange or pineapple juice
50 g (2 oz) wholewheat flour
25 g (1 oz) ground almonds
grated rind ½ lemon
½ teaspoon bicarbonate of soda
2 tablespoons corn oil
4 tablespoons sugar-free strawberry jam

Soak the apricots in the fruit juice overnight. Put them through a blender or food processor with 3 tablespoons of the juice.

Heat the oven to 180°C/350°F/Gas Mark 4. Roll out the pastry and line 12 small tartlet tins. Put the flour into a bowl with the almonds, lemon rind and bicarbonate of soda. Mix well and make a well in the centre. Put in the oil and blended apricots and mix everything together. Put 1 teaspoon jam into each tartlet case and pile the apricot mixture on top. Bake the tarts for 15 minutes or until they are just turning golden.

FIG ROLLS

The grapefruit juice prevents these little cakes from being too sweet.
Makes about 30

225 g (8 oz) wholewheat flour
½ teaspoon bicarbonate of soda
pinch fine sea salt
125 g (4 oz) butter, or margarine
90 ml (3 fl oz) milk
1 egg
225 g (8 oz) dried figs
125 g (4 oz) raisins
90 ml (3 fl oz) unsweetened grapefruit juice

Heat the oven to 200°C/400°F/Gas Mark 6. Put the flour into a bowl with the bicarbonate of soda and salt. Rub in the butter or margarine and mix to a dough with the milk and beaten egg. Leave the dough in a cool place for 30 minutes.

Remove the stalks from the figs and finely chop them. Put them into a food processor with the raisins and grapefruit juice and work until they are minced together. If you do not have a food processor, mince the raisins and figs together and gradually beat in the grapefruit juice after.

Divide the pastry into two halves and work with one piece at a time. Roll it out until it measures about 40 × 7.5 cm (16 × 3 in). Put half the fig mixture down the centre and fold in the sides. Cut the roll into short lengths and lay them on a floured baking sheet with their joins downwards. Repeat with the rest of the pastry and fig mixture. Bake the rolls for 15 minutes or until just beginning to colour. Lift them on to wire racks to cool.

APRICOT MACAROONS

Ⓓ Ⓖ Ⓦ Makes 12

125 g (4 oz) dried whole apricots
275 ml (10 fl oz) unsweetened orange
or pineapple juice
150 g (5 oz) desiccated coconut
1 egg
rice paper
6 glacé cherries

Put the apricots into a saucepan with the juice, bring to the boil and remove them from the heat. Soak for 4 hours. Drain, and purée the apricots without their juice.

Heat the oven to 180°C/350°F/Gas Mark 4. Mix the apricot purée with the coconut and beaten egg. Line a baking sheet with rice paper. Form the apricot and coconut mixture into 12 small balls and flatten them on to the rice paper. Put half a cherry on top of each one. Bake for 15 minutes or until they just begin to brown. Lift on to a wire rack, and when cold neatly cut round the macaroons with scissors.

HONEY AND CURRANT BISCUITS

Makes about 20

175 g (6 oz) wholewheat flour
pinch fine sea salt
½ teaspoon ground cinnamon
40 g (1½ oz) butter
50 g (2 oz) honey
1 egg
50 g (2 oz) currants

Heat the oven to 170°C/325°F/Gas Mark 3. Put the flour, salt and cinnamon into a bowl and make a well in the centre. Gently melt the butter and honey together and pour them into the flour. Beat the egg and add it to the well. Beat everything to a glossy dough and mix in the currants.

Bring the mixture together with your hands, coat it with a light dusting of flour and roll it out on a floured board to a thickness of about 6 mm (¼ in). Stamp it into rounds with a 5 cm (2 in) biscuit cutter and lay the rounds on buttered baking sheets. Bake the biscuits for 25 minutes and lift on to wire racks to cool.

SESAME OATCAKES
D E Makes about 30

75 g (3 oz) medium oatmeal
125 g (4 oz) wholewheat flour
40 g (1½ oz) sesame seeds
1 teaspoon bicarbonate of soda
pinch fine sea salt
3 tablespoons oil
6 tablespoons boiling water

Heat the oven to 180°C/350°F/Gas Mark 4. In a bowl, mix together the oatmeal, flour, sesame seeds, bicarbonate of soda and salt. Make a well in the centre and pour in the oil and water. Mix everything together well and form the mixture into a dough with your fingers. Turn it on to a floured board and roll out to a thickness of about 3 mm (⅛ in). Stamp it into 4 cm (1½ in) rounds with a pastry cutter and lay them on floured baking sheets. Bake the oatcakes for 12 minutes or until firm but not coloured. Lift them on to a wire rack to cool.

Serve these with cheese, spread with a savoury dip or with sugar-free jam. They are also good plain.

DATE AND PEANUT BISCUITS
D Makes about 24

125 g (4 oz) stoned dates
125 g (4 oz) wholewheat flour
125 g (4 oz) Peanut Butter (page 120)
4 tablespoons oil
1 egg

Heat the oven to 180°C/350°F/Gas Mark 4. Very finely chop the dates. Put the flour into a bowl and mix in the dates. Make a well in the centre and put in the peanut butter, oil and beaten egg. Beat first with a wooden spoon, then bring the mixture together with your fingers to make a smooth, glossy dough. Turn on to a floured board and roll out to a thickness of about 5 mm (³⁄₁₆ in). Stamp it into 5 cm (2 in) rounds with a biscuit cutter, and lay them on a floured baking sheet. Bake the biscuits for 15 minutes or until firm and just beginning to darken. Cool them for 2 minutes on the baking sheet then lift on to a wire rack to cool completely.

OATY CHEESE BISCUITS
Makes about 20

75 g (3 oz) wholewheat flour
50 g (2 oz) medium oatmeal
1 teaspoon bicarbonate of soda
50 g (2 oz) butter
75 g (3 oz) Cheddar cheese, finely grated
1 egg

Heat the oven to 170°C/325°F/Gas Mark 3. Put the flour, oatmeal and bicarbonate of soda into a bowl and rub in the butter as though you were making pastry. Mix in the cheese. Beat the egg and pour it into a well in the centre. Mix together well, kneading until the mixture becomes smooth. Turn the dough on to a floured board and roll out to a thickness of 3 mm (⅛ in). Stamp it into 4 cm (1½ in) rounds with a biscuit cutter. Lay the rounds on a floured baking sheet and bake them for 20 minutes or until they are just firm but not coloured. Leave them on the baking sheet for 5 minutes to firm completely, then lift on to a wire rack to cool.

BANANA BISCUITS
D Makes about 30

2 dried bananas
6 tablespoons unsweetened orange juice
175 g (6 oz) wholewheat flour
50 g (2 oz) medium oatmeal
4 tablespoons corn oil
1 egg

Heat the oven to 180°C/350°F/Gas Mark 4. Finely chop the bananas, put them into a saucepan with the orange juice and bring to a gentle boil. Simmer for 10 minutes or until soft, then put them through a blender or food processor with the juice.

Mix the flour and oatmeal in a bowl and make a well in the centre. Put in the oil, beaten egg and blended bananas. Mix everything to a smooth dough. Turn on to a floured work surface and roll out to a thickness of about 3 mm (⅛ in). Stamp it into 4–5 cm (1½–2 in) rounds, and lay them on floured baking sheets. Bake the biscuits for 20 minutes or until firm and just beginning to colour. Turn on to a wire rack to cool.

CHAPTER EIGHT

PORTABLE FOOD

Ideas for Picnics and Packed Meals, Snacks for Long Journeys

There is nothing quite like the fun
of a picnic. Children and adults love the break from
normal routines, and food always tastes better in the fresh air.
Food for picnics should be simple to prepare, easily transported
and suitable for eating without a lot of plates or cutlery. The same
goes for packed lunches and food for long journeys. It is all too
easy to get round the problems with convenience foods – the
inevitable packets of crisps, bars of chocolate, bought fruit
pies. But it can be just as easy, and is certainly cheaper
and more satisfying, to come up with delicious,
nutritious alternatives that both children
and adults will enjoy.

The store cupboard

A well-stocked store cupboard is
always an advantage when you have
to think of a different lunch every
day, find a snack food quickly or
prepare food for a picnic or car
journey. Bread is the first essential. If
you bake your own wholewheat bread
or buy it daily, there should always be
some on hand, but it is still a good
idea to store wholewheat rolls and
pitta bread in the freezer for
emergencies. Cut bread thaws within
ten to fifteen minutes if removed from
its wrapping, and pitta bread can be
freshened or thawed by wetting it
under the tap and grilling it until
soft, though not toasted.

For fillings and spreads, different
varieties of cheese are ideal,
especially cottage cheese and curd or
low fat soft cheese. Peanut butter and
tahini (pages 120 and 121) are good for
spreads, and tins of fish such as tuna
and sardines in brine are invaluable.

The other essential stand-by is fresh
fruit and vegetables. Fruits can be
eaten as they are or put into salads.
Vegetables can be cut into slices,
grated for salads, sliced for
sandwiches, and cooked into easy and
nutritious hot or cold soups.

Keep plenty of dried fruits and nuts
in store too. These can be mixed and
used as snacks or desserts or in
salads. Another snack can be made
from mixtures of nuts and dried fruits;
these are sold ready mixed or you can
make your own from banana chips,
toasted coconut, papaya pieces,
pineapple snacks, nuts and raisins.

Packed lunches

Many children take a packed lunch to school every day and this can become less of a chore in the morning with some forward planning and a well-stocked cupboard.

Equip your child with a special lunchbox, cup and flask. Use sandwich-size plastic bags, plastic wrap or greaseproof paper to wrap the food in and encourage your child to bring it home if possible so that you can recycle it.

Cheese sandwiches might be easy for you to prepare in the few minutes that you have in the morning, but stop and think. Is this the sort of meal you would want for lunch five days a week? Deciding what to do for a packed lunch in the few minutes between breakfast and rushing out of the door is not the best way. Do a little forward planning at the weekend. Plan the week's lunches and perhaps do some preparation in advance.

You could plan lunches around one or more basic ingredients such as a small joint of ham or bacon, cooked pulses or a chicken. These can turn up in different guises throughout the week and the stocks resulting from the cooking can be used for soup.

Soups On cold days, a flask of hot soup and buttered bread or rolls will provide a warming and nourishing meal without any extra accompaniment. The first three recipes on page 118 are for thick, substantial soups. The quick soups make warming starters and need to be followed by something more filling.

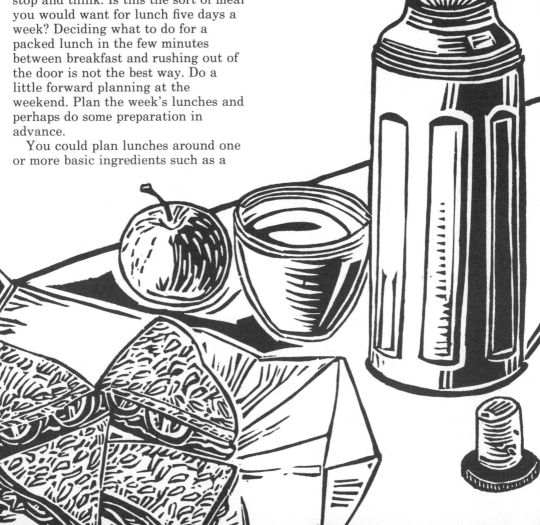

Sandwiches have always been the favourite packed lunch. They are easy to carry and easy to eat and, if they are made with wholewheat bread and include or are eaten with raw vegetables or fruit, they can make a complete and well-balanced meal. To save you time and trouble in the mornings, most of the suggestions on pages 119 to 121 can be made up the night before – the exceptions are Tuna and Tomato (the tomato may go soggy) and the mashed banana fillings. Wholewheat sliced bread will make your job easier still. If you want to make interesting shapes with the sandwiches see page 136 in the party foods chapter.

The recipes for dips and pâtés (pages 123–4) can also be used as sandwich fillings.

Filled rolls Bread rolls often give too much bread and not enough filling and when they are halved, filled and sandwiched back together they are difficult to handle. To solve both problems, hollow them out and put the filling inside.

Buy wholemeal rolls. Cut them in half crossways. Scoop out enough crumb to leave bread shells about 1 cm ($\frac{3}{8}$ in) thick. Fill the shells with a substantial mixture that is on the sticky side; slices of tomato, or cucumber, chopped celery, lettuce leaves, watercress sprigs or tufts of mustard and cress can also be added. If necessary, use elastic bands to hold the rolls closed. Recipes for fillings are on page 122.

Pitta bread is flat and oval, and can be slit to make a pocket into which you can put any number of ingredients. Either make the slit down the whole length of one side, or cut each pitta across into two, to make small pockets which are opened from the cut side. To slit pitta bread effectively, heat it very lightly under the grill, then hold it down on a work surface with the flat of one hand, whilst slitting with a sharp, preferably pointed knife with the other hand.

If you enjoy bread-making, pitta bread is very easy to make at home (page 122) and is usually easier to slit. It can be stored in the refrigerator for up to a week or in the freezer. Pitta fillings (pages 122–3) can be made the night before and stuffed into their pocket in the morning.

Picnics

Some of the best picnics require a number of containers: cheese, dips or pâtés (pages 123–4) in small covered pots; plastic bags full of washed, sliced raw vegetables – such as celery, carrot, cucumber, red and green pepper and cauliflower florettes; easily eaten fruits such as grapes and apples; pots of olives; bags of dried fruits and nuts. Wrap sandwiches or bread rolls spread with butter or margarine and long, filled French rolls in cling film. Or you can prepare all-in-one salads (pages 124–5), where all the ingredients for a balanced meal are mixed in one container.

If your family enjoys frequent picnics, buy an insulated food box or cold bag. If food is taken straight from the refrigerator and the box is not opened until lunchtime, a certain degree of coolness can be maintained.

Drinks

Provided that you have good-quality, non-breakable flasks, you can make ice-cold drinks in the summer and hot drinks in the winter. Natural fruit juices are favourites for cold drinks, or you can make barley waters (page 141) with citrus fruits and honey.

For hot drinks, heat fruit juices and barley waters or dilute concentrated apple juice with hot water. Rosehip tea is a favourite with many children and hot milk drinks are also successful: simply heat milk and sweeten it with a little honey, or use a carob drink or coffee substitute.

Spur-of-the-moment food

Bread Make standard loaves into sandwiches or simply spread slices with butter. French loaves and bread rolls can be split, the crumb removed and replaced with scrambled eggs or omelettes, salads, or any other ingredients that you may have handy.

Cold potatoes Make them into a salad with a dressing of half yoghurt and half mayonnaise and perhaps any other cold summer vegetables (carrots, peas) you may have left over from the day before.

Cold rice Make it into a salad.

Eggs Hard-boil them for finger food. Scramble them or make them into omelettes to fill hollowed bread rolls. Mash hard-boiled eggs with mayonnaise, tomato purée or grated cheese for sandwich fillings.

Cheese Grate for sandwiches. Cut into chunks or wedges to serve as finger food with salad vegetables, or with cake or apples after the meal.

Cooked beans Make into a salad or mash to make a sandwich filling.

Sausages Grill and serve whole.

Cold meats Slice or dice. Use for sandwiches or rolled up as finger foods.

Tins of tuna or sardines Use for sandwiches or pâtés or put into hollowed rolls.

Smoked mackerel fillets Cut into quarters for finger food. Mash for sandwiches or pâté.

Salad vegetables Cut the harder ones into pieces for simply chewing or for dipping into pâtés. Leave tomatoes whole. Wash and separate lettuce leaves. If you like mixed salads, chop the leaves and mix with other salad vegetables, then put into containers and package a dressing separately.

Fresh fruit Leave as it is. If it is soft fruit, make sure that the containers are not squashable.

Home-flavoured yoghurts Put into individual containers.

Cake Cut up and either wrap each piece singly or wrap the whole cut cake in plastic.

Travelling food

A supply of nourishing and appropriate food can give a much-needed boost to flagging spirits on a long journey. Keep the food simple, easy to prepare and easy to eat without creating a lot of mess; and remember that before you get to eat it, the food will probably have been sitting in its wrappings and in a warm place for several hours.

Cheesy Bread, Nutty Brioches and Nutty Scone Rolls (pages 131–2) all travel well. Some of the recipes for sandwich, roll and pitta fillings (pages 119–23) might also fit the bill, depending on how much preparation you have time to do. Simplest, and I find best of all, are yeast extract sandwiches. They last well, suffer little from the heat, and make almost no mess at all. Hard-boiled eggs make a good accompaniment.

Fruit and washed, cut up vegetables are always refreshing, particularly whole tomatoes, sticks of celery and hunks of cucumber. For something sweet, stock up with muesli bars or take bags of Oat Crunch (page 31) and dried fruit and nut mixtures.

It's important to take plenty to drink. Small 200 ml (7 fl oz) cartons of fruit juices can be invaluable, but they are expensive and you may need a large number if the journey is going to be a long one. Instead take orange juice, diluted and decanted into large plastic bottles.

GREEN PEA AND POTATO SOUP

D E G W Makes 1.15 litres (2 pints)

125 g (4 oz) green split peas
1 medium potato
1 large onion
2 celery sticks
2 tablespoons oil
850 ml (1½ pints) ham stock (opposite)
1 bayleaf

Peel and finely chop the potato. Finely chop the onion and celery. Heat the oil in a saucepan on a low heat. Stir in the potato, onion and celery and cook them gently for 5 minutes, stirring occasionally. Add the split peas and cook, stirring, for 1 minute. Pour in the stock and bring to the boil. Add the bayleaf. Cover and simmer for 50 minutes or until the peas are very soft and almost disintegrating. Remove the bayleaf.

When cool, store in a covered container in a refrigerator. Reheat just before pouring into a vacuum flask.

LENTIL MINESTRONE

D E Makes 1.15 litres (2 pints)

125 g (4 oz) small brown lentils
225 g (8 oz) carrots
4 celery sticks
125 g (4 oz) mushrooms
1 large onion
1 clove garlic (optional)
125 g (4 oz) wholewheat spaghetti
3 tablespoons oil
1.15 litres (2 pints) stock (page 19)
1 × 400 g (14 oz) tin tomatoes
2 teaspoons dried mixed herbs

Finely chop the carrots, celery, mushrooms, onion and garlic if using. Break the spaghetti into 2.5 cm (1 in) lengths. Heat the oil in a large saucepan on a low heat. Add the carrots, celery, onion and garlic and cook gently for 5 minutes. Add the mushrooms and lentils and stir. Pour in the stock and tomatoes and bring to the boil. Add the spaghetti and herbs. Cover and simmer for 50 minutes or until the lentils are completely tender.

CHICKEN AND BUTTERBEAN SOUP

D E G W Makes 850 ml (1½ pints)

75 g (3 oz) cooked chicken (opposite)
575 ml (1 pint) reserved chicken stock
175 g (6 oz) cooked butterbeans (page 12)
1 tablespoon Peanut Butter (page 120)

Chop the chicken into pieces and put all the ingredients into a blender or food processor. Work until smooth. Heat to boiling before putting into flask.

QUICK CREAM OF TOMATO SOUP

E G W Makes 425 ml (15 fl oz)

1 × 400 g (14 oz) tin tomatoes
75 g (3 oz) curd cheese

Work the tomatoes and their juice in a blender or food processor. Add the cheese and blend again. Heat slowly without boiling.

QUICK THICK VEGETABLE SOUP

D E G W Makes 425 ml (15 fl oz)

1 × 330 ml (11 fl oz) tin tomato and vegetable juice
175 g (6 oz) cooked butterbeans (page 12)
2 tablespoons chopped parsley (optional)

Work the vegetable juice and butterbeans in a blender or food processor until they are smoothly blended. Heat gently, without boiling, and finally add the parsley.

SANDWICH FILLINGS

WHITE SAUCE

This sauce is included in some of the sandwich fillings. It is easy to make and keeps well in a covered container in the refrigerator.

E

25 g (I oz) butter
2 tablespoons wholewheat flour
275 ml (10 fl oz) milk

Melt the butter in a saucepan over a medium heat. Stir in the flour, cook for 2–3 minutes, then gradually add the milk. Bring to the boil, stirring. Simmer, stirring, for 2 minutes, or until you have a smooth, thick sauce. Cool before putting into a covered container.

HAM FOR SANDWICHES

Buy a 450–675 g (1–1½ lb) piece of lean ham or bacon for boiling. Soak it overnight in cold water. Drain it, put it into a saucepan and cover with 1.5 litres (2½ pints) fresh water. Add 1 onion, halved but not peeled, 1 carrot split lengthways, 1 celery stick, broken, 1 teaspoon black peppercorns, 1 teaspoon cloves and 1 bayleaf. Bring to the boil, cover and simmer for 1 hour or until tender. Lift out the ham. Cut off any rind. Strain and reserve the stock.

For the sandwich fillings below, the ham has to be minced. This can be done as soon as it is cool.

CHICKEN FOR SANDWICHES

Buy a 1.125 kg (2½ lb) roasting chicken. Put it into a saucepan with 1 carrot, split lengthways, 1 small onion, halved but not peeled, 1 celery stick, broken, 1 teaspoon black peppercorns and a bouquet garni. Pour in enough cold water to cover the legs but leave the breast above the surface. Bring it to the boil. Cover and simmer for 50 minutes or until the chicken is tender. Lift out the chicken and cool it completely. Strain and reserve the stock.

Store both in covered containers in the refrigerator.

CHICKEN AND CUCUMBER SANDWICH FILLING

D For 4 rounds

125 g (4 oz) cooked chicken (below)
2 tablespoons mayonnaise
cucumber slices

Finely chop the chicken and mix it with the mayonnaise. Spread it on the bread and lay cucumber slices over the top.

HAM AND TOMATO SANDWICH FILLING

E For 3 rounds

75 g (3 oz) minced ham (left)
3 tablespoons white sauce (left)
2 tablespoons tomato purée

Mix all together well.

HAM AND BEAN SANDWICH FILLING

E For 3 rounds

40 g (1½ oz) minced ham (left)
50 g (2 oz) cooked haricot beans
or flageolets (page 12)
I tablespoon white sauce (above)
2 tablespoons chopped parsley

Mash the beans to a purée. Thoroughly mix them with the ham, sauce and parsley.

BEAN AND CHEESE SANDWICH FILLING

E For 4 rounds

125 g (4 oz) cooked haricot beans
or flageolets (page 12)
50 g (2 oz) mature Cheddar
cheese, finely grated
4 tablespoons white sauce (above)
I teaspoon yeast extract

Mash the beans to a purée. Thoroughly mix in the cheese, sauce and yeast extract.

TUNA AND TOMATO SANDWICH FILLING
D For 3 rounds

1 × 100 g (3½ oz) tin tuna fish
1 tomato
1 tablespoon mayonnaise

Drain and flake the tuna. Scald, skin and chop the tomatoes. Mash them with the tuna using a potato masher and mix in the mayonnaise.

CELERY AND SUNFLOWER SANDWICH FILLING
E For 3 rounds

50 g (2 oz) curd cheese,
or other low fat soft cheese
3 celery sticks
40 g (1½ oz) sunflower seeds

Cream the cheese in a bowl. Chop the celery very finely and grind the sunflower seeds. Mix into the cheese.

CHEESE SPREAD
E For 3 rounds

125 g (4 oz) grated cheese – use any of the hard cheeses, such as Cheddar, Double Gloucester, Red Leicester or Lancashire
3 tablespoons water, or tomato juice, or tomato and vegetable juice

Put the cheese into a bowl, bring the water or juice to boiling point and quickly beat it into the cheese to make a smooth paste.

NUTTY-DATE SANDWICH FILLING
E For 4 rounds

50 g (2 oz) unsalted peanuts
50 g (2 oz) dates
50 g (2 oz) curd cheese,
or other low fat soft cheese

Finely grind the nuts and finely chop the dates. Mix them into the cheese.

CREAMED APRICOT SANDWICH FILLING
E For 4 rounds

50 g (2 oz) dried whole apricots
150 ml (5 fl oz) unsweetened orange juice
50 g (2 oz) curd cheese,
or other low fat soft cheese

Soak the apricots in the orange juice for 2 hours. Bring them gently to the boil and simmer until tender. Cool them in the juice and drain. Purée the apricots in a blender or food processor. Add the cream cheese and mix well.

BANANA SANDWICHES

These are always popular. Mash the bananas and use them plain or mixed with honey, sugar-free jam, chopped dates, raisins or grated apple. Or try one of the following combinations (quantities for 1 banana):
- mixed with 2 teaspoons tahini plus 2 teaspoons lemon or orange juice;
- mixed with 2 tablespoons Peanut Butter and 1 tablespoon sugar-free jam, plus up to 1 tablespoon lemon juice, if liked;
- spread or mashed with 50 g (2 oz) curd cheese or low fat soft cheese;
- sprinkled with ground nuts.

PEANUT BUTTER
These quantities will three-quarters fill a 450g (1 lb) jam jar.
D E G W

225 g (8 oz) unroasted peanuts
2 tablespoons peanut or sunflower oil
pinch fine sea salt (optional)

Heat the oven to 120°C/250°F/Gas Mark ½. Spread the nuts on a baking tray and put them into the oven for 20 minutes. Cool them and rub off as much of the skins as possible. Put the nuts into a blender or food processor and work them until they are finely ground, stopping and easing them from the sides whenever necessary. Add the oil and work to a smooth paste. Add salt if required.

PEANUT BUTTER SANDWICHES
E

Peanut butter should be spread directly on to the bread: since it is itself oily, butter or margarine is unnecessary. Use it plain, top it with low fat soft cheese or yeast extract, or with slices of tomato, watercress or sprouted seeds; or try adding something sweet like sugar-free jam, sliced banana or chopped apple.

Peanut Butter Mixtures
Mix any of the following into 4 tablespoons peanut butter (enough for 4 rounds):
- 1 tablespoon tomato purée plus 1 small carrot, finely grated;
- 1 tablespoon tomato purée plus 1 celery stick, finely chopped;
- 1½ teaspoons yeast extract plus 4 tablespoons chopped watercress;
- 1½ teaspoons yeast extract plus generous handful mustard and cress, finely chopped;
- 50 g (2 oz) low fat soft cheese, plus 1½ teaspoons yeast extract and 2 tablespoons chopped parsley;
- juice ½ lemon and 2 tablespoons natural yoghurt, plus 5 cm (2 in) piece cucumber, finely chopped;
- 4 tablespoons natural yoghurt, plus 50 g (2 oz) dates, finely chopped;
- 2 tablespoons natural yoghurt plus 2 tablespoons sugar-free jam (top with banana slices if wished);
- 4 tablespoons natural yoghurt plus 25 g (1 oz) dates, finely chopped, and 25 g (1 oz) walnuts, finely chopped;
- 50 g (2 oz) low fat soft cheese plus 2 tablespoons sugar-free jam or honey.

TAHINI SPREAD
D E

The basic mixture is 275 ml (10 fl oz) tahini plus 2 tablespoons tamari or shoyu sauce (these are natural soya sauces available from wholefood or healthfood shops). Mix them together well. This basic mixture can be stored in a covered container in the refrigerator for up to one week. There is no need to spread the bread with butter or margarine. Tahini spread can be used in sandwiches just as it is, topped with sliced tomatoes, watercress, mustard and cress, sprouted alfalfa seeds or sliced cucumber; or you can mix in other ingredients such as diced salad vegetables, tomato purée and orange or lemon juice. For sweet sandwich fillings, combine tahini spread with honey, banana, dried fruits and nuts.

Tahini Spread Mixtures
Add the following to 4 tablespoons basic tahini mixture (enough for 4 rounds):
- 2 tablespoons finely diced cucumber, 2 tablespoons finely diced celery and 2 teaspoons tomato purée;
- 1 small carrot, finely grated, grated rind ½ small orange and 4 tablespoons orange juice.

Tahini can also be made into sweet sandwich fillings, in which case leave out the tamari or shoyu sauce:
- 4 tablespoons tahini, juice ½ orange, 125 g (4 oz) finely chopped dates and 1 banana, mashed into the mixture or sliced and placed on top;
- 2 tablespoons tahini, juice ½ lemon, 2 tablespoons honey, 50 g (2 oz) raisins and 25 g (1 oz) chopped walnuts.

EGG AND TOMATO FILLING FOR ROLLS
D For 4 rolls

4 eggs, hard-boiled
2 tablespoons mayonnaise
1 tablespoon tomato purée
2 or more tomatoes

Mash the eggs and mix in the mayonnaise and tomato purée. Fill the rolls and put them back together with slices of tomato.

SCRAMBLED EGG FILLING FOR ROLLS

As this filling has to be cooled completely before using it is a good idea to make it the night before.

For 4 rolls

3 eggs
15 g (½ oz) butter, or margarine
2 tomatoes
25 g (1 oz) Cheddar cheese, grated

Melt the butter or margarine in a saucepan on a low heat. Finely chop the tomatoes and cook them in the butter for 2 minutes. Beat the eggs and add them with the cheese.

CHICKEN FILLING FOR ROLLS

For 4 rolls

75 g (3 oz) cooked chicken,
chopped (page 119)
75 g (3 oz) cottage cheese
1 tablespoon tomato purée
1 tablespoon mayonnaise
1 tablespoon chopped chives

This forms the basic mixture. Diced green or red pepper or chopped celery can be added if wished.

WHOLEWHEAT PITTA BREAD
D E Makes 6

450 g (1 lb) wholewheat flour
25 g (1 oz) fresh yeast, or 15 g (½ oz) dried
1 teaspoon honey
275 ml (10 fl oz) warm water
2 teaspoons fine sea salt

Put the flour into a bowl. Cream the yeast with the honey and half the water and leave it in a warm place until it begins to froth – about 15 minutes. Dissolve the salt in the remaining water.

Make a well in the flour. Mix in the yeast and then the salt water. Mix everything to a dough. Cover it with a clean tea cloth and leave in a warm place for 1 hour or until doubled in size.

Heat the oven to 230°C/450°F/Gas Mark 8. Divide the dough into 6 pieces and roll each one into an oval about 12 × 20 cm (5 × 8 in) and 6 mm (¼ in) thick. Put them on to a floured board, cover them with the tea cloth again and leave in a warm place for 20 minutes.

Flour 1 large or 2 small baking sheets and put them into the oven to become really hot. Lay the pittas on the hot baking sheets and bake for 15 minutes so they are just beginning to brown.

If the pittas are to be served hot immediately, wrap them in a clean, thick napkin to keep them warm. Otherwise cool them completely on a wire rack and serve with one of the cold fillings that follow.

EGG AND HAM FILLING FOR PITTA
D For 1 pitta

1 egg, hard-boiled
15–25 g (½–1 oz) cooked ham (page 119)
handful mustard and cress
½ tablespoon mayonnaise

Chop the ham, mustard and cress very finely. Mash the egg with the mayonnaise and mix all the ingredients together.

TUNA AND BEAN FILLING FOR PITTA

D E For 1 pitta

½ × 100 g (3½ oz) tin tuna fish
1 spring onion (optional)
50 g (2 oz) cooked cannellini, butter
or haricot beans (page 12)
1 tablespoon chopped parsley
freshly ground black pepper
1 tablespoon oil
1 teaspoon lemon juice,
or white wine vinegar
2 tomatoes

Chop the onion, if using, drain the tuna and mix them with the beans, parsley and pepper. Beat the oil and lemon juice or vinegar together and mix into the rest.

Serve the tomatoes separately as they tend to make the bread soggy.

CRUNCHY SALAD FILLING FOR PITTA

For 1 pitta

½ celery stick
2 tablespoons finely shredded white cabbage
1 tablespoon coarsely grated carrot
1 tablespoon unsalted peanuts
½ tablespoon mayonnaise
½ tablespoon natural yoghurt

Chop the celery finely and mix with the cabbage, carrot and peanuts. Mix together the mayonnaise and yoghurt and fold them into the rest.

BEAN AND CHEESE FILLING FOR PITTAS

E For 2 pittas

75 g (3 oz) cooked haricot
beans (page 12)
1 large celery stick
25 g (1 oz) Cheddar cheese, finely grated
2 tablespoons oil
1 tablespoon cider vinegar

Finely chop the celery and mix with the beans and cheese. Beat together the oil and vinegar and mix them in.

BUTTERBEAN DIP

E G W

175 g (6 oz) cooked butterbeans (page 12)
4 cm (1½ in) piece cucumber
1 small carrot
2 tablespoons white wine vinegar
2 tablespoons natural yoghurt

Chop the cucumber very finely, and grate the carrot. Mash the butterbeans to a purée or put them through a blender or food processor. Mix in the remaining ingredients.

CHICKEN LIVER DIP

E G W

125 g (4 oz) chicken livers
1 small onion
1 small clove garlic
15 g (½ oz) butter
125 g (4 oz) low fat soft cheese

Finely chop the chicken livers, onion and garlic. Melt the butter in a frying pan over a low heat and soften the onion and garlic in it. Raise the heat to medium. Put in the livers and stir them for 2 minutes or until they are just cooked through. Take from the heat and cool for 5 minutes.

Put the cooled livers into a blender or food processor and work to a smooth paste. Add the cheese and blend again until it is well incorporated.

KIPPER DIP

E G W

125 g (4 oz) kipper fillets
50 g (2 oz) low fat soft cheese
grated rind and juice ½ lemon
2 tablespoons chopped parsley
1 tablespoon tomato purée

Put the kipper fillets into a saucepan and cover them with water. Bring to a gentle boil and simmer for 2 minutes. Drain, skin and flake the fish, mashing it well if you like a smooth texture. Add the cheese and mix well. Beat in the lemon juice, parsley and tomato purée.

DIPS · PÂTÉS · ALL-IN-ONE SALADS

SARDINE DIP
E G W

1 × 125 g (4 oz) tin sardines in oil
125 g (4 oz) low fat soft cheese
juice ½ lemon

Drain the sardines and mash them well.
Add the cheese and beat until smooth. Mix
in the lemon juice.

TUNA AND SARDINE PÂTÉ
E G W

1 × 100 g (3½ oz) tin tuna
2 sardines
50 g (2 oz) low fat soft cheese

Drain the tuna. Mash it with the sardines
and mix in the cheese.

LENTIL AND TOMATO DIP
This makes a substantial dish for a vege-
tarian picnic.
D E G W Serves 4

225 g (8 oz) split red lentils
1 medium onion
1 × 400 g (14 oz) tin tomatoes in juice
150 ml (5 fl oz) stock (page 19)
1 bayleaf
4 tablespoons oil
2 tablespoons white wine vinegar
1 clove garlic
4 tablespoons chopped parsley

Thinly slice the onion. Put the lentils into
a saucepan with the tomatoes, stock,
onion and bayleaf. Bring to the boil,
cover, and cook very gently for 45 minutes, or until the lentils are very soft.
Remove the bayleaf and beat to a thick
purée. Cool. Beat together the oil, vinegar
and crushed garlic. Mix into the lentils
and add the parsley.
Serve the dip with wholewheat bread
rolls or pitta bread and a selection of salad
vegetables.

ALL-IN-ONE BURGHUL SALAD
E Serves 1

50 g (2 oz) burghul wheat
1 tablespoon oil
½ tablespoon white wine vinegar
small piece garlic (optional)
freshly ground black pepper
1 small carrot
1 celery stick
¼ bunch watercress
25 g (1 oz) Cheddar, or similar hard cheese
25 g (1 oz) ham (page 119),
or other cold meat (optional)
1 tomato
15 g (½ oz) unsalted peanuts
few raisins or sultanas (optional)

The night before, soak the wheat in warm
water for 20 minutes. Drain, and squeeze it
dry. Beat together the oil, vinegar,
crushed garlic, and pepper. Mix them into
the wheat. Grate the carrot and chop the
celery and watercress. Put these 3 ingredients in a polythene bag in the refrigerator.
Finely chop the cheese and meat.
In the morning, chop the tomato and
mix all the ingredients into the wheat.
This is just an example of what can go
into this type of salad. You could use all
cheese or all meat, or replace them both
with 50–75 g (2–3 oz) cottage cheese.
Chopped hard-boiled egg could also be
added, in which case omit the carrot and
add another tomato.

ALL-IN-ONE SALADS

BROWN RICE AND BEAN SALAD

Beans and rice together make a high-protein meal.

D E G W Serves 1

50 g (2 oz) brown rice, cooked
50 g (2 oz) cooked black kidney beans, red kidney beans, pinto or aduki beans (page 12)
1 celery stick
½ dessert apple
1 spring onion (optional)

Dressing
1 tablespoon oil
½ tablespoon white wine vinegar
1 teaspoon tamari sauce
1 teaspoon tomato purée
small piece garlic (optional)

The night before, mix together the rice and beans and leave them in a covered container in the refrigerator. The next morning finely chop the celery. Core and chop the apple. Chop the onion. Mix them into the rice. Beat the oil, vinegar, tamari sauce, tomato purée and crushed or chopped garlic together to make the dressing. Fold them into the salad.

ALL-IN-ONE BURGHUL, CELERY AND APPLE SALAD

D Serves 1

50 g (2 oz) burghul wheat
50 g (2 oz) walnuts
1 celery stick
1 small dessert apple
1 tablespoon oil
½ tablespoon cider vinegar

The night before, soak the wheat in warm water for 20 minutes. Drain, squeeze it dry and put it into a container. Chop the walnuts.

In the morning chop the celery and apple and mix these and the walnuts into the wheat. Add the oil and vinegar and mix well.

ALL-IN-ONE COTTAGE CHEESE SALADS

These salads are not as complete as those based on grains but they are still an excellent way of packing a salad. Serve them with bread, biscuits or crispbreads to complete the meal.

E G W Serves 1

Peanut and Raisin
125 g (4 oz) cottage cheese
25 g (1 oz) peanuts
25 g (1 oz) raisins
2 tomatoes, chopped
1 celery stick, chopped
generous handful mustard and cress, chopped
1 satsuma, divided into segments

Celery, Apple and Walnut
125 g (4 oz) cottage cheese
2 celery sticks, chopped
1 small dessert apple, chopped
25 g (1 oz) walnuts, chopped
25 g (1 oz) dates, chopped

Bean and Beetroot
125 g (4 oz) cottage cheese
50 g (2 oz) cooked haricot or butterbeans (page 12)
1 medium-sized cooked beetroot, chopped
2 tomatoes, chopped

Carrot, Celery and Raisin
125 g (4 oz) cottage cheese
1 garlic clove, crushed (optional)
1 medium carrot, finely grated
1 celery stick, finely chopped
40 g (1½ oz) raisins

PASTIES

SARDINE FILLING FOR PASTIES
For 4 pasties

2 × 125 g (4 oz) tins sardines in oil
150 g (5 oz) potato
2 tomatoes
1 small onion
½ teaspoon paprika
3 tablespoons chopped parsley

Mash the sardines with their oil. Peel and finely chop the potato. Scald, skin and chop the tomatoes. Finely chop the onion. Mix all together and add the paprika and parsley.

PORK FILLING FOR PASTIES
For 4 pasties

225 g (8 oz) lean pork
½ medium cooking apple
1 small onion
3 sage leaves, chopped
freshly ground black pepper

Heat the oven to 180°C/350°F/Gas Mark 4. Very finely dice the pork. Peel, core and finely dice the apple. Finely chop the onion. Mix them together, add the sage and season with the pepper.

MIXED VEGETABLE FILLING FOR PASTIES
For 4 pasties

125 g (4 oz) swede
50 g (2 oz) carrot
125 g (4 oz) potato
50 g (2 oz) leek
1 small onion
125 g (4 oz) cooked haricot beans (page 12)
2 sage leaves, chopped
1 teaspoon chopped thyme
1 tablespoon chopped parsley
2 tablespoons tomato purée
2 tablespoons stock (page 19)

Finely chop the swede, carrot, potato, leek and onion. Mix them with the haricot beans and add the herbs. Mix together the tomato purée and stock. Mix them into the vegetables.

PASTIES
Makes 4

shortcrust pastry made with 300 g (10 oz) wholewheat flour (page 79)
chosen filling (see below)
beaten egg for glaze

Divide the pastry into 4 equal-sized pieces and roll each one into a round. Put a quarter of the chosen filling on one side of the pastry. Fold over the other side and seal the edges neatly. Lay the pasties on a floured baking sheet and brush them with beaten egg. Put them into a preheated 180°C/350°F/Gas Mark 4 oven for 45 minutes. If they look as though they are going to brown too quickly, cover them with damp greaseproof paper after the first 25 minutes. Lift the pasties carefully on to a wire rack to cool.

When cold, store in a covered container in the refrigerator. Pasties can also be frozen on a flat tray and then packed separately into polythene bags. Thaw them overnight at room temperature.

CHEESE FILLING FOR PASTIES
For 4 pasties

1 medium onion, or 125 g (4 oz) leek
3 celery sticks
150 g (5 oz) potato
125 g (4 oz) mature Farmhouse Cheddar cheese, grated
1 egg
4 tablespoons chopped parsley

Heat the oven to 180°C/350°F/Gas Mark 4. Finely chop the onion or leek and celery. Peel and finely chop the potato. Beat the egg and mix in the cheese. Add the vegetables and parsley.

SUBSTANTIAL PICNIC DISHES

FISHERMAN'S EGGS
Serves 6 or 12

6 eggs, hard-boiled
1 medium onion
675 g (1½ lb) potatoes
4 tablespoons milk
1 × 200 g (7 oz) tin tuna
4 tablespoons chopped parsley
50 g (2 oz) wholewheat flour
1 egg
50 g (2 oz) dried wholewheat breadcrumbs
oil for deep frying

Thinly slice the onion, and boil it with the potatoes in their skins. Drain and skin the potatoes and mash them with the onion and milk; mash in the drained tuna. Cool the mixture completely.

Coat each egg with the potato mixture: it is easier if you use slightly dampened hands and rinse them when they start getting sticky. Roll each coated egg in the flour, then in the beaten egg and finally in the breadcrumbs. Heat a deep pan of oil to 185°C/360°F. Put in the eggs two or three at a time, depending on the size of the pan. Fry them for about 4 minutes or until they are golden brown, turning them once. Lift them on to crumpled kitchen paper to drain.

The eggs can be boiled and the coating prepared in advance, but they are best coated and cooked on the morning of the picnic.

MEAT LOAF
Ⓓ Serves 6

450 g (1 lb) minced beef
40 g (1½ oz) wholewheat bread
50 g (2 oz) mushrooms
1 medium onion
25 g (1 oz) vegetable margarine
2 teaspoons Worcestershire sauce
2 teaspoons tomato purée
4 chopped sage leaves, or ½ teaspoon dried
1 egg

Soak the bread in water. Heat the oven to 190°C/375°F/Gas Mark 5. Put the beef into a bowl, squeeze out the bread and mix it into the beef. Finely chop the mushrooms and onion. Melt the margarine in a frying pan over a low heat. Put in the onion and soften it. Raise the heat, put in the mushrooms and cook for 1 minute. Mix the mushrooms and onions, Worcestershire sauce, tomato purée and sage into the beef. Gradually add the beaten egg. Put the mixture into a 900 g (2 lb) loaf tin and bake for 1 hour, or until firm. Cool the loaf completely in the tin. Turn it out and cut it into 1.5 cm (½ in) slices.

EGG-WRAPPED BEEF SAUSAGES
Ⓓ Makes 8

mixture for meat loaf as above
8 eggs
4 tablespoons fresh chopped mixed herbs, or
1 tablespoon dried
oil for frying

Make up the beef loaf mixture and form it into 8 small sausage shapes. Heat the grill to high and if you have an open wire rack, cover it with foil perforated with a fork or skewer. Grill the sausages until they are browned and cooked through.

Beat each egg separately with a portion of the herbs. For each one, pour about ½ tablespoon oil into a small pan over a medium heat. Pour in the egg and cook it, turning it once, to make a thin, flat omelette. Turn it out on to a plate. Cook the rest in the same way.

Roll each sausage up in an omelette, folding in the sides, and secure with a cocktail stick.

SUBSTANTIAL PICNIC DISHES

EGGY POTATO SQUARES
G W Makes about 30

6 eggs
350 g (12 oz) potatoes
1 small onion
6 tablespoons milk
50 g (2 oz) mature Cheddar cheese,
finely grated
4 tablespoons chopped parsley
4 small tomatoes

Heat the oven to 200°C/400°F/Gas Mark 6. Cut the potatoes into chunks and thinly slice the onion. Steam them until tender. Skin the potatoes and mash them with the milk and onion. Mix in the cheese and parsley. Beat the eggs together and mix them into the potatoes a little at a time, making a smooth thick batter. Pour into a buttered 18 × 28 cm (7 × 11 in) baking tin. Thinly slice the tomatoes and arrange them in even rows on top. Bake the batter for 25 minutes or until it is set and beginning to turn golden. Leave it in the tin to cool. Cut it into squares, with a tomato in the centre of each piece. Lift them out and let them get quite cold.

OAT-COATED DRUMSTICKS
D

12 chicken drumsticks
150 g (5 oz) porridge oats
15 g (½ oz) grated Parmesan cheese
2 teaspoons dried mixed herbs
3 tablespoons oil
2 eggs
50 g (2 oz) wholewheat flour

Heat the oven to 200°C/400°F/Gas Mark 6. Mix together the oats, Parmesan cheese, herbs and oil. Dip the chicken drumsticks in the beaten egg, roll them in the flour and dip them again into the egg. Roll them in the oats to coat them completely. Lay the drumsticks on a wire rack in a roasting tin. Put them into the oven for 45 minutes or until they are golden brown. Cool them completely on a rack.

SESAME-COATED DRUMSTICKS
D E G W

12 chicken drumsticks
1 tablespoon tahini
4 tablespoons sesame or olive oil
1 tablespoon tomato purée
1 tablespoon white wine vinegar
pinch chilli powder
50 g (2 oz) sesame seeds

Heat the oven to 200°C/400°F/Gas Mark 6. Beat together the tahini, oil, tomato purée, vinegar and chilli powder. Coat the chicken pieces in the mixture and then roll them in the sesame seeds. Lay them on a rack in a roasting tin. Roast them for 30 minutes or until they are golden brown.

Leave the chicken pieces on the rack for about 10 minutes so the coating begins to set on them. Lift them on to a plate or rack to cool completely.

PORKIES
A delicious and wholesome substitute for bought sausages.
D Makes 8

450 g (1 lb) lean pork (use a cheap cut such as hand or shoulder)
1 egg
4 sage leaves, chopped
freshly ground black pepper
25 g (1 oz) wholewheat flour

Finely mince the pork. Mix in the beaten egg, sage and pepper: the mixture will be quite moist. Divide it into 8 equal portions. With floured hands make each portion into a sausage shape and coat it in flour. Heat the grill to high and if you have an open wire rack, cover it with foil perforated with a fork or skewer. Lay the 'sausages' on the hot rack or foil and grill until they are well browned on each side and cooked through – about 12 minutes. Lift the porkies on to a plate and cool them completely before packing.

Celery and apples are a good accompaniment.

FALAFEL
(SPICY CHICKPEA BALLS)

D E Makes about 20

225 g (8 oz) cooked chickpeas (page 12)
4 tablespoons water
2 tablespoons tahini
juice 1 lemon
25 g (1 oz) fresh wholewheat breadcrumbs
4 tablespoons chopped parsley
1 teaspoon ground cumin
$\frac{1}{2}$ teaspoon ground coriander
pinch cayenne pepper
1 clove garlic
50 g (2 oz) wholewheat flour
oil for deep frying

Mash the chickpeas well, mince them twice, or purée them in a blender or food processor. Beat in the water, tahini and lemon juice. Mix in the breadcrumbs, parsley, spices and crushed garlic. Form the mixture into small balls about 2.5 cm (1 in) in diameter. Roll them in the flour. Heat a deep pan of oil to 185°C/360°F. Fry the balls 5 or 6 at a time for about $2\frac{1}{2}$ minutes or until they are lightly browned. Drain them on kitchen paper.

These balls can be prepared in advance but are best fried on the morning of the picnic.

YOGHURT DIP FOR FALAFEL
E G W

275 ml (10 fl oz) natural yoghurt
4 tablespoons chopped parsley
1 clove garlic, crushed

Mix all the ingredients together. Refrigerate in a covered container until needed.

CHEESY BEAN STRUDEL
Serves 4–6

Pastry
225 g (8 oz) wholewheat flour
pinch fine sea salt
150 ml (5 fl oz) water
6 tablespoons corn oil
beaten egg for glaze

Filling
225 g (8 oz) cooked red
kidney beans, (page 12)
225 g (8 oz) tomatoes
1 medium onion
1 clove garlic
3 tablespoons oil
1 teaspoon dried mixed herbs
75 g (3 oz) Cheddar cheese, grated

Glaze
beaten egg

Make the pastry first. Put the flour and salt into a bowl. Bring the water to the boil in a small saucepan and add the oil. Boil until the mixture begins to look opaque and the oil and water are well incorporated. Pour the mixture into the flour and beat it in with a wooden spoon until it forms a soft dough. Knead to make it smooth and shiny, then wrap the dough in foil and a clean tea cloth and put it in the refrigerator for at least 30 minutes.

Scald, skin and chop the tomatoes. Thinly slice the onion and chop the garlic. Soften them in the oil over a low heat. Mix in the tomatoes, herbs and beans. Cover and cook gently for 5 minutes. Cool the mixture completely.

Heat the oven to 200°C/400°F/Gas Mark 6. Divide the dough into 2. Roll out one piece to a very thin oblong, spread it with half the bean filling and scatter half the cheese over the top. Roll it up from one narrow end, and lay it on a floured baking sheet with the end of the dough on the underside. Make another roll using the remaining pastry and filling. Brush the rolls with beaten egg and bake them for 30 minutes. Cool completely on the baking sheet.

For easy carriage, cut each roll in half crossways and pack them in a lidded plastic container. Cut them into slices 2–2.5 cm ($\frac{3}{4}$–1 in) thick when serving.

VEGETARIAN PICNIC SAVOURIES

CHEESE AND VEGETABLE PIES
E Makes 8

shortcrust pastry made with 300 g (10 oz)
wholewheat flour (page 79)
350 g (12 oz) small new potatoes
6 small or 4 large celery sticks
125 g (4 oz) shelled peas, fresh or frozen
1 small onion
50 g (2 oz) mushrooms
25 g (1 oz) butter
4 tablespoons milk
125 g (4 oz) Cheddar cheese, finely grated

Roll out the pastry and line 8 individual
tartlet tins 7.5 cm (3 in) across and 5 cm (2
in) deep. Heat the oven to 200°C/400°F/Gas
Mark 6.

Scrub and thinly slice the potatoes.
Finely chop the celery. Steam the potatoes
and celery together for 15 minutes or until
tender. If using fresh peas, boil or steam
the peas separately; thaw frozen peas.
Thinly slice the onions and mushrooms.
Melt the butter in a frying pan on a low
heat and soften the onions in it. Raise the
heat, add the mushrooms and cook for 1
minute. Take the pan from the heat. Mix
all the vegetables together. Add the milk
and half the cheese. Fill the tartlet cases
with the mixture and put the remaining
cheese on top. Put all the pies on a baking
sheet and bake for 20 minutes or until the
cheese on top has melted but not browned.
Lift the pies, still in their individual cases,
on to a wire rack to cool.

When they are quite cold, enclose each
one individually in plastic wrap.

OATY SAUSAGES
D E Makes about 5

175 g (6 oz) porridge oats
50 g (2 oz) green split peas
50 g (2 oz) split red lentils
425 ml (15 fl oz) water
1 medium carrot
1 medium onion
1 clove garlic
2 tablespoons oil
1 teaspoon yeast extract
1 tablespoon tomato purée
4 tablespoons chopped parsley
1 teaspoon dried sage
1 teaspoon dried thyme
75 g (3 oz) fresh wholewheat breadcrumbs
freshly ground black pepper
50 g (2 oz) wholewheat flour

Put the split peas and lentils into a
saucepan with the water. Bring them to
the boil, cover and simmer for 20 minutes.
Grate the carrot and onion and crush the
garlic. Add them to the pan and simmer for
a further 20 minutes or until the peas and
lentils are soft. Stir in the porridge oats
and cook, stirring, for 5 minutes. Take the
pan from the heat. Add the oil, yeast
extract, tomato purée, herbs and
breadcrumbs and season to taste with the
pepper. Leave to cool completely.

Form the mixture into small sausage
shapes and roll them in the flour. To cook,
heat the grill to high and if you have an
open wire rack, cover it with foil. Grill the
'sausages' until they are browned all over
– about 7 minutes altogether.

NUTTY BRIOCHES
D Makes 8

350 g (12 oz) wholewheat flour
25 g (1 oz) fresh yeast, or 15 g ($\frac{1}{2}$ oz) dried
1 teaspoon honey, if using dried yeast
4 tablespoons warm water
1 teaspoon fine sea salt
3 eggs
6 tablespoons oil
beaten egg for glaze

Filling
75 g (3 oz) split red lentils
1 small onion
150 ml (5 fl oz) vegetable or tomato juice
150 ml (5 fl oz) water
1 bayleaf
$\frac{1}{2}$ teaspoon dried mixed herbs
25 g (1 oz) walnuts
50 g (2 oz) unsalted peanuts
4 tablespoons chopped parsley

Put the water into a bowl and crumble in the fresh yeast. If using dried yeast, dissolve the honey in the water and sprinkle the yeast on top. Leave the mixture in a warm place until it is frothy – about 15 minutes.

Put the flour and salt into a bowl and make a well in the centre. Pour in the yeast mixture and stir a little of the flour into it. Stir in the beaten eggs and oil and mix everything to a dough. Turn it on to a floured board and knead until it is smooth. Return it to the bowl and cut a cross in the top. Cover the bowl with a clean tea cloth and leave it in a warm place for 1 hour or until the dough has doubled in size.

To make the filling, finely chop the onion and put it into a saucepan with the lentils, vegetable juice, water and herbs. Bring to the boil and cook gently for 45 minutes or until all the liquid has been absorbed and the lentils can be beaten to a purée. Take the pan from the heat. Finely chop or grind the nuts and mix them into the purée with the parsley.

Heat the oven to 200°C/400°F/Gas Mark 6. Knead the dough. Divide it into 8 portions and roll out each piece to a thickness of about 6 mm ($\frac{1}{4}$ in). Put a portion of the filling in the centre. Bring the edges of the dough together and seal by squeezing them. Turn the dough packet over and form it into a round bun with the sealed edges underneath. Lay the buns on a floured baking sheet, brush with beaten egg and leave them in a warm place for 15 minutes or until they have almost doubled in size. Bake the brioches for 20 minutes or until they are golden. Lift them on to a wire rack to cool.

CHEESY BREAD

basic bread dough (page 104) made with
225 g (8 oz) wholewheat flour, risen once
175 g (6 oz) Cheddar cheese, grated
2 teaspoons dried mixed herbs
beaten egg for glaze
2 teaspoons sesame seeds

Heat the oven to 200°C/400°F/Gas Mark 6. Knead the dough and roll it into an oblong 6 mm ($\frac{1}{4}$ in) thick. Scatter a quarter each of the cheese and herbs over two-thirds of the dough. Fold the dough into 3 and roll it out again. Repeat this 3 times, the final time leaving the dough folded and not rolled.

Place the loaf in a greased baking tin. Brush it with the beaten egg and scatter it with sesame seeds. Leave it to prove for 15 minutes, then bake in the oven for 40 minutes. Lift it on to a wire rack to cool completely.

Serve the loaf sliced and spread with butter or margarine, or a little cottage or other low fat soft cheese.

NUTTY SCONE ROLLS
E Makes about 12

basic scone mixture (page 98) made with
450 g (1 lb) wholewheat flour with
1 teaspoon dried mixed herbs added to
the flour before rubbing in the fat
150 g (5 oz) crunchy Peanut
Butter (page 120)
4 tablespoons tomato juice
1 tablespoon tomato purée

Heat the oven to 200°C/400°F/Gas Mark 6.
Roll the scone mixture out to a rectangle
1.5 cm ($\frac{1}{2}$ in) thick.

Put the peanut butter into a bowl and
gradually mix in the tomato juice. You
should have a moist, spreadable paste.
Beat in the tomato purée: you may have to
adjust the amount, as peanut butters vary
considerably. Spread the peanut butter
mixture over the scone dough. Roll it up
from one narrow end, cut it into slices
2.5 cm (1 in) thick and lay them on a
floured baking sheet. Bake for 20 minutes
or until the rolls are firm but not coloured.
Lift them on to a wire rack to cool.

OAT AND SUNFLOWER FINGERS
D E W Makes about 20

225 g (8 oz) porridge oats
50 g (2 oz) sunflower seeds
50 g (2 oz) raisins
125 g (4 oz) apple and pear spread
50 g (2 oz) honey
6 tablespoons corn oil

Heat the oven to 180°C/350°F/Gas Mark 4.
In a bowl, mix together the oats, sunflower
seeds and raisins. Put the apple and pear
spread, honey and corn oil into a saucepan
and stir over a low heat until the spread
and honey melt – it will be quite a thick
mixture. Stir into the oats, making sure
that it is well incorporated. Press the
mixture into an oblong tin, about 18 × 25
cm (7 × 10 in). Bake for 20 minutes or
until golden brown. As soon as it comes
out of the oven, cut into fingers. Leave
them in the tin until they are quite cold.

DATE AND ALMOND FINGERS
D E Makes about 14

125 g (4 oz) stoned dates
6 tablespoons water
175 g (6 oz) porridge oats
50 g (2 oz) wholewheat flour
25 g (1 oz) ground almonds
1 tablespoon honey
6 tablespoons concentrated apple juice
6 tablespoons corn oil
few drops almond essence (optional)

Heat the oven to 180°C/350°F/Gas Mark 4.
Finely chop the dates. Put them into a
saucepan with the water, bring to the boil
and stir over a low heat until you have a
thick purée – about 2 minutes. Cool.

Mix the oats, flour and almonds in a
bowl, and make a well in the centre. Melt
the honey and mix it in with the apple
juice, corn oil and almond essence, if
using. Make sure the dry ingredients
become evenly coated. Put half the mixture in an even layer in a greased 18 cm
(7 in) square tin. Spread the dates over the
top and put in the remaining mixture.
Spread it evenly and press down. Bake for
20 minutes or until golden. Cut into fingers in the tin, and leave until quite cold
before lifting them out.

These store well in an airtight
container.

PORTABLE CAKES

CARROT CAKE

225 g (8 oz) carrots
1 × 225 g (8 oz) tin pineapple in natural juice
75 g (3 oz) walnuts
300 g (10 oz) wholewheat flour
2 teaspoons bicarbonate of soda
1 teaspoon ground cinnamon
150 g (5 oz) apple and pear spread
175 ml (6 fl oz) corn oil
3 eggs

Heat the oven to 180°C/350°F/Gas Mark 4. Drain the pineapple and put just the fruit through a blender or food processor. Finely grate the carrots and chop the walnuts. In a bowl, mix together the flour, bicarbonate of soda and cinnamon and make a well in the centre. Melt the apple and pear spread in a small saucepan and gradually beat it into the flour with the oil, beaten eggs and pineapple purée. Beat to a smooth batter. Mix in the carrots and walnuts and put the mixture into an oiled 20 × 27 × 5 cm (8 × 11 × 2 in) baking tin. Bake for 30 minutes or until it is firm and springy. Cool for 5 minutes in the tin and then turn the cake on to a wire rack to cool completely.

Cut the cake into small squares and pack in an airtight container.

MOLASSES GINGER CAKE

225 g (8 oz) wholewheat flour
2 teaspoons ground ginger
½ teaspoon ground nutmeg
1 teaspoon baking powder
175 g (6 oz) butter
75 g (3 oz) apple and pear spread
75 g (3 oz) molasses
(or use 150 g (5 oz) molasses)
3 eggs
75 g (3 oz) sultanas

Heat the oven to 180°C/350°F/Gas Mark 4. Sift the flour into a bowl with the spices and baking powder, and make a well in the centre. Gently melt together the butter, apple and pear spread and molasses. Cool them a little and stir them into the flour together with the beaten eggs. Fold in the sultanas. Put the mixture into a greased 900 g (2 lb) loaf tin and bake for 1 hour or until a skewer inserted in the centre comes out clean.

BANANA CAKE

3 bananas
175 g (6 oz) vegetable margarine
grated rind 1 medium orange
175 g (6 oz) wholewheat flour
1 teaspoon bicarbonate of soda
1 teaspoon ground mixed spice
3 eggs

Heat the oven to 180°C/350°F/Gas Mark 4. Mash the bananas and either purée them in a blender or food processor or rub them through a sieve. Beat them into the margarine. Beat in the orange rind. Mix the flour with the baking powder and spice. Beat it into the banana mixture alternately with the beaten eggs. Put the mixture into a well-greased, 20 cm (8 in) diameter cake tin and bake for 30 minutes or until firm. Cool the cake in the tin for 5 minutes then turn it on to a wire rack to cool.

For a Banana and Apple Cake, add 2 peeled, cored and finely chopped dessert apples to the mixture after the flour and eggs.

CHAPTER NINE

PARTY TIME

Fun Food for Festive Occasions

Parties are fun, not just for children
but for parents too. However, children can be very fussy
and this can lead to disappointment for you, so the golden rule
is to keep everything as simple as possible. You may be sure that
your child will eat everything on the menu, but the party guests
could shy away from anything new, so stick to the familiar
ingredients children like and present them as
attractively as possible.

Preparation

A few days before the party, make a list of the foods that you intend to serve and go out and buy the ingredients. Children's tastes vary widely, so your list of foodstuffs should cover as wide a range as possible. Don't, for example, have all the savoury dishes made with eggs and all the sweet things with carob. On your shopping list you should also include all those things that make parties go with a swing: paper tablecloths with matching plates and cups, party hats, streamers, whistles, balloons and candles for the cake. This helps to set the theme of the party and is enjoyed by the children, no matter what age, as much as the food.

Do most of the preparation the day before. Even sandwich fillings can be prepared and stored in the refrigerator in sealed containers. Keep jobs on the day of the party to a minimum so that you don't neglect the party girl or boy and tire yourself.

If the party is for very young children, you will probably be entertaining the parents too, so provide suitable food and drink.

Reducing mess

If you are worried about your floor covering, put a large sheet of polythene beneath the table. Spilt drinks will need to be mopped up quickly, but crumbs and paper napkins can wait.

Presentation

To minimize wastage and mess, make sandwiches, tarts, pizzas and cakes small – enough for one or two bites only. There will then be no need for knives and spoons. With young children especially, most of the party food should be presented as finger food (page 137). Children do, however, appreciate attractive presentation. Make sandwiches into pinwheels and double deckers (page 136), mix the colours in the tart fillings (page 137), and decorate the plates with wedges of tomato or lemon, leafy pieces of celery and watercress. They will help to make the table look cheerful and full of colour and may even be eaten. Make flags with the names of the fillings on them for each plate of sandwiches.

Put all the savoury foods on the table before the guests arrive. Let them start on the food, and after about fifteen minutes gradually replace the savoury dishes with plates of cakes and biscuits, and keep the jug of juice filled up. As the grand

finale, bring on the cake. It doesn't
have to be a fancy shape with masses
of sugar icing to look spectacular.
Two round cakes sandwiched
together, covered liberally with low-
sugar frosting (pages 142–3) and
decorated with dried fruits can have
just as much impact. If you are feeling
ambitious, adapt the recipe on page
142 to make an animal shape or
number cake: cover it with frosting.

Party drinks
Most children like natural fruit
juices. Small children will probably
not appreciate cocktails and milk
shakes, which tend to be too heavy, so
the rule is to stick to the plain and
simple. Orange juice is usually the
favourite, with apple and pineapple
next. Dilute all fruit juices with cold
water to taste, or with carbonated
mineral water.

If you aren't sure how much drink
to provide, buy concentrated fruit
juices. Make up one jug according to
the manufacturer's instructions and
see how far it goes.

For an outdoor party for older
children, you could heat the juice, or
serve it spiced as punch.

Something fresh
Not all children enjoy salads, but it is
still a good idea to put a small
selection of salad vegetables on the
table, cut into lengths or fancy shapes
with the aid of tiny stainless steel
cutters. When the cakes and sweet
things are put on the table, swap the
vegetables for a bowl of seasonal
fruits: strawberries, plums or
satsumas.

Special parties
From the age of about three, children
begin to develop a sense of occasion
and enjoy taking part in traditional
festivities such as Christmas and
Hallowe'en. Because of the dangers of
firework parties, Hallowe'en parties
are now very popular. You can keep
the food warm in the oven or light a
barbecue. The fire will provide a focus
of attention and it makes the food
smell delicious. A barbecue in
midsummer is also a wonderful way to
have a party and the children are
then encouraged to play outside.

If you are serving hot food,
remember to let it cool off as eager
young fingers and mouths could be
burnt if food is too hot.

SANDWICHES FOR TEA PARTIES

SANDWICHES

Sandwiches are a familiar food for even the most conservative eaters, so include several platefuls of different types on the party table. Try some fancy variations, such as those suggested below. You will find it much easier if you use ready sliced wholewheat bread, and butter or margarine at room temperature.

Double Decker Skewers Use thin-sliced bread. Put it into the freezer for 2 hours. Take it out and remove the crusts from the slices. Spread two-thirds of the slices on one side with butter or margarine, the remaining third on both sides. Spread one type of filling on half the single-buttered slices. Top with a double-buttered slice. Spread on the second filling and top with the remaining single-buttered slices. Cut the sandwiches into cubes and push a cocktail stick through each one to keep it together.

Open Sandwiches Use sliced bread. Cut off the crusts. Spread with butter and then cut into squares or triangles. Spread with filling and decorate with small pieces of salad vegetable (one piece on each), such as tomato, cucumber, celery, cress, watercress, diced pepper or one sweetcorn kernel.

Sandwich Shapes Cutting sandwiches into elaborate animal shapes takes time; you also waste a great deal of bread and in the end the shapes may fall apart (if the bread is soft) or be unrecognizable. If you want shapes, keep them open and simple – stars or trees can be quite successful, for example, and appropriate for a party. Simpler still, and safer, is to use an ordinary round pastry cutter. With one 4 cm (1½ in) in diameter you can get 4 shapes per large slice with little waste apart from a wide crust and a small centre piece. If you are making a sandwich with 2 slices of bread, finish it before stamping out. With open sandwiches you can make the filling

go further by stamping the shapes out after buttering but before spreading. Decorate open sandwich shapes with small pieces of salad vegetable.

Pinwheels Put an uncut loaf in the freezer for about 2–3 hours. When you take it out, cut off all the crusts and cut the loaf lengthways into slices 6 mm (¼ in) thick. Roll each one with a rolling pin to flatten it slightly. Butter the slices, spread them with filling and roll up: if you have a small or medium loaf roll from the short side; roll a large slice from the long edge. Cut the roll into slices about 1 cm (⅜ in) thick.

Sweet Open Sandwiches Use a malt loaf, sliced very thinly and then cut into quarters. Spread with butter.

Suggestions for Fillings

Use a different filling for each shape or type:
- hard-boiled eggs mashed with 1 tablespoon mayonnaise per egg;
- hard-boiled eggs mashed with 1 tablespoon grated cheese plus 1 tablespoon mayonnaise per egg;
- as above but substitute 1 tablespoon sweet pickle for the mayonnaise;
- mild red cheese such as Double Gloucester or Red Leicester, finely grated and mixed with 1 tablespoon milk and 2 teaspoons tomato purée per 25 g (1 oz);
- cooked ham (page 119), finely minced and moistened with 1 tablespoon mayonnaise per 25 g (1 oz);
- tuna, drained and mashed with 50 g (2 oz) curd cheese per 200 g (7 oz) tin;
- tinned salmon, drained and mashed with a squeeze of lemon juice plus 2 tablespoons tomato purée per 200 g (7 oz) tin;
- crunchy Peanut Butter (page 120);
- Banana and Peanut Butter filling (page 120);
- Creamed Apricot filling (page 120).

Right: No-cook Carob Fudge, top (p. 94); Fig, Date and Brazil Nut Sweets, centre (p. 92); Apricot, Apple and Sunflower Seed Bars, bottom (p. 93).

Overleaf from left to right: Birthday Cake (p. 142), Tiny Pizzas (p. 137), Apricot and Almond Cakes (p. 139), Orange and Lemon Barley Water (p. 141), Sandwich Shapes (p. 136).

TARTS · PIZZAS FOR TEA PARTIES

LITTLE TARTS

Use shortcrust pastry (page 79) made with butter or margarine and wholewheat flour: if you are using a 5 cm (2 in) pastry cutter, 225 g (8 oz) flour will make 24 tartlet cases. Roll out the pastry and line tartlet or bun tins. Prick the rounds of pastry all over with a fork.

The tart cases can either be cooked empty to be filled later with a cold filling; or they can be filled before cooking to make miniature quiches that can be served either hot or cold. To cook them empty, put them into a preheated 200°C/400°F/Gas Mark 6 oven for 12–15 minutes or until they are crisp but not coloured. Take them from the tins immediately and cool completely on wire racks. These can be made up to 2 days in advance and filled on the morning of the party. Filled quiches are also cooked for 12–15 minutes or until the filling is set and the pastry crisp. Lift them on to wire racks to cool. These can be made a day in advance.

Cold Fillings
Each of these following combinations will fill 12 tartlet cases:
- 1 × 200 g (7 oz) tin tuna mixed with 2 tablespoons mayonnaise. Decorate each tart with ¼ cucumber slice;
- 1 × 200 g (7 oz) tin salmon mixed with squeeze lemon juice and 1 tablespoon tomato purée. Decorate with cucumber or small pieces of tomato;
- 3 hard-boiled eggs, mashed and mixed with 2 tablespoons finely grated Cheddar cheese and 2 tablespoons mayonnaise. Decorate with mustard and cress, chopped chives or small parsley sprigs;
- 1 × 175 g (6 oz) tin sweetcorn, drained, plus ½ × 400 g (14 oz) tin cooked red kidney beans, drained, mixed together and coated with 2 tablespoons oil and 1 tablespoon white wine vinegar.

Left: Frozen Yoghurt (p. 72).

Miniature Quiche Fillings
Each of the following combinations will fill 24 tartlets:
- 3 eggs beaten with 2 tablespoons milk and 1 tablespoon tomato purée, then mixed with 75 g (3 oz) finely grated cheddar cheese;
- 3 eggs beaten with 2 tablespoons milk, then mixed with 125 g (4 oz) cooked lean ham (page 119), finely diced.

TINY PIZZAS
E Makes 16

Dough
225 g (8 oz) wholewheat flour
1 teaspoon fine sea salt
1 teaspoon bicarbonate of soda
3 tablespoons olive oil
150 ml (5 fl oz) natural yoghurt

Topping
2 × 400 g (14 oz) tins tomatoes
1 teaspoon dried mixed herbs
75 g (3 oz) Edam cheese
2 anchovy fillets (optional)

Heat the oven to 200°C/400°F/Gas Mark 6. Put the flour into a bowl with the salt and bicarbonate of soda. Make a well in the centre and add the oil and yoghurt. Mix everything to a dough. Turn on to a floured work surface and knead lightly until smooth. Roll out to a thickness of 6 mm (¼ in) and stamp it into 16 rounds. Use these to line shallow tartlet tins. Prick them all over with a fork and bake for 5 minutes; cool.

For the topping, drain and chop the tomatoes. Put them in a saucepan with the herbs, bring to the boil and simmer for 10 minutes or until thick. Take them from the heat and cool them. Divide between the pizzas. Cut the cheese into tiny dice and scatter them over the top of the tomatoes. If using, cut each anchovy fillet into 8 small pieces and put one in the centre of each pizza.

These can be made in advance up to this stage and stored on plates in the refrigerator under plastic wrap. Bake the pizzas for a further 5 minutes at the same oven temperature just before serving.

SAVOURY DISHES FOR TEA PARTIES

NUTTY CHICKEN SAUSAGES
E Makes about 25

1 × 1.574 kg (3½ lb) roasting chicken,
cooked (page 119)
50 g (2 oz) unsalted peanuts
1 medium onion
15 g (½ oz) butter
1 tablespoon wholewheat flour
150 ml (5 fl oz) milk
4 tablespoons chopped parsley
1 tablespoon Worcestershire sauce
sea salt and freshly ground black pepper

Finely grind the peanuts. Spread them on a baking sheet and put them into a preheated 200°C/400°F/Gas Mark 6 oven for 4 minutes or until golden brown. Tip them on to a plate to cool.

Remove the chicken meat from the bones and finely mince it. Chop the onion very finely and soften it in the butter over a low heat. Stir in the flour, cook it gently for 2–3 minutes and then gradually add the milk. Bring to the boil, stirring, and simmer for 1 minute. Mix the sauce into the chicken. Beat in the parsley, Worcestershire sauce and seasonings to taste and cool the mixture completely.

Form the mixture into tiny sausage shapes about 4 cm (1½ in) long and 1 cm (½ in) thick. Roll them in the peanuts. Leave for 30 minutes to firm up, then roll them in the nuts again.

Store in the refrigerator in single layers on plates covered with plastic wrap for up to 2 days. Skewer with cocktail sticks before serving.

SAVOURY NUTTY ROLLS
D Makes about 16

shortcrust pastry made with 225 g (8 oz)
wholewheat flour (page 79)
1 large onion
4 tablespoons oil
50 g (2 oz) yellow split peas
50 g (2 oz) green split peas
275 ml (10 fl oz) stock (page 19)
1 teaspoon dried mixed herbs
1 tablespoon tomato purée
1 bayleaf
25 g (1 oz) hazelnuts
25 g (1 oz) unsalted peanuts
beaten egg for glaze

Finely chop the onion and soften it in 3 tablespoons oil over a low heat. Stir in the split peas. Pour in the stock and bring to the boil. Add the mixed herbs, tomato purée and bayleaf. Cover and simmer for 45 minutes or until all the stock has been absorbed and the peas can be beaten to a thick purée. Grind the nuts and mix them in. Beat in the remaining 1 tablespoon oil. Leave the mixture until it is quite cold.

Heat the oven to 200°C/400°F/Gas Mark 6. Divide the pastry into 2 and roll each piece into a strip about 7.5 cm (3 in) wide. Put half the nutty filling in a sausage shape just off centre of each of the strips. Fold the other side of the strip over and seal the edges together with water. Cut small diagonal slashes all the way down the roll and cut into lengths of about 4 cm (1½ in). Lay the lengths on floured baking sheets, brush them with beaten egg and bake for 20 minutes or until they are golden brown. Lift them on to a wire rack.

Serve warm, either immediately or reheated in a 180°C/350°F/Gas Mark 4 oven for 10 minutes.

SMALL CAKES FOR TEA PARTIES

CAROB CRUNCHIES
D E W Makes about 20

2 × 40 g (1½ oz) sugar-free carob bars
25 g (1 oz) vegetable margarine
175 g (6 oz) crunchy oat cereal or granola
glacé cherries for decoration

Break up the carob bars and put them into a saucepan with the margarine. Set the pan over a low heat and stir continuously until the carob has melted, taking great care not to let it boil. Take the pan from the heat and stir in the crunchy cereal, making sure that every part becomes well coated with carob. Spoon the mixture into paper cake cases, or on to a large oiled baking sheet in heaps of about two teaspoons. Halve the glacé cherries and put half on top of each heap. Put the cakes into the refrigerator or a cool place to set.

These are best stored in the refrigerator, where they will keep for up to one day.

APRICOT AND ALMOND CAKES
E Makes about 18

50 g (2 oz) dried whole apricots
275 ml (10 fl oz) unsweetened orange juice
50 g (2 oz) wholewheat flour
25 g (1 oz) ground almonds
½ teaspoon bicarbonate of soda
3 tablespoons corn oil
2 drops of almond essence

Topping
125 g (4 oz) curd cheese
2 tablespoons sugar-free apricot jam, plus extra for decorating
flaked almonds

Put the apricots into a saucepan with the orange juice. Bring to the boil, take the pan from the heat and soak the apricots for 2 hours. Drain, and put them through a blender or food processor with 3 tablespoons of the juice.

Heat the oven to 180°C/350°F/Gas Mark 4. In a bowl, mix together the flour, ground almonds and bicarbonate of soda. Make a well in the centre and add the apricots, oil and almond essence. Beat well to make a thick batter. Use the mixture to half-fill about 18 oiled bun tins. Bake the cakes for

12 minutes or until firm and just beginning to brown. Lift them on to wire racks to cool completely.

Make the topping by creaming together the cheese and jam. Spread teaspoonfuls on each little cake, add a small dollop of jam and scatter them all with the flaked almonds.

STRAWBERRY BISCUITS
Makes about 24

225 g (8 oz) stoned dates
125 g (4 oz) walnuts
50 g (2 oz) wholewheat flour
1 egg
4 tablespoons corn oil

Topping
4 tablespoons sugar-free strawberry jam
225 g (8 oz) curd cheese
up to 6 tablespoons milk
as many small strawberries as biscuits

Heat the oven to 180°C/350°F/Gas Mark 4. Very finely chop the dates and walnuts. Mix them in a bowl with the flour and make a well in the centre. Add the beaten egg and the oil and mix well, kneading with your fingers until you have a smooth, shiny dough. Turn on to a floured board and roll out to a thickness of about 6 mm (¼ in). Stamp it into 5 cm (2 in) rounds with a biscuit cutter. Lay them on a floured baking sheet and bake for 20 minutes or until firm and just beginning to colour. Cool the biscuits on the baking sheet for 1 minute and then lift them on to a wire rack to cool completely.

Beat the jam into the cheese. Beat in enough milk to give the consistency of whipped cream and spread over the biscuits. Top each one with a strawberry.

You can make peach biscuits when strawberries are not available. Use the same biscuit base, apricot jam instead of strawberry and top with slices of peach tinned in natural juice.

BROWNIES
Makes about 35

225 g (8 oz) wholewheat flour
50 g (2 oz) carob powder
125 g (4 oz) walnuts
6 tablespoons oil
175 g (6 oz) apple and pear spread
6 tablespoons apple juice
3 eggs

Frosting
2 × 75 g (3 oz) plain carob bars
275 ml (10 fl oz) natural yoghurt
flaked almonds, or flaked coconut (optional)

Heat the oven to 180°C/350°F/Gas Mark 4. Put the flour into a bowl and sieve in the carob powder. Chop the walnuts, add them to the flour and toss all together. Make a well in the centre and pour in the oil. Melt the apple and pear spread in the apple juice in a saucepan over a low heat. Pour into the well and begin to mix in flour from the sides. Beat the eggs together and beat them in until you have a thick cake mixture. Put it into an oiled 18 × 25 cm (7 × 10 in) cake tin. Bake for 25 minutes or until firm. Cool the cake for 2 minutes in the tin and then turn it on to a wire rack to cool completely.

To make the icing, break up the carob bars and put them into a bowl in a saucepan of cold water. Set over a low heat until the carob melts, taking care not to let the water boil or splash into the bowl. Take the bowl from the pan and quickly beat in the yoghurt. Immediately spread the icing over the cake and scatter it with flaked almonds or coconut as a decoration. Leave the cake until the icing is cold and firm. Cut it into pieces approximately 4 cm (1½ in) square.

Without the frosting, Brownies can be stored in an airtight container for up to 2 days, or can be frozen in plastic wrap. They can be frosted and decorated the day before the party and stored in the refrigerator.

JELLIES

For every 425 ml (15 fl oz) fruit juice you will need 1 envelope powdered gelatine, or just under 15 g (½ oz). Heat the juice to just under boiling point and take it from the heat. Pour about 150 ml (5 fl oz) of the hot juice into a jug and add the gelatine, stirring vigorously until it dissolves completely. Stir the mixture back into the rest of the juice. Cool the juice, pour it into moulds and put it into the refrigerator or other cool place to set. To be on the safe side, allow at least 3 hours for setting. Once set, jellies can be covered with plastic wrap and kept in the refrigerator for up to 2 days.

Cheap but effective plastic jelly moulds can be bought from most cookware shops. Small ones, holding around 150 ml (5 fl oz), come in the shape of teddy bears, cars and traditional 'blancmange' shapes; larger moulds include rabbits and fish. A single moulded jelly standing alone in the centre of a plate looks rather bare, so make up another jelly in a contrasting colour and set it in a flat dish.

Make the jellies well in advance, and prepare them for serving about 2 hours before the party. First find a suitable serving dish – a large flat dish with 4–5 cm (1½–2 in) high sides is best. If you have one large mould, dip it into a bowl of hot water for about 10 seconds (no more or details such as ears and noses will melt away), invert the serving dish over the top, turn both over together and give a sharp sideways shake: the jelly should come free of the mould and you will hear a 'squelch' as it settles into the dish. Dip small moulds into the water for 6 seconds. You will probably have two or more of these on a dish together, so inverting the dish is impossible; instead, carefully and quickly turn the moulds on to the dish. Hold them all down together and give a sharp sideways shake.

The jelly in the flat dish should be immersed in the water for 10 seconds, then shaken out on to a chopping board. Chop it finely, and put the chunks around the jelly shapes. It turns something quite plain into a picture, besides giving an extra flavour.

JELLIES · DRINKS FOR TEA PARTIES

Vegetarian Jellies

For a vegetarian family or vegetarian guest, jellies can be set with agar-agar, which is available from most health food shops. It makes a firm but soft-textured jelly, more cloudy than one set with gelatine and with no obtrusive flavour. The amount of agar-agar needed to set a given quantity of liquid varies according to brand, so refer to the manufacturer's instructions. For the basic method, follow the recipe on this page.

PINK RABBIT IN A PURPLE FIELD
E G W

1 × 400 g (14 oz) tin raspberries in natural apple juice
575 ml (1 pint) unsweetened red grape juice
40 g (1½ oz) gelatine
275 ml (10 fl oz) natural yoghurt

Drain the raspberries and reserve the juice in a saucepan. Rub the raspberries through a sieve and mix them back into their juice. Put the grape juice into a separate saucepan. In a third pan, soak the gelatine in 6 tablespoons water for 5 minutes. Gently warm the raspberries and the grape juice. Melt the gelatine over a low heat, pour half into each saucepan and stir until it dissolves completely. Take the pans from the heat and let the contents cool.

Pour the grape juice into a flat dish (such as a large lasagne dish). Put the yoghurt into a bowl and gradually mix in the raspberry mixture. Pour the mixture into a 575 ml (1 pint) rabbit mould. Put both jellies into the refrigerator or cool place for 2–3 hours to set.

When both jellies are set completely, turn the rabbit out into the centre of a serving plate. Using a fork, rough up the grape juice jelly (or chop it on a board). Spoon it round the rabbit. Keep the jellies in the refrigerator until you are ready to serve them.

VEGETARIAN ORANGE, PINEAPPLE AND GRAPEFRUIT JELLY
D E G W

500 ml (18 fl oz) unsweetened orange juice
225 ml (8 fl oz) unsweetened pineapple juice
225 ml (8 fl oz) unsweetened grapefruit juice
agar-agar to set 1 litre (1¾ pints) liquid

Pour all the juices into a saucepan. Mix in the agar-agar and set the pan on a medium heat. Stir until the agar-agar has dissolved, getting the juices hot but not letting them boil. Cool, pour into moulds and leave the jelly in a cool place for 2 hours to set.

ORANGE AND LEMON BARLEY WATER
Makes about 1.15 litres (2 pints)

50 g (2 oz) pearl barley
1.5 litres (2½ pints) water
2 oranges
1 lemon
2 tablespoons honey

Put the barley into a saucepan with the water. Bring it to the boil and simmer for 1 hour or until tender. Grate the rinds of the oranges and lemon into a large jug. Cut away and discard the pith. Thinly slice the flesh and add it to the rinds. Strain the boiling water from the barley into the jug. Stir in the honey and leave to cool.

Stir well and press down on the fruits before serving straight from the jug.

Variations
Lemon Barley Water Use 3 lemons and 3 tablespoons honey.

Orange Barley Water Use 3 oranges and 1 tablespoon honey.

Grapefruit Barley Water Use 2 grapefruit and 3 tablespoons honey.

Grapefruit and Orange Barley Water Use 1 grapefruit, 2 oranges and 2 tablespoons honey.

THE CAKE

A BIRTHDAY CAKE

175 g (6 oz) wholewheat flour
1 teaspoon bicarbonate of soda
175 g (6 oz) butter, softened, or margarine
175 g (6 oz) apple and pear spread
3 eggs
flavouring (optional, see below)
frosting (see below)

Heat the oven to 180°C/350°F/Gas Mark 4. Mix together the flour and bicarbonate of soda. Cream the butter or margarine and gradually beat in the apple and pear spread. Beat the eggs together and beat them into the mixture, alternating with the flour. Add one of the flavourings (below), if using. Divide the mixture between 2 greased sandwich tins, 18 cm (7 in) diameter, and bake the cakes for 20 minutes or until they are firm and springy and have shrunk slightly from the sides of the tins. Turn them on to wire racks to cool completely.

Frost the cake with one of the suggestions below.

Flavourings

Orange Cake Add the grated rind and juice 1 medium orange.

Lemon Cake Add the grated rind and juice 1 lemon.

Almond Flavoured Cake Add $\frac{1}{4}$ teaspoon almond essence.

Vanilla Flavoured Cake Add $\frac{1}{4}$ teaspoon vanilla essence.

Frostings

Soft Cheese Frosting Into 225 g (8 oz) low fat soft cheese or curd cheese beat 75 g (3 oz) sugar-free jam or 3 tablespoons concentrated apple juice. If the mixture is too stiff, beat in up to 2 tablespoons natural yoghurt, but remember that this frosting will not become any firmer when it is left.

Carob Frosting I Break up 2 × 75 g (3 oz) plain or flavoured carob bars or 4 × 40 g (1½ oz) sugar-free carob bars. Put them into a basin in a saucepan of cold water, and set over a low heat until the carob melts, stirring frequently. Do not let the water boil and do not splash any water into the bowl: either will turn the carob hard and grainy. Take the bowl from the pan and gradually beat in 275 ml (10 fl oz) natural yoghurt. Sandwich the cakes together with about one-third of the frosting while it is still warm, and then quickly spread the remainder over the top and sides. The frosting will become firm as it cools, so leave the cake for at least two hours before serving.

Carob Frosting II Prepare carob bars as above. Cream 225 g (8 oz) low fat soft cheese or curd cheese in a bowl and beat in 4 tablespoons natural yoghurt. Gradually beat in the melted carob. Use immediately as the frosting will firm up on cooling. Leave the cake for at least 2 hours before serving.

Decorations
- glacé cherries, halved or cut into fine strips for lettering
- tiny currants (good for lettering)
- angelica, finely chopped or in strips
- whole pieces of candied peel, finely chopped or cut into strips
- almonds, blanched or flaked
- walnuts, halved or chopped
- any other nuts, chopped or whole
- chopped toasted hazelnuts or mixed nuts
- crunchy oat cereal or granola (looks good sprinkled over light-coloured frostings)

Non-edible decorations
- small plastic toys
- plastic letters and numbers if small enough
- shiny cake board
- artificial flowers (silk ones look better but may get in more of a mess than plastic)
- don't forget the candles.

THE CAKE

ORANGE CAKE

This flavoured cake has a choice of frostings.

175 g (6 oz) wholewheat flour
I teaspoon bicarbonate of soda
175 g (6 oz) margarine
175 g (6 oz) apple and pear spread
3 eggs
grated rind and juice I medium orange

Carob Frosting II (opposite), using
orange-flavoured carob bars

or Orange and Apricot Frosting:
225 g (8 oz) low fat soft cheese
75 g (3 oz) sugar-free apricot jam
grated rind I medium orange

Heat the oven to 180°C/350°F/Gas Mark 4. Mix the flour with the bicarbonate of soda. Cream the margarine with the apple and pear spread. Beat in the flour alternately with the beaten eggs, the orange rind and juice and mix well. Divide the mixture between 2 greased sandwich tins 18 cm (7 in) in diameter. Bake the cakes for 20 minutes or until they are firm and springy, and have shrunk slightly from the sides of the tins. Turn on to wire racks to cool completely.

Make the Carob Frosting II and use immediately, or try Orange and Apricot Frosting: cream the cheese in a bowl and beat in the jam a tablespoon at a time. Beat in the orange rind. This frosting does not have to be used quickly, and there is no need to leave it to set: it will only firm up if spread thinly.

Whichever frosting you use, sandwich the cakes together with about one-third of the mixture and spread the rest over the top and sides.

FROSTED APPLE CAKE

50 g (2 oz) dried apple rings
7 tablespoons concentrated apple juice
275 ml (10 fl oz) water
175 g (6 oz) wholewheat flour
I teaspoon bicarbonate of soda
I teaspoon ground cinnamon
3 eggs
6 tablespoons corn oil

Frosting
225 g (8 oz) curd cheese
3 tablespoons concentrated apple juice
2 tablespoons natural yoghurt, if necessary
walnuts, halved or chopped (optional)

Put the apple rings into a saucepan with 1 tablespoon of the concentrated apple juice and the water. Bring to the boil, take from the heat and soak for 2 hours. Drain and put them through a blender or food processor with 4 tablespoons of the liquid.

Heat the oven to 180°C/350°F/Gas Mark 4. Put the flour into a bowl and toss in the bicarbonate of soda and cinnamon. Make a well in the centre and put in the blended apple rings, beaten eggs, oil and remaining apple juice. Beat everything to a thick batter. Divide the mixture between 2 greased sandwich tins, 18 cm (7 in) in diameter. Bake for 20 minutes or until the cakes are firm and have shrunk slightly from the sides of the tins. Turn them on to wire racks to cool.

For the frosting, put the cheese into a bowl and beat it to a cream. Beat in the concentrated apple juice and add the yoghurt if the mixture is very stiff: it should be the consistency of butter cream.

Sandwich the cake together using half the frosting. Spread the remaining frosting on top and decorate with halved or chopped walnuts.

CAKES FOR CHRISTMAS PARTIES

GOOEY CAROB CAKE

175 g (6 oz) wholewheat flour
1 teaspoon bicarbonate of soda
50 g (2 oz) carob powder
175 g (6 oz) margarine
175 g (6 oz) apple and pear spread
3 eggs
Carob Frosting 1 (page 142)

Heat the oven to 180°C/350°F/Gas Mark 4. Mix the flour with the bicarbonate of soda and sieve in the carob powder. Beat together the margarine and apple and pear spread. Beat in the flour mixture, alternating with the beaten eggs. Divide the mixture between 2 greased sandwich tins, 18 cm (7 in) in diameter. Bake the cakes for 20 minutes or until they are firm and springy and have shrunk slightly from the sides of the tin. Turn them on to wire racks to cool completely.

Make the frosting and while it is still warm use one-third of the mixture to sandwich the cakes together. Cover it completely with the rest. Leave for 2 hours to set.

CHRISTMAS YULE LOG

75 g (3 oz) wholewheat flour
pinch fine sea salt
1 teaspoon ground mixed spice
3 eggs
75 g (3 oz) apple and pear spread
1 tablespoon hot water

Filling and Coating
350 g (12 oz) curd cheese, or low fat soft cheese, at room temperature
2 × 75 g (3 oz) sugar-free carob bars

Decoration
coloured almond paste (page 92)

Heat the oven to 200°C/400°F/Gas Mark 6. Line a 33 × 23 cm (13 × 9 in) Swiss roll tin with buttered greaseproof paper. Leave a narrow strip overhanging at one end, to help you roll up the cake. Swiss rolls are best mixed with an electric beater, but if you do not have one, half-fill a large saucepan with water, bring it to the boil and remove it from the heat.

Mix the flour with the salt and spice. Put the eggs into a bowl and whisk them lightly. Whisk in the apple and pear spread. Either put the bowl into the pan of water and whisk by hand, or use an electric beater. When ready the mixture should be light and foamy and if you trail a little of it over the surface of the rest it should stand out for about 3 seconds. Remove the bowl from the pan and fold in the flour, a little at a time, and then 1 tablespoon hot water. Pour the mixture into the prepared tin and spread it out lightly. Bake the cake for 8–10 minutes or until it is set and firm but not coloured. Roll up the cake still with the greaseproof paper adhering to one side. Lift it on to a wire rack and leave it for 5 minutes or until it is only just cool.

While the cake is resting, prepare the filling. Beat the cheese in a bowl until it is soft. Break up the carob bars and put them into a small bowl in a pan of cold water. Set it over a low heat and stir until the carob has just melted, taking care not to let the water boil or splash into the carob. Quickly beat the carob into the cheese. Use immediately as the frosting will firm up as it cools.

Unroll the cake on a clean tea cloth. Spread the inside with half the cheese mixture. Carefully roll the cake up again, this time without the paper: use the cloth to help you ease the cake over. Set the roll on a serving plate or cake board and trim the ends if necessary to make them flat. Spread the remaining cheese and carob mixture over the outside of the cake. Make a ridged 'bark' pattern on it with the prongs of a fork.

Make robins, sprigs of holly or anything that takes your fancy out of coloured almond paste, and use them to decorate the log.

CAKES FOR CHRISTMAS PARTIES

CHRISTMAS BISCUIT TREE
D E Makes about 20 biscuits

125 g (4 oz) vegetable margarine
50 g (2 oz) honey
175 g (6 oz) wholewheat flour
I teaspoon ground mixed spice

Heat the oven to 180°C/350°F/Gas Mark 4. Put the margarine into a bowl and beat in the honey. Toss the flour with the spice and gradually beat them into the margarine and honey. Using your fingers, bring the mixture into a ball of smooth dough. Dust it with flour.

Roll the dough out to a thickness of about 6 mm ($\frac{1}{4}$ in). Stamp it into star shapes about 6 cm ($2\frac{1}{2}$ in) across (if you do not have a star-shaped cutter, use a round one). With an apple corer, make a hole in the centre of each biscuit, gathering up the little round pieces and using them to make more biscuits. Lay all the biscuits on floured baking sheets. Bake for 20 minutes or until they are firm but not coloured. Cool them on the sheets for 5 minutes, then lift on to wire racks to cool completely.

Enclose each biscuit in plastic wrap, snipping it in the middle and wrapping the plastic round the inner edge of the biscuit. With red and green paper ribbon about 1.5 cm ($\frac{1}{2}$ in) wide, or coloured string or thick wool, make loops of ribbon through each one, stapling or tying the ends together.

Wrap a flowerpot in coloured paper. Find a large, branchy twig and either leave it as it is or spray or paint it white. Put it in the centre of the flowerpot and pack it round with heavy stones, small stones or damp sand, or a combination – it needs to be quite firm. Hang the biscuits on it and decorate with tinsel or other decorations.

CHRISTMAS PUDDING CAKES
Makes 24

50 g (2 oz) prunes
150 ml (5 fl oz) unsweetened orange juice
50 g (2 oz) stoned dates
125 g (4 oz) wholewheat flour
$\frac{1}{2}$ teaspoon ground mixed spice
75 g (3 oz) butter, softened, or margarine
2 eggs
50 g (2 oz) raisins
50 g (2 oz) sultanas

Decoration
40 g ($1\frac{1}{2}$ oz) ground almonds
$1\frac{1}{2}$ tablespoons concentrated apple juice
red and green food colouring

Soak the prunes in the orange juice for 4 hours. Drain them, reserving the juice. Stone and finely chop them. Finely chop the dates. Put the prunes and dates into a saucepan with the reserved juice, bring to a gentle boil and simmer for 5 minutes. Cool slightly and put them through a blender or food processor with the juice.

Heat the oven to 180°C/350°F/Gas Mark 4. Mix the flour with the spice. Cream the butter or margarine and gradually add the beaten eggs, alternating with the flour. Beat in the blended dried fruits. Fold in the sultanas and raisins. Divide the mixture between 24 greased, individual cake or bun tins. Bake the cakes for 15 minutes or until firm and turn on to wire racks to cool.

For the decoration, mix together the almonds and concentrated apple juice so you have a stiff, marzipan-like paste. Colour one-third with red food colouring and roll it into small holly berries. Colour the rest with green food colouring. Dampen a work surface and a rolling pin and roll out the green paste. Cut it into 24 small leaf shapes. Turn the cakes rounded side up and stick on the berries and leaves.

BONFIRE SALAD
E G W Serves 6

450 g (1 lb) carrots
1 head celery
1 cucumber
225 g (8 oz) uncooked beetroot
1 box mustard and cress
225 g (8 oz) curd or cottage cheese
4 tablespoons natural yoghurt
4 tablespoons chopped parsley

Cut the carrots, celery, cucumber and beetroot into matchstick pieces. Arrange in rings on a serving plate, with a rosette of mustard and cress in the centre.

Beat the cheese. Gradually beat in the yoghurt and parsley. Serve as a dip.

HOT POTATO CAKES
Makes about 24 of each type

1.125 kg (2½ lb) potatoes
125 g (4 oz) butter, or margarine
175 g (6 oz) wholewheat flour
1 teaspoon bicarbonate of soda
150 g (5 oz) lean back bacon rashers
75 g (3 oz) Cheddar cheese, finely grated
4 tablespoons chopped parsley
beaten egg to glaze

Cook the potatoes in lightly salted boiling water until soft. Drain and peel them as soon as they are cool enough to handle. Mash them with butter or margarine. Gradually beat in the flour and bicarbonate of soda. Divide the mixture into 2. Grill the bacon rashers until they are well done. Finely chop them. Mix them into one portion of the potatoes. Mix the cheese into the other portion. Divide the parsley between each portion.

Heat the oven to 200°C/400°F/Gas Mark 6. Roll out each portion of the potato mixture to a thickness of 1.5 cm (½ in) and stamp it into 5 cm (2 in) rounds with a biscuit cutter. Lay them on floured baking sheets. Brush with beaten egg and bake for 30 minutes or until golden brown.

Either serve the potato cakes immediately, or cool them on wire racks and reheat in a preheated 180°C/350°F/Gas Mark 4 oven for 5 minutes.

BAKED POTATOES

Warm potatoes in their jackets are perfect for outdoor parties in October or November. Cook them as described on page 90, split them in half and serve wrapped in foil or a double layer of kitchen paper so that they can be eaten in the hand. Add butter, a sausage or some cheese, or make up one of the recipes that follow. (There are more suggestions on page 90, but they are less suitable for eating in the hand and you will probably need to supply plates, knives and forks if serving one of them.)

CHEESE AND TOMATO POTATO TOPPING
E G W For 10–12 potatoes

6 tablespoons tomato juice
225 g (8 oz) Red Leicester cheese, finely grated

Heat the tomato juice to just below boiling point and quickly beat it into the cheese to obtain a smooth consistency. Cool completely. Put about 2 teaspoons of the mixture on each potato half.

SAUSAGE STUFFED POTATOES
E G W Serves 12

12 potatoes, long shaped if possible, each weighing approximately 125–175 g (4–6 oz)
12 chipolata sausages, or 6 large sausages
175 g (6 oz) Cheddar cheese, grated
6 tablespoons chutney

Heat the oven to 200°C/400°F/Gas Mark 6. Scrub and bake the potatoes (page 90) and put the sausages into the oven for the final half-hour of the cooking time. While both are cooking, mix the chutney with the cheese. When the potatoes are done, slit them lengthways not quite all the way through. Cut large sausages in half lengthways but leave the chipolatas whole. Put a portion of the cheese and half a sausage or a whole chipolata into each potato. Wrap in foil or a double layer of kitchen paper for eating in the hand.

HOT BEAN BAPS
D E

Make up a double quantity of Baked Beans (page 86). Split 12 wholemeal baps and remove some of the crumb. Put them in a preheated 180°C/350°F/Gas Mark 4 oven for 5 minutes to warm through. Fill them with the beans. A small slice of cheese or a square of grilled bacon could be added if wished.

HOT APPLE CAKE
This warming cake is perfect for a bonfire or Hallowe'en party.
D Serves 16

450 g (1 lb) dessert apples
450 g (1 lb) wholewheat flour
½ teaspoon salt
1 teaspoon bicarbonate of soda
¼ nutmeg, freshly grated
225 g (8 oz) vegetable margarine
225 g (8 oz) apple and pear spread
2 eggs

Heat the oven to 180°C/350°F/Gas Mark 4. Peel, core and chop the apples. Put the flour into a bowl with the salt, bicarbonate of soda and nutmeg. Rub in the margarine and make a well in the centre. Melt the apple and pear spread in a saucepan over a low heat. Tip it into the flour, add the beaten eggs and mix well to a stiff consistency. Fold in the chopped apples. Put the mixture into a 20 × 30 cm (8 × 12 in) tin lined with oiled greaseproof paper. Bake the cake for 45 minutes, or until a skewer inserted in the centre comes out clean. Turn out on to a wire rack.

Serve the cake warm, cut in small squares: to reheat a cold cake, carefully return it to the tin and put it into a preheated 180°C/350°F/Gas Mark 4 oven for 5 minutes.

HOT SPICED APPLE JUICE
Serves 12

2 oranges
2 lemons
4 dessert apples
225 ml (8 fl oz) concentrated apple juice
1.725 litres (3 pints) water
1 cinnamon stick

Thinly slice the oranges and lemons. Halve the apples lengthways, core and slice them. In a large saucepan mix together the apple juice and water and add all the other ingredients. Heat to just below simmering point and keep at this temperature for 15 minutes. Cool slightly before serving.

BOB APPLE PUNCH
Serves 16

1 orange
12 cloves
1.15 litres (2 pints) unsweetened
red grape juice
575 ml (1 pint) unsweetened grapefruit juice
575 ml (1 pint) unsweetened orange juice
2 cinnamon sticks
125 g (4 oz) honey
6 crisp eating apples
lemon juice

Stick the cloves into the orange and bake it in a moderate oven – 180°C/350°F/Gas Mark 4 – for 15 minutes. Take it out and slice it. Mix the juices in a large saucepan and put in the orange, cinnamon sticks and honey. Set the pan over a moderate heat and bring the juices to just below simmering point. Leave them at this temperature for 10 minutes.

Core the apples. Quarter them lengthways and then cut them across into thin slices. Sprinkle with lemon juice to stop the flesh turning brown and add the slices to the punch just before serving.

CHAPTER TEN

ILLNESS AND FOOD SENSITIVITY

Ingredients and Special Recipes for Allergy Diets

All children become ill at some time and it does
help to know how to feed your child if she is off colour with a
common ailment such as influenza or diarrhoea. For some children,
certain foodstuffs can be the cause of the illness if they lead to an
allergic reaction, which can manifest itself as a skin rash,
diarrhoea or asthmatic wheezing.

Illness

With any childhood illness such as
chickenpox, a common cold or
influenza, the first thing to do is to
follow your child's lead. A sick child
will usually be indifferent to food and
it will do no harm to give her nothing
at all but water or freshly squeezed,
diluted fruit juice for a day or two.
Give small drinks hourly. Staying off
food will help her body fight for itself.
When she is hungry again she is
probably on the mend, so begin by
giving fresh fruit and a little plain
yoghurt. Commercial glucose drinks
are expensive. Fresh orange juice well
diluted with carbonated mineral
water will do as well, or add a
teaspoonful of honey to your child's
favourite drink. A sick child needs
food that is digestible, fairly bland
and mushy in texture. She will also
need some calories for energy.

Vomiting and diarrhoea

Your child will probably not want any
food at all. Even if she does, or if the
diarrhoea or vomiting continues, keep
her off solid foods. It is essential that
you don't let her become dehydrated.
Give water with a little honey and a
pinch of salt dissolved in it every
hour or so. After a day of liquids only
(but not cow's milk) you can start
solid food gradually. Begin with plain
things and watch for an adverse

reaction. Try yoghurt, wholewheat
toast or biscuits, oatcakes and
porridge plus fresh fruit.

If you are in any doubt about the
cause of your child's vomiting or
diarrhoea, consult your doctor and
don't attempt to diagnose it yourself.

Allergy

It is a sensible precaution when
weaning your baby off milk feeds
(pages 36–41) to introduce new foods
slowly and one at a time; you will
then be better able to spot any
reaction and identify the foodstuff.

Your baby's immature digestive
system needs time to adapt to certain
foodstuffs; the foods most commonly
associated with problems are dairy
foods, egg white, wheat products and
citrus fruits. Allergic reactions can be
persistent outbreaks of hives, skin
rashes, diarrhoea, eczema, colic,
asthmatic wheezing, vomiting, and in
severe cases such as gluten
sensitivity, a failure to thrive and
foul-smelling, fatty stools.

There is no need to be unduly
anxious about allergy unless there is
a family history of allergic diseases
such as eczema, asthma and hayfever.
Your doctor or health visitor will be
the best person to guide you if this is
the case. Even if your child has a
slight rash or a loose bowel motion
after eating strawberries, for example,

the foodstuff can be introduced again after a period of time and there may well be no reaction. All children get spots and diarrhoea from time to time. There is no need to suspect allergy unless the symptoms are severe or persistent. A bad allergic reaction is very distressing; if your child seems unperturbed, don't worry about it.

In the recipes in this book we have indicated those suitable for a specific allergy diet by the use of the letters D (dairy-free), E (egg-free), G (gluten-free) and W (wheat-free). In some people the allergy may be to wheat only, in others it may be to all products which contain gluten. There are many substitute foods and if your doctor advises you to remove a certain foodstuff from your child's diet, you will find it easy to cook this way with delicious results.

Remember when buying commercially prepared food to read the labels carefully. For example, margarine is rarely a totally vegetable product – there may be whey solids from cow's milk in it (see page 156 for a brand of vegetable margarine) and mustards and sauces often contain wheat products. In all cases, you should not impose any dietary limits on your child without medical advice.

Ingredients used in allergy recipes
Goat's milk
In some cases children with an allergy to cow's milk can drink goat's milk without any adverse reaction. It is available in fresh and dried forms or frozen. Cheese and yoghurt from goat's milk are widely available.

Soya milk
This is available dried and in tins and cartons. It is made from the soya bean and can be used like ordinary milk, though the flavour is milder. Some soya milks have sugar added. If your doctor agrees, you can try it, though bear in mind that your child may not be able to tolerate it either.

Tofu
This is a non-dairy substitute for yoghurt and soft cheeses. It is made from soya milk set with rennet and comes in the form of a solid, creamy block packed in water to keep it fresh. It should be drained before use and whipped to a purée. Its flavour is similar to low fat cheeses such as quark. Thinned with soya milk, it becomes the consistency of yoghurt. It has a bland taste and is useful as a protein and calcium supplement in savoury and sweet dishes as well as moistening dry dishes.

Flours
If your child is allergic to wheat only, simply use wholegrain rye or barley flour, and oatmeal as a thickener.

With a gluten allergy your child will need to avoid all the common cereals – wheat, oats, barley and rye. Some useful substitutes are cornmeal (page 14), rice flour, made by grinding brown rice, soya flour from soya beans, and buckwheat flour from buckwheat seeds. The latter has a rich, nutty flavour and is often used for pancakes and muffins; it can be substituted for wholewheat flour in the recipe for bread on page 104. Potato flour can be used to make a batter and, like arrowroot and tapioca, makes an excellent thickener.

Some of these flours have an obtrusive flavour and it is often not possible simply to substitute the wholewheat flour in a recipe with the same amount of a gluten-free one, particularly when baking. Follow special recipes whenever you can, and use the flours in combination to dilute their flavours.

SAVOURIES

MUSHROOM SOUP

This is just an example of how potato flour can be used as a thickener.

D E G W Serves 4

225 g (8 oz) open mushrooms
2 medium onions
3 tablespoons oil
2 tablespoons potato flour
850 ml (1½ pints) stock (page 19)
1 bayleaf
4 tablespoons chopped parsley
4 tablespoons chopped watercress

Finely chop the mushrooms and onions. Heat the oil in a saucepan over a low heat and stir in the mushrooms and onions. Cover and cook gently for 10 minutes. Stir in the potato flour and then the stock. Bring to the boil, stirring. Add the bayleaf and parsley and simmer, uncovered, for 10 minutes. Remove the bayleaf and add the watercress just before serving.

CHEESE AND ONION QUICHE

E Serves 4

shortcrust pastry made with 175 g (6 oz) wholewheat flour (page 79)
1 × 300 g (10 oz) pack tofu
125 g (4 oz) Cheddar cheese, finely grated
4 tablespoons milk
2 medium onions
3 tablespoons oil

Heat the oven to 200°C/400°F/Gas Mark 6. Use the pastry to line a 20 cm (8 in) diameter tart tin.

Put the tofu into a blender or food processor and work it until smooth; alternatively, rub it through a sieve. Mix in the cheese and milk. Chop the onions and fry them in the oil over a low heat until golden. Put them in the tart tin in an even layer and pour the tofu mixture on top. Bake the quiche for 30 minutes or until the top is golden. Serve hot or cold.

DAIRY-FREE CHEESE

D E G W

125 g (4 oz) vegetable margarine
125 g (4 oz) soya flour
1–2 teaspoons yeast extract

Melt the margarine in a saucepan over a low heat. Stir in the soya flour and cook gently, stirring, for 1 minute. Take the pan from the heat. Beat in 1 teaspoon yeast extract, taste and add more if required. Pour the mixture into a shallow, 18 cm (7 in) square non-stick tin. Cover with plastic wrap and put the cheese in the refrigerator for 2 hours to set.

Remove the cheese from the tin and cut it into squares. Enclose each one separately in greaseproof paper or foil and store in the refrigerator.

TUNA QUICHE

D E Serves 4

shortcrust pastry made with 175 g (6 oz) wholewheat flour (page 79)
1 × 300 g (10 oz) pack tofu
2 tablespoons tomato purée
1 × 200 g (7 oz) tin tuna

Heat the oven to 200°C/400°F/Gas Mark 6. Use the pastry to line a 20 cm (8 in) tart tin.

Put the tofu into a blender or food processor with the tomato purée and work until you have a soft, pink mixture. Alternatively, rub the tofu through a sieve and beat in the tomato purée. Drain and flake the tuna. Put it into the pastry case in an even layer. Pour the tofu over the top and spread it out evenly. Bake the quiche for 30 minutes or until the top is beginning to brown.

To make Tomato Quiche, substitute 225 g (8 oz) sliced tomatoes for the tuna.

BUCKWHEAT PANCAKES
D G W Makes 8

125 g (4 oz) buckwheat flour
15 g (½ oz) fresh yeast, or 2 teaspoons dried
275 ml (10 fl oz) warm water
1 teaspoon honey, if using dried yeast
pinch fine sea salt
1 egg, beaten
2 tablespoons oil
oil for frying

If you are using fresh yeast, crumble it into a bowl and pour in half the water. If using dried, dissolve the honey in half the water and sprinkle in the yeast. Leave in a warm place until frothy – about 15 minutes.

Put the flour and salt into a bowl and make a well in the centre. Gradually beat in the egg, the remaining water, oil and yeast. Cover the bowl with a clean tea cloth and leave it in a warm place for 1 hour for the batter to become bubbly.

Heat 1 tablespoon of the oil in a frying pan on a high heat. Spoon in 3 tablespoons of the batter and tip the pan to spread it evenly. Cook the pancake until the underside is golden. Turn it over and brown the other side. Cook the remaining pancakes in the same way.

Buckwheat pancakes can be served with honey and lemon, with sugar-free jam or stewed fruit, or topped with natural yoghurt or tofu whipped until it is creamy. You can also serve them with savoury fillings such as those on page 89.

SCRAMBLED TOFU
D E G W Serves 2

1 × 300 g (10 oz) pack tofu
1 small onion
2 tablespoons oil
pinch ground turmeric (for colour)
½ tablespoon soy sauce

Drain the tofu and mash it with a fork. Chop the onion finely and soften it in the oil over a low heat. Put in the tofu and the turmeric. Add the soy sauce and cook for 2 minutes or until the tofu looks like scrambled egg.

TOFU MAYONNAISE

This recipe uses Dijon mustard: check the label to make sure it contains no wheat or edible starch.

D E G W

1 × 300 g (10 oz) pack tofu
2 tablespoons oil
juice ½–1 lemon
2 teaspoons Dijon mustard

Put the tofu into a blender or food processor and work it to a smooth cream; alternatively, rub it through a sieve. Add the oil, lemon juice and mustard and mix well. Taste and add more lemon juice if required.

APPLE CRUMBLE
D E G W Serves 4

450 g (1 lb) apples
75 g (3 oz) raisins
50 g (2 oz) apple and pear spread

Topping
75 g (3 oz) rice flour
50 g (2 oz) desiccated coconut
25 g (1 oz) ground almonds, or ground mixed nuts
25 g (1 oz) apple and pear spread
75 g (3 oz) vegetable margarine

Heat the oven to 200°C/400°F/Gas Mark 6. Peel, core and chop the apples. Mix them with the raisins and apple and pear spread and put them into an ovenproof dish.

To make the topping, put the rice flour, desiccated coconut and ground nuts into a bowl. Rub in the apple and pear spread and margarine until the mixture resembles fine breadcrumbs. Spread the mixture evenly on top of the apples, and bake the crumble for 25 minutes or until the top is browned.

You can use the same crumble topping for other types of fruits.

BANANA AND DATE PUDDING
D G W Serves 4

2 bananas
50 g (2 oz) stoned dates
1 tablespoon oil
50 g (2 oz) millet
150 ml (5 fl oz) water
grated rind and juice 1 medium orange
2 eggs, separated

Heat the oil in a small frying pan on a low heat. Stir in the millet and cook it for $\frac{1}{2}$ minute. Pour in the water, bring to the boil, cover and cook gently for 20 minutes or until the millet is soft and fluffy and all the water has been absorbed. Turn the millet into a bowl.

Heat the oven to 190°C/375°F/Gas Mark 5. Mash the bananas and finely chop the dates. Add these and the orange rind and juice to the millet. Mix in the egg yolks. Whip the egg whites in a separate bowl until they are stiff, then fold them into the banana mixture. Tip into a greased ovenproof dish and bake for 20 minutes or until the top is beginning to brown.

CUSTARD
D E G W Serves 4

5 tablespoons oil
5 tablespoons soya flour
425 ml (15 fl oz) soya milk
pinch fine sea salt
$\frac{1}{2}$ teaspoon vanilla essence
3 tablespoons honey, or 4 tablespoons
concentrated apple juice

Heat the oil in a saucepan over a low heat. Stir in the soya flour. Gradually add the soya milk, add the salt and bring to the boil, stirring. Simmer, stirring continuously, until the sauce thickens – about 3 minutes. Take the pan from the heat and beat in the vanilla and honey or concentrated apple juice.

Leave the custard for 5 minutes before serving, stirring several times. It will thicken as it stands; should it go lumpy, rub it through a sieve.

RICE PUDDING
D E G W Serves 4

125 g (4 oz) short grain brown rice
175 ml (6 fl oz) soya milk
6 tablespoons concentrated apple juice
$\frac{1}{2}$ teaspoon vanilla essence
grated rind $\frac{1}{2}$ lemon (optional)

Cook the rice in unsalted water for 45 minutes or until tender. Drain, and put it into a bowl. Heat the oven to 170°C/325°F/Gas Mark 3. Mix the soya milk, concentrated apple juice, vanilla essence and lemon rind into the rice. Put the mixture into an oiled ovenproof dish and bake for 50 minutes or until the pudding is firm and the top browned.

Sliced dessert apples or pears or fruits tinned in natural juice (drained first) can be put into the dish under the rice mixture to make a Fruity Rice Pudding.

FRUITY RICE PORRIDGE
D E G W Serves 2

3 tablespoons rice flour
275 ml (10 fl oz) water
2 tablespoons raisins
2 tablespoons chopped figs, or dates
15 g ($\frac{1}{2}$ oz) ground almonds,
or ground mixed nuts

Put the rice flour into a saucepan and gradually mix in the water to make a smooth, thin paste. Add the fruits, bring to the boil and cook for about 3 minutes, stirring constantly, until the mixture thickens. Stir in the ground almonds or nuts.

COLD DESSERTS

BANANA ICE-CREAM
D E G W Serves 4

4 large ripe bananas
juice ½ lemon
25 g (1 oz) arrowroot
850 ml (1½ pints) soya milk
75 g (3 oz) sugar-free apricot jam, or honey

Mash and sieve the bananas with the lemon juice, or work them to a purée in a blender or food processor. Put the arrowroot into a bowl and stir in about 150 ml (5 fl oz) of the soya milk to make a thin smooth paste. Put the remaining soya milk into a saucepan and add the jam or honey. Stir over a low heat until the sweetener has dissolved, and bring to just below boiling point. Stir the soya milk into the arrowroot paste. Return the mixture to the saucepan and bring it to the boil, stirring constantly. Boil for about 2 minutes for the mixture to thicken. Take the pan from the heat and stir in the bananas. Cool and chill.
Freeze as for ice-cream, page 74.

CAROB ICE-CREAM
D E G W Serves 4

25 g (1 oz) carob powder
25 g (1 oz) arrowroot
850 ml (1½ pints) soya milk
125 g (4 oz) sugar-free apricot jam, or honey

Sieve the carob powder into a bowl and toss it with the arrowroot. Mix in 150 ml (5 fl oz) of the soya milk to make a thin, smooth paste. Put the remaining soya milk into a saucepan and add the jam or honey. Stir over a low heat until the sweetener has dissolved, and bring to just below boiling point. Stir the soya milk into the carob mixture.
Return the mixture to the saucepan and bring it to the boil, stirring constantly. Boil for about 2 minutes until the mixture thickens. Cool and chill.
Freeze as for ice-cream, page 74.

HOT CAROB SAUCE FOR ICE-CREAM OR PUDDINGS
D E G W

2 tablespoons oil
3 tablespoons soya flour
2 tablespoons carob powder
275 ml (10 fl oz) soya milk
1–2 tablespoons honey

Heat the oil in a saucepan over a low heat. Stir in the soya flour and sieved carob powder. Stir in the soya milk and bring to the boil, stirring. Add the honey and simmer, stirring, for about 3 minutes or until the sauce is thick.

SWEET DREAM TOPPING OR FLAVOURED YOGHURT SUBSTITUTE
D E G W Serves 3 as a yoghurt, 4 as a topping

1 × 300 g (10 oz) pack tofu
3 tablespoons sugar-free jam

Drain the tofu and cream it in a blender or food processor. Add the jam and blend again. Alternatively, rub both tofu and jam through a sieve, and mix well. Chill for about half an hour.

TOFU AND STRAWBERRY WHIP
You can adapt this recipe for other soft fruits.

D E G W Serves 4

1 × 300 g (10 oz) pack tofu
3 tablespoons sugar-free strawberry jam
225 g (8 oz) strawberries

Drain the tofu and cream it in a blender or food processor, add the jam and blend again; or rub the drained tofu and the jam through a sieve and mix well. Chill for 30 minutes. Quarter the strawberries and mix them into the whip.

CORN BREAD
E G W

175 g (6 oz) cornmeal
50 g (2 oz) soya flour
½ teaspoon fine sea salt
½ teaspoon bicarbonate of soda
4 tablespoons corn oil
150 ml (5 fl oz) natural yoghurt, or sour
milk, or buttermilk

Heat the oven to 200°C/400°F/Gas Mark 6. Put the cornmeal into a bowl with the soya flour, salt and bicarbonate of soda, make a well in the centre and pour in the oil and yoghurt, sour milk or buttermilk. Mix everything to a moist dough. Press into an oiled, 18 cm (7 in) diameter cake tin. Bake for 20 minutes or until firm and beginning to colour. Cool on a wire rack.

This bread tends to be rather crumbly, but it has a delicious flavour and can be served plain or buttered, or with sweet or savoury spreads.

CORN AND APRICOT CAKES
D G W Makes 15

75 g (3 oz) cornmeal
125 g (4 oz) dried whole apricots
275 ml (10 fl oz) unsweetened orange juice
25 g (1 oz) soya flour
1 teaspoon bicarbonate of soda
2 eggs
4 tablespoons corn oil

Put the apricots into a saucepan with the orange juice, bring to the boil and soak them for 4 hours. Drain them, reserving the juice, and purée the apricots in a blender or food processor.

Heat the oven to 180°C/350°F/Gas Mark 4. Put the cornmeal and soya flour into a bowl with the bicarbonate of soda and make a well in the centre. Beat the eggs and pour them into the well. Add the apricot purée. Gradually begin to beat in flour from the sides of the well. Add the oil plus 4 tablespoons of the reserved apricot juice and beat to make a thick batter. Half-fill 15 oiled bun tins, and bake for 20 minutes or until the cakes are firm and risen.

BROWNIES I

This and the following recipe are variations of the Brownies on page 140, and show how an ordinary recipe may be adapted to suit children on special diets.
D E Makes about 35

225 g (8 oz) wholewheat flour
175 g (6 oz) tofu
125 g (4 oz) walnuts
50 g (2 oz) carob powder
6 tablespoons corn oil
6 tablespoons apple juice
175 g (6 oz) apple and pear spread

Heat the oven to 180°C/350°F/Gas Mark 4. Put the tofu through a blender or food processor to make it smooth, or rub it through a sieve. Chop the walnuts. Sieve the flour and carob powder into a bowl, toss in the walnuts and make a well in the centre. Put in the oil, apple juice, apple and pear spread and blended tofu. Gradually mix in flour from the sides of the well and then beat to make a smooth mixture. Pour into an oiled 18 × 30 cm (7 × 10 in) cake tin and bake for 30 minutes or until a skewer stuck in the centre comes out clean. Turn the cake on to a wire rack to cool.

Serve cut in small squares.

CAKES · BISCUITS

BROWNIES II
D E G W Makes about 35

175 g (6 oz) soya flour
50 g (2 oz) rice flour
50 g (2 oz) carob powder
125 g (4 oz) walnuts
6 tablespoons corn oil
6 tablespoons apple juice
175 g (6 oz) apple and pear spread
175 g (6 oz) tofu

Heat the oven to 180°C/350°F/Gas Mark 4. Put the tofu through a blender or food processor to make it smooth, or rub it through a sieve. Put the soya flour and rice flour into a bowl. Sieve the carob powder in. Chop the walnuts, add them to the flour and toss with your fingers to mix all together. Make a well in the centre and put in the corn oil, apple juice, apple and pear spread and tofu. Gradually beat in flour from the sides of the well until it is all mixed in. Put the mixture into an oiled 18 × 30 cm (7 × 10 in) cake tin and bake for 30 minutes or until a skewer stuck in the centre comes out clean. Turn the cake on to a wire rack to cool.
Serve cut in small squares.

SPICE BISCUITS
E G W Makes about 16

75 g (3 oz) cornmeal
50 g (2 oz) soya flour
25 g (1 oz) rice flour
2 teaspoons ground mixed spice
4 tablespoons corn oil
50 g (2 oz) apple and pear spread
4 tablespoons natural yoghurt

Heat the oven to 180°C/350°F/Gas Mark 4. Put the cornmeal, soya flour, rice flour and mixed spice into a bowl. Rub in the oil and apple and pear spread. Make a well in the centre, put in the yoghurt and mix everything to a soft dough.

Using soya flour to coat your board and rolling pin, roll or press the dough out to a thickness of 6 mm ($\frac{1}{4}$ in). Stamp it into 5cm (2 in) rounds with a biscuit cutter and lay them on a baking sheet that you have sprinkled with soya flour. Bake for 20 minutes or until the biscuits are firm but not coloured. Lift them on to wire racks to cool.

HONEY FRUIT CAKE
D E

225 g (8 oz) wholewheat flour
125 g (4 oz) vegetable margarine
75 g (3 oz) raisins
75 g (3 oz) sultanas
125 g (4 oz) honey
1 teaspoon bicarbonate of soda
90 ml (3 fl oz) soya milk
$1\frac{1}{2}$ tablespoons cider vinegar

Heat the oven to 180°C/350°F/Gas Mark 4. Put the flour into a bowl and rub in the margarine. Toss in the raisins and sultanas. Put the honey into a saucepan and melt it gently. Put the bicarbonate of soda into a bowl and mix in 2 tablespoons of soya milk. Mix the remaining milk in a jug with the vinegar and add the bicarbonate of soda mixture. Make a well in the flour. Pour in the honey and the milk mixture, and mix to a stiff consistency. Put the mixture into a greased 450 g (1 lb) loaf tin and bake for 1 hour or until a skewer inserted in the centre comes out clean. Turn the cake on to a wire rack to cool.

INDEX